DIODORUS SICULUS: THE REIGN OF PHILIP II

The Greek and Macedonian narrative from Book XVI

Also available in the Classical Studies series

Euripides: Medea and Electra, J. Ferguson
Homer: Odyssey, P. Jones
Catullus to Ovid: Reading Latin Love Elegy, J. Booth & G. Lee
Sophocles: Antigone & Oedipus the King, J. Wilkins & M. Macleod
Tacitus: Annals XIV, N. Miller
Virgil: Aeneid, R.D. Williams

In Bristol Classical Paperbacks:

Alexander the Great: King, Commander and Statesman, N. Hammond

Published by Duckworth:

Philip of Macedon, N. Hammond
The Genius of Alexander the Great, N. Hammond

DIODORUS SICULUS:
THE REIGN OF PHILIP II

The Greek and Macedonian Narrative
from Book XVI

A Companion

E.I. McQueen

Published by Bristol Classical Press
General Editor: John H. Betts

First published in 1995 by
Bristol Classical Press
an imprint of
Gerald Duckworth & Co. Ltd
61 Frith Street
London W1D 3JL
e-mail: inquiries@duckworth-publishers.co.uk
Website: www.ducknet.co.uk

Reprinted 2001

A catalogue record for this book is available
from the British Library

ISBN 1-85399-385-9

Printed in Great Britain by
Antony Rowe Ltd, Eastbourne

Contents

Preface

In the light of the prominence of the reign of Philip II in the A-level and university undergraduate syllabus, a convenient edition and English translation of the Sixteenth Book of Diodorus has long been a desideratum. There is as yet no Penguin Diodorus, and the only translation readily available in English is that in the Loeb Classical Library. The seventh volume in the Loeb Diodorus series, translated by Charles L. Sherman, containing chapters 1-65 (along with the whole of Book 15), appeared in 1952, and the eighth volume, which is translated by C. Bradford Welles and contains chapters 66-95 together with Book 17, was published in 1963. Split as it is between two volumes, the Loeb translation is both inconvenient to use and expensive to purchase. Though both volumes (and the latter in particular) provide notes that are likely to be of assistance to the reader, the lack of a commentary on such an important source for Philip's reign has long disadvantaged students. It is the hope that the present work will to some extent fill the gap.

This edition contains an introduction, translation and historical commentary on the greater part of Book 16, covering all the sections Diodorus devotes to the history of Macedonia, Greece and Asia Minor. The only omissions are passages dealing with events in Italy and Sicily, together with the lengthy section (chapters 40.3-52.8) on the Persian recovery of Phoenicia and Egypt in 344-3 which is distinctly peripheral to the history of the Greek world. Since this edition is intended to be of use to sixth formers and undergraduates who have no knowledge of Greek, I have not included in my commentary any discussion of grammatical or textual problems. The text translated is that which is printed in the two Loeb volumes cited above. My translation is fairly literal and, since it is aimed merely at communicating to the student the meaning of Diodorus' Greek, it makes no pretensions to literary merit. If it be thought inelegant, this is deliberately contrived, at least in the (not infrequent) places where Diodorus' Greek is itself inelegant. In the translation, the term "the King" invariably refers to the king of Persia (the 'Great King') as opposed to "the king" in lower case letters, which refers to all other monarchs mentioned in the text, be they kings of Sparta or even Philip himself. Unless otherwise indicated, all dates are B.C. In the bibliography I confine myself to citing books and articles written in English.

Introduction

1. The Life and Works of Diodorus

Diodorus the historian, surnamed in later times Siculus or the Sicilian from his native island (distinguishing him from other literary figures who bore this common name, such as the comic poet from Sinope, Diodorus Cronus of Iasos the philosopher, Diodorus Periegetes 'the Topographer', and the first century Alexandrian mathematician) was born at Agyrium, the modern Agira, some 50-60 km. inland from Catana on the east coast of the island and situated on the ancient road from Catana to Panormus and Segesta. Under Timoleon's settlement in the fourth century, the city had been a place of some importance, (16.85.2, 16.83.3), but it had declined somewhat since then, and its impoverishment in Diodorus' own day is attested in Cicero's *Second Action Against Verres* (3.18.47, 3.27.67, 3.31.73, 3.51.120-1).

Neither Diodorus himself nor any other ancient writer tells us much about his life or background, but his ability to travel and to support himself in the course of a prolonged stay abroad would indicate that he had no financial problems. His life in Agyrium was presumably quiet and uneventful, for there is nothing in his work to suggest either political or administrative experience even at municipal level, nor does he make reference to the tenure of any military or political office among his qualifications for writing history. Travels outside his native Sicily are attested only to Egypt (1.22.2-7, 1.44.1 and 4, 1.83.8-9, 3.11.2-3, 3.38.1, 17.52.6) and to Rome (1.4.2-4). The claim he makes in his Preface (1.4.1) to have travelled widely in both Europe and Asia (not without some hardship and personal danger) is not supported by the facts: certainly he can have visited neither the Red Sea nor the site of Niniveh, since in both descriptions (3.38.1; 2.2.2 and 7.1) he is able to cite only earlier writers, and in the latter case (2.7.2) locates the site on the Euphrates instead of the Tigris. Similarly anyone who had visited Chalcidice can hardly have believed it to be near the Hellespont (16.53.2).

His residence in Egypt in the 180th Olympiad (60-56) in the reign of Ptolemy Auletes (1.44.1) witnessed the arrival of the Roman embassy of 59 (1.83.8-9). His visit to Egypt was made at least in part to undertake some of the preliminary research necessary for his projected historical work (see

1

3.11.3, where we are told of his conversations with native priests and Ethiopian ambassadors in which he sought to check the veracity of existing works, and 3.38.1, where he mentions his consultation of records in Alexandria and his cross- examination of eye-witnesses.) His lengthy stay in Rome had much the same purpose (1.4.3-4). Such libraries as were possessed by Agyrium and other Sicilian cities were inadequate for his purposes, and, since he had already acquired some familiarity with Latin while still living in Sicily (1.4.4), he soon became convinced of the need for a protracted period of residence in Rome. His claim to have spent some thirty years researching his subject, which presumably covers his stay in Egypt as well as in the capital, will have lasted roughly from 60 to 30. In the course of those thirty years, Diodorus read widely among the writers whom he selected as his authorities, while he also claims familiarity with what he calls *hypomnemata* or official records, which he consulted in both Alexandria (3.38.1) and Rome (1.4.3). In actual fact his text betrays no obvious knowledge of either Alexandrian or Roman official material (except perhaps at 40.4), though he may have obtained some information about such records in the historical authors he read in the course of his research. On the assumption that the thirty years of study included the time spent on writing up the fruits of his research, the *Library of History* (*Bibliotheke Historike*) will have been completed in 30.

In form, the work was a Universal History in forty books, embracing the history of the known world from mythological times down to his own day, with particular emphasis on events in Greece, Asia, Sicily and Italy, the scale of treatment gradually becoming more detailed as he approached the events of his own lifetime. The terminal date of the work is variously given as 60, the year of the formation of the First Triumvirate (1.4.7) and 46 (1.5.1). In support of the latter date is Diodorus' promise at 5.21.2 and 22.1 to include in its proper context a description of Caesar's invasion of Britain, but what remains of his final book (the latest surviving fragment of which concerns the Catilinarian conspiracy of 63) suggests that he cut the work short at 60. The change of plan may have been made to avoid the potential pitfalls inherent in composing a narrative of what was regarded in the 30s as the risky and politically sensitive period of the fall of the republic. Of the forty books of the original, there survive *in toto* only Books 1-5 and 11-20, of which the first pentad provides an *archaeologia* of the various nations of Asia, North Africa and Europe, and Books 11-20 a history of the Greek-speaking world from Xerxes' invasion of 480/79 till the eve of the Battle of Ipsus in 302/1.

Diodorus' History achieved such popularity in his own day that he even refers to the appearance of pirated editions of some of his earlier books (40.8). Yet in the earlier part of the imperial period it suffered much from the neglect of serious writers, of whom only the Elder Pliny (*NH* 25, Preface) cites him by name, though the work was probably known to both Athenaeus (12.541F) and Cephalion (*FGH* 93, Frag. 1B, Jacoby). From the fourth century A.D. onwards, it recovered much of its former popularity, as was only to be expected in an age when long historical works went out of fashion and abridgments and epitomes came into their own. Among the writers who quote Diodorus with some frequency are Porphyry, Eusebius, Malalas, Syncellus and Tzetzes, while Photius (*Bibl.* 244 p. 393a 12) even excerpts passages ascribed to Diodorus which cover the period 59 BC to 14 AD. Unless Photius is guilty of error, there must have been in existence in the Byzantine era an edition of Diodorus' work, which some later writer had carried down to the death of Augustus and appended to the genuine text. His popularity in this period was so great that his work contributed, however unintentionally, to driving out of circulation the more detailed histories which he had used as his authorities, and which are now unfortunately lost.

2. Diodorus' Purpose in Writing

In his preface to Book 1, Diodorus praises historiography as a literary genre in extravagant terms. For him it is the transmitter of experience, which is itself the supreme teacher of mankind (1.1.1-2). It is therefore the benefactor of the human race and a prime factor in the advancement of civilisation. Moreover its narration of the good deeds of individuals not only inspires humanity to undertake activities beneficial to the whole of mankind, such as the foundation of cities and the drafting of law codes, but also promotes the cause of progress in both science and the arts (1.2.1-2). So too the historian himself is the benefactor of mankind, since it is his task to preserve the memory of, and thereby to encourage the undertaking of the good deeds which contribute so much to the enrichment of civilisation (1.2.4).

In his belief that history must serve as the teacher of mankind, Diodorus is not at all unusual among the historians of antiquity, but his aim is something very different from the didactic purposes of a Thucydides or a Polybius. He takes it for granted that it is the desire for immortality that leads man to benefit his fellow men (e.g. 1.2.2, 11.38.6, 15.1.1) and that the historian, by offering moral judgments on the deeds of those whose *acta* he is recording, has the power to stimulate the cultivation of virtue and to discourage vice (e.g. 1.1.5, 1.2.1-5, 11.3.1). Thus in his preface (1.2.2) he states that:

> the purpose of history is to preserve the nobility of eminent men and to report the evil of the wicked, and thereby to serve the good of mankind. History is the best means of conferring noble integrity on the characters.

3

In the preface to Book 15 (1.1) he writes in similar vein:

> Throughout the course of my work it has been my practice to
> eulogise the good and to criticise the evil. We shall thereby
> induce those whose nature inclines to virtue to perform noble
> deeds because of the immortality they are granted by fame, and
> by appropriate censures we shall divert the wicked from their
> propensity to evil.

Time and time again Diodorus inserts personal judgments of praise or
censure when he sees an opportunity for edifying the reader, a habit which
brings him closer to the biographical tradition inherited by Plutarch than to
the Thucydidean concept of historiography.

Closely linked to his didactic purpose is his belief in the workings of
heavenly justice both to reward the good and to punish the evil. Thus at
11.46.4 he sees a connection between the loss of Spartan supremacy at sea
and the divine punishment of the regent Pausanias, whose crimes are described at length in the two preceding chapters. In Book 16 the most sustained
example is the lengthy account of the fate of the sacrilegious Phocians at the
end of the Third Sacred War (chapters 61-64) which is narrated (61.1)

> to put on record the punishment inflicted by the god on those
> who had sinned against the oracle. For the implacable vengeance
> of the gods pursued not only the actual perpetrators of the
> sacrilege but all who were even minimally connected with the
> transgression.

And, he continues,

> on those who had dared to show contempt for the god punish-
> ment was visited upon them in the manner I have related.

Conversely the gods rewarded Philip, their chosen instrument of vengeance (64.3):

> He continued to consolidate his strength from that time because
> of his piety towards the god, was designated supreme com-
> mander of the whole of Greece and won the greatest of all the kingdoms
> of Europe. In seeing Philip's appointment as *hegemon* of the
> League of Corinth as a divine reward for his role in the Sacred
> War, Diodorus' moral purpose gets the better of him, as it does
> in tarring all Spartans with the same brush in the passage on the
> baseness of Pausanias in Book 11. Elsewhere he ascribes Philip's

4

power to his own abilities (16.1.1, 4 and 6) and to his acts of goodwill in Greece (16.89.2).

Diodorus' second major purpose in writing was the less utilitarian and more informative one of creating a Universal History conceived as a work of scholarship aimed at the more discerning type of reader (*philanagnostountes*, literally 'those who love to read' [1.3.6]). Though such readers would naturally have preferred to peruse the more detailed works of the major historians, Diodorus seems be catering for those who either lack the time or do not have access to large numbers of voluminous texts:

> from such a work anyone will be able to obtain what is needed for
> his special purpose, as it were drawn from a great fountain. (1.3.6).

At the same time, if it is true, as he claims, that pirated editions of his work were circulated in his lifetime (40.8), a more popular readership is indicated. The title of Diodorus' work, the *Bibliotheke Historias* or *Library of History* also suggests a work aimed at the man in the street: the only other literary work containing the word *Library* in its title that is known prior to the end of the Graeco-Roman world is the uncritical handbook of mythology incorrectly attributed to Apollodorus of Athens in the second century but in fact a later production. Diodorus' work has every appearance of being directed less at the serious academic than at the general reader, whom he sought to provide with what he needed without having to go to the trouble of changing source. In one passage (16.1.1) he expresses the hope that his work will be clear to the reader and its contents easy to remember. The passage continues with a censure of historians who offer incomplete narratives which are in his view likely only to interrupt the reader's concentration and interest (16.1.2, cf. 20.1.1 and 4). Since serious readers are unlikely to allow their attention to wander or to be discouraged from further study by lack of clarity or failure on the part of the writer to produce what is in Diodorus' opinion an incomplete action, his comments are much more apposite to an amateur readership.

In order to embrace the events of such a lengthy period of time within the confines of his forty books, Diodorus is unable to supply the wealth of detail to be found in universal histories devoted to much shorter periods. Consequently he provides the reader with what is in effect a manual or handbook containing what in his opinion the man in the street needs to know about history. The scale of treatment is therefore far from generous, though it varies from book to book and shows a tendency to become more ample for the Hellenistic Age, as the following table will indicate:

BOOK	YEARS COVERED	NO. OF CHAPTERS DEVOTED TO EVENTS OF GREECE & ASIA	NO. OF YEARS	AVERAGE NO. OF CHAPTERS PER YEAR
11	480/79-451/0	67	28	$2^1/_2$
12	450/49-416/5	56	34	$1^1/_2$
13	415/4-405/4	46	10	$4^1/_2$
14	404/3-387/6	45	17	$2^1/_2$
15	386/5-361/0	84	25	$3^1/_2$
16	360/59-336/5	65	24	$2^1/_2$
17	335/4-324/3	117	11	$10^1/_2$
18	323/2-318/7	75	5	15
19	317/6-311/0	86	6	$14^1/_2$
20	310/09-302/1	53	8	$6^1/_2$

Fluctuations in scale of treatment between contiguous books is accounted for by the choice of starting and culmination points, which are in turn determined by the need to produce books that are sufficiently self-contained to be capable of standing by themselves as individual homogeneous units. Thus in order to construe Book 16 as an artistic unity centred on the reign of Philip, Diodorus is compelled to compress the events of 24 years into one such unit, even if it produces a book that contains a smaller amount of material than the other books devoted to the history of the fourth century.

In view of the limitation of length imposed by his scheme, Diodorus' account of the reign of Philip is brief, and has more in common with abridgments and compendia than with full-scale historiographical works. However the scale of abridgment varies from passage to passage: in Book 16, for instance, events like the Persian reconquest of Phoenicia and Egypt (ch.43-51) and Philip's siege of Perinthus (ch.74-6) are described in so much detail that source abridgment must be minimal. Such passages are invaluable, but there is a price to be paid for their inclusion: they can only be accommodated in such a work by the exclusion of other material no less significant.

Such omissions would not adversely affect the value of the book if only material of lesser historical importance were selected for excision, but unfortunately Diodorus' criteria for selectivity are not always those of the modern historian. He is not particularly interested in diplomatic negotiations or constitutional settlements, which contain little in the way of human interest or stories for the moral edification of the reader. Consequently such crucial events as the signing of the Peace of Philocrates in 347/6 and the establishment and constitution of the League of Corinth in 338/7 were dispensable, even though his reference at 89.3 to the common synedrion of the Greeks is unintelligible to the reader who has no information on the League's formation. In like manner Diodorus begins to lose interest in what was for him the interminable series of campaigns of the Third Sacred War by the time he gets around to narrating the events of 351/0, which he contents himself by describing in one sentence:

> The Boeotians and the Phocians continued to skirmish and raid one another's territory , but no activities worthy of mention took place in the course of this year. (40.2)

Even worse is his narrative of the three following campaigning years, which are telescoped together in one chapter with no attempt to separate the events of each of the campaigning seasons (see my note on 56.1 in the Commentary). It is perhaps the need for drastic condensation that leads him to record nothing of the events of the Greek mainland for the archon years 350/49 and 339/8, though it is also possible that the omissions were due to carelessness and caused by his total absorption in simultaneous events elsewhere (in the former instance by the Persian reconquest of Egypt and in the latter by particulars of Timoleon's settlement of Sicily. The omission of the events on the mainland for the year 339/8 is particularly serious, since Diodorus provides us with no account of the outbreak of the Fourth Sacred War, and his transition from the (unhistorical) conclusion of peace between Philip and the Athenians in 340/39 (77.3) to Philip's seizure of Elatea in 339/8 (84.2) is sudden, unmotivated and, as it stands in Diodorus' narrative, incomprehensible. Lack of interest or the need for compression may also lie behind the summary accounts of the fighting in Euboea in 358/7 between the Boeotians and Athenians (7.2) and of Philip's Illyrian War of 356/5 (22.3).

The sacrifice of such important material is achieved in order to find sufficient space for the inclusion of items which, though historically insignificant, for one reason or another aroused Diodorus' interest, such as the totally unhistorical account of the origins of the Delphic oracle (ch. 26), the edifying tale of Tennes the king of Sidon who paid the penalty for his treachery (ch. 45), the anecdote of Dionysius of Syracuse and Athenian impiety (ch. 57), the fate of the sacrilegious Phocians (ch. 61-4) and anecdotes such as the tale of Satyrus, illustrative of Philip's generosity (ch. 55), the chastening by Demades of the drunken Philip (ch. 87), and the sensational story of the indignities suffered by Pausanias, Philip's assassin (ch. 93-4). It is easy to deplore Diodorus' lack of discrimination in his choice of material, but this would be to judge him by our standards rather than by his own.

3. Diodorus' Chronological Scheme

The chronological scheme followed by Diodorus for his synchronisation of Athenian archontic and Roman consular years differed from the traditional ('Varronian') scheme drawn up in the first century B.C. and regularly used by chronographers thereafter. In fact the consuls whom Diodorus equates with most of the Athenian archons in Book Sixteen are those who under the 'Varronian' system held office some 3-4 years earlier. Thus at 2.1 he synchronises the archon of 360/59 with the consuls whom the Varronian scheme dated to 363, and, at the end of the book, the archon of 336/5 with the consuls traditionally dated to 339. This three year discrepancy is maintained throughout the book except at 66.1, where a transposition in Diodorus' consular list has produced a synchronisation between the archon of 345/4 with the consuls of 345. The three year gap in synchronisation that occurs elsewhere in the book is not due to carelessness on his part, but to his use of a Roman chronological tradition that was different from, but not necessarily superior to the Varronian scheme which eventually came to supersede it. It is clear from Polybius 1.6.1 that the capture of Rome by the Gauls, which Varronian chronology dates to 390, actually took place in 387/6, the archon year under which it is recorded by Diodorus (14.11.5-6). The existence of more than one chronological system indicates some confusion in the list of Roman magistrates transmitted from the early republic to later times, and various devices were resorted to in order to regulate it, such as the belief that there was a five year period when there were no curule magistrates (Livy 6.35.10) or the postulation of so-called 'dictator years', for which the *Fasti Capitolini* record the existence of *dictatores sine consule* (dictators without a consul).

4. The Sources of Diodorus in the Sixteenth Book

Among the many claims made by Diodorus in his Preface is his undertaking, as a preliminary to writing his *Library*, of a period of study lasting thirty years. If true, it would imply familiarity with a vast range of authors. Unfortunately neither in the Preface nor elsewhere in the text does he provide a systematic list of sources or any discussion of how he may have handled them. He does however refer by name in the course of his narrative to a large number of earlier writers, including Cleitarchus, Ctesias, Dionysius Scytobrachion, Ephorus, Euhemerus, Hecataeus of Abdera, Megasthenes, Poseidonius and Timaeus, without any indication of the extent of his debt. As with most ancient historians, he tends to refer to a predecessor by name as his authority only for some small detail, without revealing how much of the immediate context derives from that same source. Occasionally two sources are cited in instances of major disagreement (e.g. Ephorus and Timaeus for Sicilian matters at 13.54.5, 13.60.5, 13.80.5, 13.109.2, 14.54.5, 20.89.5). For most of the time however Diodorus acknowledges no indebtedness to any source at all, but, given the vast range of subject matter embraced within his work, the number of writers consulted by him must have been large, though perhaps not quite so large as he would have us believe.

Diodorus also inserts from time to time information on the historians who have written on specific periods, including the number of books into which their work was divided, together with starting and terminal points. Such passages occur at 11.37.6, 12.37.2, 13.42.5, 13.103.3, 14.46.6, 14.87.7, 14.117.8, 15.37.3, 15.60.6, 15.89.3, 15.94.4, 15.95.4, 16.3.8, 16.14.3-5, 16.71.3, 16.76.5 and 21.5: the historians mentioned are Herodotus, Thucydides, Antiochus, Ctesias, Xenophon, Theopompus, Philistus, Callisthenes, Hermias, Duris, Anaximenes, Athanas, Dionysodorus, Anaxis, Ephorus, Demophilus, Diyllus and Psaon. Some historians include these writers among Diodorus' sources, and indeed a few of them, such as Ctesias and Ephorus, really did serve him as authorities. However it is unlikely that he read every single one of these eighteen writers, nor does he make any claim to have done so. In fact his account of the period covered by the extant historians Herodotus, Thucydides and Xenophon is so different from theirs that he cannot possibly have used them to any meaningful extent. In my view he may have included them for the benefit of those of his readers who wanted information beyond what he himself saw fit to supply: in other words the passages were intended to fulfil the function of a modern guide to further reading and inserted at the most appropriate point as an aid to the reader. The information he may have gathered himself from a cursory perusal of the relevant texts or may have been taken over from the chronological handbook of Apollodorus of Athens whom he cites specifically for the information on non-historical literary authors that appears at 13.105.4-5 and 108.1. The same source may also lie behind the dates he cites at 11.26.8 for the *floruit* of Pindar, at 14.46.6 for the *floruit* of the poets Philoxenus, Timotheus, Telestes and Polyeidus and at 15.71.4 for that of Isocrates, Aristotle, Anaximenes, Plato, Xenophon, Aristippus and Aeschines the Socratic.

Both in Book Sixteen and elsewhere, this same Apollodorus of Athens, whose versified chronological tables (*Chronike Syntaxis*) covered the period from the fall of Troy to 144 B.C., provided Diodorus with his chronological framework (perhaps including the names of the Athenian archons, Roman consuls and winners of the footrace at Olympia, by which he regularly

9

introduces his account of the events of each year), as well as with the frequent brief statements he makes on matters such as the outbreak and end of wars (e.g. 16.45.8 and 69.1), the foundation of new cities (e.g. 16.3.7) and the death and accession to power of kings and other rulers (e.g.16.31.6, 36.2, 46.7, 52.10, 69.2, 72.1, 74.2, 90.2). Such passages are usually to be found at the beginning of Diodorus' account of the events of the archon year, though occasionally they occur at the end (e.g. 16.3.7, 31.6, 36.2). In addition to the two passages from Book Thirteen already cited in the previous paragraph, Diodorus also names Apollodorus as a source at 1.5.1.

Occasionally Diodorus fails to integrate the material from his handbook with that derived from his main narrative source, as at chapter 31.6, where he makes a brief mention (from the handbook) of Philip's capture of Methone under the year 354/3, only to repeat the statement, this time from his historical source, at 35.4-5, among the events of 353/2. Similarly at 34.3 (from the handbook?) he mentions under the archon year 353/2 the battle fought between the Argives and Spartans near Orneae, then describes the same event in much greater detail, presumably from his principal historical source, at 39.1-7, where he dates it among the events of 352/1. In like manner at 31.6, under the year 354/3, he takes out of context and notes briefly, probably echoing an entry in his handbook, Philip's capture of Pagasae, which surely belongs to the campaign he fought against Lycophron of Pherae, narrated in chapter 35 under the archon year 353/2.

In the matter of Diodorus' use of sources for the narrative portions of his work, scholars disagree on whether he followed one single source slavishly for lengthy passages or sought to supplement his principal authority with information drawn from one or more secondary writers. Was he so lacking in originality that he amounted to little more than a copyist or an epitomator, or did he seek to compare one source with another when he had reason to question one authority's accuracy or veracity? For his Sicilian narrative in Books 13 and 14 it is clear that he consulted both the fourth century universal historian Ephorus of Cumae and Timaeus of Tauromenium, the third century writer on Sicily and Magna Graecia, since he notes discrepancies between them at 13.45.4, 60.5, 80.5 and at 14.54.5-6. However in his corresponding narrative of the events of the Greek mainland, the only authority cited is Ephorus (e.g. 12.41.1, 13.41.3, 14.22.2, 15.60.5): Timaeus wrote only on the west, and there is no indication that Diodorus actively sought a second source on Greece with which to compare him.

Diodorus manifestly admired Ephorus, whose work he assesses favourably at 5.1-4:

> Ephorus the universal historian achieved success not only in his style of composition but also in the arrangement of his work. For he has constructed each of his books in such a way as to embrace

events topic by topic. Therefore we too, since we prefer this kind of treatment, adhere to the best of our ability to the same plan.

Such praise does not prevent Diodorus from attacking Ephorus' account of Egypt for inaccuracy and falsehood, which he seeks to correct from personal autopsy (1.39.4-13):

> He attempts to argue from probability but he is seen to have by no means hit upon the truth.... This writer seems to us not only not to have witnessed the character of the places in Egypt, but not even to have carefully interrogated those who have knowledge of the situation in this land.... Under no circumstances would one look for accuracy in Ephorus when he sees that in many topics he shows scant regard for the truth.

However if Diodorus could not resist the temptation to parade his knowledge of the country with which he can claim some personal familiarity, he realised that Ephorus' understanding of the Greek world was superior to his own. The extent of his debt to Ephorus can be determined from a study of his account of Cimon's campaigns in Cyprus and of the Eurymedon at 11.59-61, which can be compared directly with a mutilated papyrus fragment of Ephorus' *History* (Ephorus Fragment 191, Jacoby). In this passage he follows Ephorus' narrative closely, even to the extent of taking over some of the phraseology of the original. Though too sweeping a generalisation should not be made about Diodorus' method of work on the evidence of such a short passage, it is at least suggestive.

Even if there is disagreement on how far, if at all, Diodorus used other sources, it is widely accepted that Ephorus was his principal authority for the historical section of the narrative of events on the Greek mainland from Book 11 down to and including Book 16. But unfortunately for Diodorus, Ephorus' account of the reign of Philip was incomplete. Since Ephorus wrote topic by topic (see Diodorus 5.1.1ff, cited in the previous paragraph), not annalistically, his stopping point varied from one geographical area to another. For events in mainland Greece, death terminated his narrative at 357/6, just before the outbreak of the Third Sacred War (16.14.3). However his son Demophilus wrote an account of the Sacred War which he published along with at least some of the 29 books into which his father's work was divided, as a supplementary Book 30 (Athenaeus 6.232D). Ephorus's work did include events contemporary with the reign of Philip that occurred in areas outside Greece, including Macedonia (Frag. 217), Thrace and Illyria (Frags. 87, 88), Italy (Frag. 42) and Sicily (Frag. 220-1), and Diodorus himself states (16.76.5) that it terminated with the siege of Perinthus in 340. Thus for the events of Macedonia, Thrace, Sicily and Italy, Diodorus had Ephorus'

History before him as he wrote, but for his Greek narrative from chapter 23 onwards, Ephorus was useless. For the first time in this decad of his work he had to look elsewhere for the bulk of his material. There is perhaps a note of irritation with Ephorus in his preface to Book 16, where he insists that historians should include actions that are self-contained from beginning to end and complains of works that are only half complete (16.1.1-2).

It is more than likely that the incomplete condition of Ephorus' *History* for this period obliged Diodorus, as a preliminary to writing Book 16, to consult other sources more frequently than was his wont in Books 11-15, and that he retained some memory of them even when he was recording events that Ephorus did mention. This seems to be the most probable explanation for the discrepancy between 16.2.2, where Philip is said to have been delivered by his father Amyntas to the Illyrians, who in turn handed him over to the Thebans, and 15.67.4 (probably from Ephorus), where he is given directly into the hands of the Thebans by his brother Alexander.

For his account of the Sacred War Diodorus probably had before him the monograph of Demophilus, which was included in the published text of Ephorus, but for his narrative of events in Greece in the last years of Philip's reign, another source was needed. Diodorus provides no hint of his authorities for these events (or indeed for any of those narrated in Books 17-20), but we know of two historians whose works covered the relevant period. The more popular of these, Duris of Samos (c.330-260), chronicled events from 370/69 (Diod. 15.60.6) till at least 281 (Frag. 55) in his *Makedonika*: in addition, his *History of Agathocles* is specifically cited as a source by Diodorus in Book 21.6.

The *Makedonika* was postulated by A.Momigliano (*Le fonti della storia greca e macedone nel libro XVI di Diodoro*, Rendiconti dell' Instituto Lombardo 65, 1932, pp. 523-43) as the source of the anecdotes that appear in chapters 55, 84-5, 87-8 and 92). Arguments for much wider use of Duris are offered by M.M.Markle in his article *Diodorus' Sources for the Sacred War* in I.Worthington (ed.), *Ventures into Greek History*, Oxford, 1994, pp. 43-69. Markle detects two distinct sources for the Sacred War narrative, one used in chapters 23-9, 56 and 58-60, the other in 30-9, 57 and 61-4. The former is seen as objective and unbiased, essentially favourable to Philomelus, sympathetic to the Phocians and realistic in its appraisal of Philip's motives for involvement, while the other is characterised by a religious fervour that manifests itself in an idealistic view of Philip's motives and in a marked bias against Philomelus and the Phocians. The former source he identifies, probably rightly, with Demophilus, the latter with either Theopompus or Duris or a combination of both (whether consulted independently or through the incorporation by Duris of material drawn from Theopompus). To my mind the rhetorical style and censorious manner of Theopompus are so strong that his influence would still be apparent in

Diodorus' text, were he a direct authority, and if Markle is correct in postulating the existence of a more biased source, an identification with Duris is more credible. Unfortunately what remains of Duris tells us nothing of his perception of Philip or his character, the single relevant fragment revealing only a taste for luxurious living that led him to keep a gold cup weighing fifty drachmas under his pillow (Fragment 37). On the other hand, in the course of a detailed examination of what remains of the work, R.B.Kebric (*In the Shadow of Macedon: Duris of Samos*, Historia, Einzelschrift 29, 1977) arrives (p. 66) at the following conclusion: 'whatever use Diodorus made of Duris (direct or indirect), it could only have been slight, and he was, at best, a minor source for Greek and Macedonian affairs.

The second historian who wrote on this period was a contemporary of Duris, Diyllus of Athens, whose First *Syntaxis* began with the outbreak of the Third Sacred War (Diod. 16.14.5), and whose Second *Syntaxis* had as its starting point the end of Ephorus' *History* at 341/0 (Diod. 16.76.6). As an alternative to Duris, Markle is perhaps unnecessarily dismissive of Diyllus' claim to be a source for Diodorus. As a continuer of Ephorus' *History*, he was an obvious choice, and, though too little remains of Diyllus to constitute proof, N.G.L.Hammond (*The Sources of Diodorus XVI, I*, CQ 31, 1937, pp. 79-91) has made out a strong case for regarding Diyllus rather than Duris as Diodorus' principal source for Greece and Macedonia in the parts of Book 16 not covered by Ephorus/Demophilus. In particular he notes the inconsistency between Diodorus' essentially favourable attitude to Philip and the markedly hostile portrait to be found in the later chapters of the book, with its emphasis on his bribery (ch. 54) and inebriation (87.1), as well as the admiration expressed both for Athenians in general and for Demosthenes in particular (54.2, 84.5). Moreover an Athenian source is likely for the series of anecdotes in which Athenian citizens figure prominently (e.g. the actors Satyrus (ch. 55) and Neoptolemus (ch. 92) and for the impressive knowledge of Attic orators (chapters 84, 87 and 88) which Diodorus does not display elsewhere. In such passages, Diyllus is no less plausible a source than Duris, and in the light of the surviving evidence, a final decision is impossible.

If correctly identified, Diodorus' sources for the activities of Philip are primarily Ephorus, Demophilus and Diyllus (or Duris). It is also probable that, for the first time in the historical part of his narrative of events of mainland Greece, he was obliged to move around from source to source, as he switched to and from Ephorus and back again. It appears to be the frequent change of source that is responsible for the scrappy, even disjointed nature of the book. In his account of the Third Sacred War, by far the most muddled and least successful portion of Book 16, he has difficulty in the simultaneous manipulation of his two sources, Demophilus and Diyllus (or Duris). The chronology is thoroughly confused: he gives three different estimates for the length of the war (11 years at 14.3; 9 years at 23.1 and 10 years at 59.1), while dating the outbreak to 355/4 (ch. 23) and its end to 346/5 (ch. 59). It is clear from a combination of Aeschines 2.131 and 3.148 with Demosthenes 19.39 that the war lasted ten years from 357/6 till 347/6. Diodorus' inability to handle two sources simultaneously is also shown by his inclusion of two distinct narratives of the outbreak of the war. Chapters 23-5 and 28-9 cover much the same ground: both relate the imposition of the Amphictyonic fine on the Phocians, who refuse to pay, the enrolment of mercenaries by Philomelus, the seizure of the oracle, the involvement of the Boeotians and the defeat of a Locrian invasion by Philomelus, while 29.1 repeats the catalogue of allies of the two belligerents already given at 27.5. An imperfect assimilation of the narratives of Demophilus and Diyllus (or Duris) is the most satisfactory explanation for the confusion.

5. Diodorus' Portrait of Philip

In Diodorus' opinion, Philip deserved the highest praise for his achievement in raising Macedonia from the status of an insignificant state to the hegemony of Greece (1.3; 8.7; 95.2): this success he ascribes to Philip's military reforms (3.1-2), his skill in increasing the economic wealth of the kingdom (8.6-7) and, above all, to his personal qualities, amongst which Diodorus picks out for mention excellent generalship (60.4), diplomatic skill (1.3, 95.3-4), brilliance of personality (1.6) and possession of a whole series of virtues, including *arete* ('courage' or , more generally, 'ability', 1.4; 1.6), piety (1.4, 60.4, 64.3), *philanthropia* (8.2, 8.5, 95.2), and *philophrosyne* ('affability' or 'cordiality', 1.3, 60.4, 89.2, 91.6, 95.2), all in all providing a combination which won him the support of both gods and men. To Diodorus, Philip's piety was perfectly genuine, and there is no hint that he may have championed Apollo against the sacrilegious Phocians for purely political motives. It is also fully in accord with Diodorus' religious convictions that the hegemony of Greece should have been conferred on him by the gods as a reward (64.3).

The combination of virtues inherent in the Philip depicted by Diodorus marks him out as being in a sense a second Epaminondas, his alleged fellow student in Pythagorean studies (2.3). The similarity in character of the two men is never made explicit, but is implied by the attribution to both men of the same good qualities: like Philip, Epaminondas possessed *arete* (15.39.3, 15.50.6, 15.63.4, 15.88.4), military shrewdness (15.52.7, 15.63.4, 15.88.1), brilliance of personality (15.88.4) and *philanthropia* (15.57.1). Diodorus was not the only writer to compare the two men. Plutarch (*Pelopidas* 26.5) also detected a similarity, though for him the comparision is rather one of contrast: Epaminondas, in his view, was far superior in possessing the additional virtues of moderation, justice, magnanimity and clemency which Philip totally lacked. The flaws in Philip's character which are mentioned by Plutarch do not appear in Diodorus, whose portrait is essentially favourable, though not uncritical. He is aware of the stories illustrative of Philip's drunkenness (e.g. 55.2), and at 87.1-2 recounts the anecdote of Demades' apposite comparision of the king to the buffoon Thersites. There are also hints of disapproval at the elevation of Philip's statue to the level of those of the Twelve Gods (95.1). Above all Diodorus makes several references to Philip's use of bribery to build up support in Greece (8.7, 53.3, 54.3-4, 55.4). Some of the inconsistencies are to be ascribed to the influence of his source material: on Markle's interpretation of the Sacred War narrative, he combined items from a source who treated Philip idealistically (Duris?) with others from a more critical writer (Demophilus?). It may not be entirely fortuitous that most of the emphasis on Philip's defects occurs in the second half of the book, where Diodorus was particularly indebted to a non-Ephoran source, whether Duris or Diyllus. Yet his source did not invent these defects: stories of Philip's bribery go back to Demosthenes, who tends to see all political leaders less anti-Macedonian than himself as Philip's hirelings (e.g. 6.34; 9.60; 18.19, 21, 36, 41, 46, 52, 61, 149, 175, 247, 284, 297; 19.28, 110, 118, 119, 139-40, 142, 145, 166-8, 178, 231, 243, 254, 259-61, 265, 292-3), and, though Demosthenes does describe the debauchery characteristic of the Macedonian court (2.18-9), stories of Philip's drunkenness were first put into general circulation by Theopompus, whose *Historiae Philippicae* established the definitive portrait of the king, and who personally witnessed this debauchery on the occasion of his visit to Philip's court in the winter of 343/2 (*FGH* 115, Jacoby, Test. 7). Theopompus was something of a puritan, who saw social decay and corruption at the heart of the contemporary world. Of the many symptoms of this decay none seems to have appalled him more than addiction to wine, of which he accuses so many of the peoples and individuals of whom he writes, including the Illyrians (Frag. 39), Thessalians (Frags 49 and 162), Byzantines (Frag. 62), Athenians (Frag. 213), Methymnaeans (Frag. 227), Tarentines (Frag. 233), Cotys of Thrace (Frag. 31), Agathocles of Thessaly (Frag. 81), Eubulus (Frag. 100), Chabrias (Frag. 105), Straton of Sidon (Frag. 114), Dionysius the Elder (Frag. 134), Charidemus (Frag. 143), the brothers Apollocrates, Hipparinus, Nysaeus and the Younger Dionysius (Frags. 185, 186, 188, 283) and Timolaus of Thebes (Frag. 210). It is not surprising either that Philip should make an appearance among this company of alcoholics (Frags. 27, 162, 163, 236, 282), or indeed that Theopompus should denounce the licentiousness of his court (Frags. 224-5) in a passage which Polybius censures (8.11.2) for exceeding the bounds of propriety. Such was the influence of Theopompus on later historiography that his portrait of Philip will have been sufficiently familiar even to writers who used him only indirectly, if at all, and the unfavourable side of Philip's character that is discernible in Diodorus need not necessarily owe everything to Diyllus or Duris. Of Philip's womanising, a major vice according to authorities such as Theopompus (Frag. 27), Satyrus (Frag. 5) and Justin (9.8.3), there is no trace in Diodorus, whose portrait is, of those that survive, easily the most sympathetic.

6. Inaccuracies in Diodorus 16

Book 16, like the other books in Diodorus' *Library of History*, is marred by a large number of errors of various kinds, which will be pointed out in the notes to the individual chapters. Many of them are caused by his inability to amalgamate harmoniously material derived from different sources into a well integrated whole. Others are the result of a failure to reconcile Ephorus' thematic treatment of his subject matter with his own annalistic scheme, while yet others are less excusable and seem to be caused by Diodorus' own ignorance or carelessness: at least some of the contradictions and inconsistencies which mar the narrative could have been avoided by a more careful check on what had already been committed to writing. Some inaccuracies I have already mentioned: others will be noted at the appropriate place in the commentary. What I give here is but a representative selection of some of the more interesting types of error to illustrate the fallibility of the writer.

Geographical ignorance is discernible in Diodorus' belief that Chalcidice is near the Hellespont (53.2) and that the major naval engagement of the Social War was fought in the Hellespont rather than off the coast of Erythrae (21.3). His poor grasp of family relationships may be seen at 56.5, where he makes Philomelus rather than Phayllus the brother of Onomarchus, and at 93.9, where Attalus is said to be the nephew rather than the uncle of Cleopatra. Factual errors include 72.1, where Diodorus records the death in 342/1 of Arybbas the Molossian, who was merely expelled from his throne, and 86.22, where the Athenians assign one wing at Chaeronea to the Boeotians and the other to themselves, though it was actually the Boeotians who exercised command of the coalition forces by land. At 77.3 Philip makes peace with the Athenians after the siege of Byzantium, when his siege actually drove the Athenians to war. At 2.2-3 Philip is handed over to the Illyrians as a hostage by his father and delivered by them to the Thebans, who entrust him to Epaminondas' father, when in fact he was handed over to the Thebans either by his brother Alexander II or by the regent Ptolemy and placed in the house of Pammenes. At 38.6 he states that the Third Sacred War was kindled by Onomarchus, apparently oblivious of his earlier statement (23.1) assigning that role to Philomelus.

Many of the mistakes are chronological, of which only a few examples are cited here. At 16.7 he dates the outbreak of the fighting in Euboea to 358/7 instead of 357/6, and contradicts himself on the duration of the Social War (three years at 7.3, but four years at 22.2). The length of the reign of Agis III of Sparta is given as fifteen years at 63.2, but nine years both at 88.4 and at 17.63.4. The twelve year period during which Lycurgus was in charge of the finances of Athens is said at 88.1 to have come to an end in 338/7, when in fact it did not even begin till the following year. Most serious of all is the predating of the Persian recovery of Phoenicia and Egypt (actual date 344-3) to the year 351/0 (chapters 40-51).

From the above examples it can be seen that there are many inaccuracies in the narrative which we can correct from other sources. At the same time for much of the information he records, he is our sole authority, and there are no alternative sources to serve as correctives. Yet for all his unreliability Diodorus preserves the only surviving narrative in Greek covering the reign of Philip, and, but for him, the king would be, given the paucity of the extent material, an even more obscure figure than he already is. The Sixteenth Book of Diodorus is, for all its faults, of inestimable value to students both of the king himself and of the events of his reign.

The Library of History of Diodorus of Sicily

Book Sixteen

1.1 In all historical expositions it is proper that historians should include in their books the actions of cities or of kings that are self-contained from beginning to end, for in this way I am of the opinion that history will be easy to remember and clear to my readers. **2** For events that are only half complete and do not have an ending that is linked to the beginning interrupt the concentration of attentive readers, but self-contained actions succeed in achieving an exposition of events that is complete in itself. Whenever the very nature of events cooperates with the historian, he above all must in no way depart from this principle. **3** For this reason I too, now that I have reached the deeds of Philip son of Amyntas, shall attempt to include the exploits of this king within the present book. For he ruled as king of Macedonia for twenty four years and from the most humble of beginnings he established his kingdom as the greatest of the powers of Europe, and, inheriting a Macedonia that was a slave to the Illyrians, he made her ruler of many tribes and cities. **4** And because of his own abilities he received the hegemony of the whole of Greece from the cities which willingly submitted to him. Moreover, having subdued those who had sacked the sanctuary at Delphi and come to the assistance of the oracle, he became a member of the Council of the Amphictyons, and, thanks to his piety towards the gods, he received as his reward the votes of the Phocians whom he had defeated. **5** And when he had subdued the Illyrians, Paeonians, Thracians, Scythians and all the tribes who were neighbours of these, he applied himself to overthrowing the Persian supremacy, and, once he had conveyed forces across to Asia, he sought to free the Greek cities. Though he was cut off by Fate, he nevertheless left behind forces so great that his son Alexander had no need of any additional allies when he came to dissolve the Persian Empire. **6** Nor did he accomplish these deeds through the indulgence of Fortune but rather by his own excellence. For this king was outstanding for the shrewdness of his leadership, for his valour and for the brilliance of his personality. But in order not to anticipate his exploits in my preface, I shall go back briefly in time and resume the continuity of my narrative.

The Events of the Archon Year 360/59

2. 1 In the archonship of Callimedes at Athens, the one hundred and fifth Olympiad was celebrated, at which Porus of Cyrene won the footrace and the Romans elected to the consulship Gnaeus Genucius and Lucius Aemilius. While they were in office, Philip, the son of Amyntas and father of the Alexander who subjugated the Persians, took over the kingdom of the Macedonians. The circumstances of his accession were as follows. **2** When Amyntas had been vanquished by the Illyrians and compelled to pay tribute to the victors, the Illyrians took his youngest son Philip as a hostage and entrusted him to the Thebans. They in turn handed him over to the father of Epaminondas and instructed him to take attentive care of the youth and to supervise his training and education. **3** Since Epaminondas had a Pythagorean philosopher as his tutor, Philip, who was reared along with him, shared in his detailed study of Pythagorean philosophy. Since both students brought their natural aptitude and industry to bear, each proved himself to be outstanding in ability. Of the two, Epaminondas endured great trials and dangers and, contrary to expectation, bestowed upon his native city the leadership of Greece, while Philip, who made use of the same educational foundation, proved himself in no way inferior to the fame of Epaminondas. **4** For, after the death of Amyntas, Alexander, the eldest of his sons, succeeded to the kingdom but was killed by Ptolemy of Alorus who took over the kingdom. In like manner Ptolemy was removed by Perdiccas who became king in turn. But when he was worsted by the Illyrians in a pitched battle and lost his life, his brother Philip, who had fled from detention, took over the kingdom which was now in a sorry state. **5** For in the battle more than four thousand Macedonians had been killed, and the remainder, struck with panic, were thoroughly terrified of the Illyrian armies and had no enthusiasm for prosecuting the war. **6** About the same time the Paeonians, who lived close to Macedonia, began to devastate their land out of contempt for the Macedonians, and the Illyrians, gathering large forces, were making preparations for an invasion of Macedonia. Moreover a certain Pausanias, who was of royal lineage, was planning to return to the Macedonian kingdom with the support of the Thracian king, and in like manner the Athenians, who were on bad terms with Philip, were seeking to restore Argaeus to the throne and had dispatched Mantias as general with three thousand hoplites and a naval force of some size.

3.1 Because of the disaster suffered in the battle and the extent of the peril threatening them, the Macedonians were reduced to the greatest despair. Nevertheless though they were encompassed by terrors and hazards of such magnitude, Philip was not alarmed at the extent of the expected

danger but, assembling the Macedonians in successive meetings and stimu-
lating their valour by skillful addresses, he renewed their confidence. In
addition, having reformed the military formations for the better and provided
his troops with the appropriate weapons of war, he held constant manoeuvres
under arms as well as competitive exercises. **2** Moreover he devised both
the close array of the phalanx and its equipment, modelling it on the close
shield formation of the heroes at Troy, and was the first to organise the
Macedonian phalanx. **3** In his conversation he was gracious and sought
by means of gifts and promises to inspire the fullest amount of goodwill in
large numbers of people, while at the same time shrewdly contriving to
neutralise the mass of dangers which were looming over them. For when he
perceived that the Athenians were directing all their ambition towards the
recovery of Amphipolis and were for this reason seeking to bring back
Argaeus as king, he withdrew of his own accord from the city and left
it independent. **4** Next he opened up negotiations with the Paeonians,
and, having corrupted some with bribes and others with generous promises,
he made an agreement with them to remain at peace for the time being.
Likewise he induced by presents the king who was intending to restore
Pausanias and so thwarted his return. **5** Mantias the Athenian general, who
had sailed into Methone, stayed there himself, while dispatching Argaeus with
mercenaries to Aegae. When Argaeus approached the city, he proceeded to call
upon the citizens of Aegae to welcome his return and to become the founders of
his kingship. **6** However, since nobody paid any attention to him, he
returned to Methone. When Philip appeared on the scene with his troops, he
joined battle with the mercenaries and killed many of them. The remainder,
who had taken refuge on a hill, he let go under truce, but received from them
the exiles whom they surrendered to him. As a result of his victory in this first
battle Philip made the Macedonians more confident in facing subsequent
conflicts. **7** While these events were taking place, the Thasians founded the
place called Crenides, which later the king named Philippi after himself and filled
with settlers. **8** Among the historians Theopompus of Chios started his
Histories of Philip at this point and wrote fifty eight books of which five
have perished.

The Events of the Archon Year 359/8

4.1 In the archonship at Athens of Eucharistus, the Romans appointed as
consuls Quintus Servilius and Quintus Genucius. While they were in office
Philip sent envoys to Athens and persuaded the people to make peace with
him now that he was no longer laying claim to Amphipolis. **2** Free of the
war with the Athenians and learning that Agis the king of the Paeonians had
died, he believed that he had an opportunity for attacking the Paeonians.
Marching therefore into Paeonia and defeating the barbarians in battle, he
compelled the tribe to obey the Macedonians. **3** Because the Illyrians still

remained hostile, he was eager to subdue them also. Therefore, as soon as he had called an assembly and with appropriate words urged his troops to war, he marched against the land of the Illyrians with no fewer than ten thousand foot soldiers and six hundred cavalry. **4** Bardylis, the Illyrian king, on being apprised of the enemy presence, immediately dispatched ambassadors concerning a settlement on terms that allowed both parties to remain masters of the cities which they at that time controlled. But when Philip said that though he wanted peace he would not agree to this unless the Illyrians withdrew from all the Macedonian cities, the ambassadors returned without achieving any result. Bardylis, putting his trust in his previous victories and in Illyrian courage, proceeded to meet the enemy with his forces, which consisted of ten thousand picked infantrymen and about five hundred cavalry. **5** When the armies drew near to one another and met with loud shouting, Philip, who directed the right wing and the pick of the Macedonians involved in the conflict, ordered his cavalry to ride past the enemy and attack them on the flank, while he himself assailed the enemy in the front and brought on a fierce struggle. **6** The Illyrians, forming themselves into a square, threw themselves into the engagement with all their might. At first the battle was equally balanced for a long time because of the surpassing valour of both sides, and, while many were being killed and still more wounded, the battle inclined first one way and then the other, as the bravery of the contestants caused the outcome to oscillate backwards and forwards. But later, as the cavalry forced their way onwards both from the flank and from the rear with Philip fighting heroically alongside the best of his troops, the bulk of the Illyrians were obliged to take to flight. **7** After pursuing them over a large amount of territory in the course of which many were slain, Philip recalled the Macedonians by means of a trumpet signal and, setting up a trophy, buried those on his own side who had fallen. The Illyrians, sending envoys, withdrew from all the Macedonian cities and gained peace. More than seven thousand of the Illyrians were killed in the course of this battle.

The Events of the Archon Year 358/7

6.1 In the archonship of Cephisodotus at Athens the Romans chose as consuls Gaius Licinius and Gaius Sulpicius. While they were in office... .

7.2 Simultaneously with these events the inhabitants of Euboea became involved in strife with one another and war erupted throughout the island when some called in the Boeotians and others the Athenians. Now the Athenians, now the Thebans prevailed: no major pitched battles took place, but once the island had been destroyed by the civil war and many had been slain on both sides, they were with difficulty chastened by the disasters and, coming to an agreement, made peace with one another. **3** While the Boeotians went home and remained inactive, the Athenians, now that the Chians, Rhodians,

Coans and Byzantians had revolted, became involved in the so-called Social War, which lasted for three years. Electing Chares and Chabrias as generals, they sent them out with troops. These, on sailing against Chios, discovered that allies had arrived from the Byzantians, Rhodians and Coans, as well as from Mausolus the ruler of Caria. When they had drawn up their troops, they proceeded to besiege the city by land and by sea simultaneously. Chares, who commanded the infantry, approached the walls by land and engaged in a conflict with the men who poured out of the city to oppose him, while Chabrias, sailing up to the harbour, became involved in a violent sea battle and got into difficulties when his ship was rammed and shattered. 4 Though those on board the other ships retired while they still could and saved their lives, he, because he preferred a glorious death to defeat, was wounded in the struggle for his ship and perished.

8.1 At about the same time, Philip, king of the Macedonians, who had prevailed over the Illyrians in a great battle and subdued all who lived as far as the lake called Lychnitis, returned to Macedonia when he had concluded a memorable peace with the Illyrians and won great repute with the Macedonians because of the successes he had gained through his valour. 2 After this, since the inhabitants of Amphipolis were on bad terms with him and afforded him many opportunities for war, he took the field against them with a sizable force. Having applied siege engines to the walls and launched continuous and vigorous attacks, he knocked down part of the wall with his battering rams. Entering the city through the breach and slaying many, he won control of the city. He exiled those who were ill-disposed towards him but treated the remainder with lenience. 3 Since this city was well situated in relation to Thrace and the adjacent regions, it made no small contribution to the increase of Philip's power. He straightway reduced Pydna and concluded an alliance with the Olynthians, by the terms of which he agreed to secure for them Potidaea, a city which the Olynthians were particularly keen on controlling. 4 Because the Olynthians inhabited a significant city with a great deal of influence in war because of its large population, the city was repeatedly fought over by those who aspired to further aggrandisement. It was for this reason that the Athenians and Philip were in competition for the Olynthian alliance. 5 Despite this, when Philip reduced Potidaea, he brought the Athenian garrison out of the city and, treating them humanely, sent them back to Athens, since he was extremely respectful of the Athenian people because of the importance and reputation of their city. Having sold the citizens of Potidaea into slavery, he handed it over to the Olynthians and at the same time gave them in addition the properties in its territory. 6 After this he went to the city of Crenides and, increasing its population with a multitude of settlers, he changed its name to Philippi, naming it for himself. Then with regard to the gold mines in its territory which were wholly paltry and unimportant, by means of new equipment he augmented their production to such an extent that they were able to produce for him a revenue of more than one thousand talents. **7** When he had quickly accumulated revenue from these, he brought the Macedonian kingdom to the height of its supremacy thanks to the abundance of money, for, by striking a gold currency named Philippeioi after himself, he assembled a significant force of mercenaries and by this means induced many Greeks to become traitors to their cities. But details of these activities will be explained by the events themselves when narrated in the proper order, and I shall now move back my account to events as they successively occurred.

The Events of the Archon Year 357/6

9.1 While Agathocles held the archonship at Athens the Romans appointed as consuls Marcus Fabius and Gaius Poplius... .

14.1 In Greece Alexander the tyrant of Pherae was murdered by his own wife Thebe and her brothers Lycophron and Tisiphonus. These at first won much approbation as tyrannicides, but later they underwent a change, and, by corrupting the mercenaries with bribes, they revealed themselves as tyrants. They put to death many of those who were opposed to them and, by building up a significant armed body of support, they proceeded to maintain their rule by force. **2** Those among the Thessalians called the Aleuadae, who enjoyed a well publicised reputation because of their aristocratic lineage, began to set themselves up in opposition to the tyrants. But since they were not capable of fighting them on their own, they acquired as an ally Philip king of the Macedonians. He then entered Thessaly and, by overcoming the tyrants and regaining freedom for the cities, showed much goodwill to the Thessalians. Consequently in subsequent events not only Philip but also after him his son Alexander acquired them as confederates. **3** Of the historians Demophilus son of Ephorus the writer of histories compiled his work on what is known as the Sacred War, which had been omitted by his father, beginning with the seizure of the Delphic temple and the plundering of the oracle by Philomelus the Phocian. This war continued for eleven years till the destruction of those who had shared in the division of the sacred monies. **4** Callisthenes wrote a History of the Greek World in ten books, ending with the occupation of the temple and the sacrilege of Philomelus the Phocian. **5** And Diyllus of Athens began his work with the sacrilege and wrote twenty six books containing all the events which occurred in this period both in Greece and in Sicily.

The Events of the Archon Year 356/5

15.1 In the archonship of Elpines at Athens the Romans elected as consuls Marcus Poplius Laenates and Gnaeus Mamilius Imperiosus, and the one hundred and sixth Olympiad was celebrated at which Porus of Malis won the footrace... .

21.1 In Greece the Chians, Rhodians, Coans and Byzantians were waging the Social War against the Athenians. Both sides were making great preparations, since they wanted to determine the war by a battle at sea. The Athenians had previously dispatched Chares with sixty ships, and then, manning a further sixty and putting in command as generals the most renowned of their citizens, Iphicrates and Timotheus, they sent them out to continue, along with Chares, the war against their revolted allies. **2** The Chians, Rhodians and Byzantines together with their allies, manning one hundred ships, ravaged Imbros and Lemnos which were Athenian possessions and, sending a sizable force on an expedition to Samos, they devastated the countryside and proceeded to besiege the city by land and sea. They also committed acts of aggression against many other islands which were under Athenian control and collected money for the necessities of war. **3** All the Athenian generals gathered together and proposed initially to lay siege to the city of the Byzantians, but later, when the Chians and their allies abandoned the siege of Samos and directed their attention to assisting the Byzantians, all the forces met in the area of the Hellespont. But just when a naval battle was on the point of taking place, a violent wind fell upon them and frustrated their purpose. **4** Though Chares wanted to engage despite the natural conditions, Iphicrates and Timotheus opposed him because of the roughness of the sea. Calling upon his troops as witnesses, Chares misrepresented his fellow generals as traitors and wrote about them to the people of Athens, accusing them of having deliberately avoided the battle at sea. The enraged Athenians accordingly brought Iphicrates and Timotheus to trial, fined them a large sum of talents and deposed them from the generalship.

22.1 Having taken over command of the entire fleet and eager to free the Athenians of the costs, Chares embarked upon an enterprise that was fraught with risk. For Artabazus, who had revolted from the King, was about to engage in battle, though he had only a few soldiers, with the satraps who had more than seventy thousand. Chares came to his aid with all his troops and defeated the King's army. Out of gratitude for his services, Artabazus gave him a large sum of money with which he was able to provision his entire force. **2** At first the Athenians approved of Chares' actions, but later, when the King sent envoys to bring accusations against Chares, they adopted the opposite viewpoint. For a story had been spread to the effect that the King had undertaken to wage war against the Athenians with three hundred ships on the side of their enemies. Accordingly the people, acting with discretion, resolved to terminate the war with their revolted allies. On learning that they too wanted peace, they had little difficulty in arriving at a settlement. The so-called Social War came to an end in this way, having lasted four years. 3 In Macedonia three kings combined against Philip, those of the Thracians, Paeonians and Illyrians. For because these had common borders with the Macedonians, they looked with suspicion on Philip's increasing power, but, since they had been defeated in the past and were by themselves no match for him, they reckoned that, if they made war in common, they would come out on top. Therefore, as they were still in the process of assembling their armies, he appeared on the scene while they were disorganised and, throwing them into a panic, compelled them to support the Macedonians.

The Events of the Archon Year 355/4

23.1 When Callistratus was archon at Athens, the Romans appointed to the consulship Marcus Fabius and Gaius Plotius. When they were in office, there broke out what was known as the Sacred War, which lasted nine years. For Philomelus the Phocian, an individual who surpassed his contemporaries in brazenness and lawlessness, occupied the shrine at Delphi and kindled the Sacred War for the following reasons. **2** When the Spartans fought against the Boeotians the war that culminated at Leuctra and were defeated, the Thebans brought a serious accusation against the Spartans before the Amphictyons for seizing the Cadmea and secured a condemnation which required them to pay a large sum of money in reparations. **3** So too the Phocians were prosecuted before the Amphictyons on the charge of having cultivated a large portion of the sacred ground called Cirrhaean and condemned to pay many talents. When they did not pay the fine, the Amphictyonic delegates proceeded to bring an accusation against the Phocians and asked the synod to consecrate the land of those who were defrauding the god unless the Phocians paid the money to the god. In like manner they stated that the other parties who had been condemned (including the Spartans) must pay the fine, and, if they refused to pay, they should incur the hatred of all the Greeks in common because of their depravity. **4** When the Greeks had ratified the decisions of the Amphictyons and the land of the Phocians was about to be consecrated, the people of his nation were addressed by Philomelus, who enjoyed the greatest reputation among the Phocians. He told them that they could not pay the money because of the vast amount of the fine and that to sit back and allow their land to be consecrated was not only spineless but would bring about the risk of ruin for the livelihood of everyone. **5** He also tried to prove to the best of his ability that the verdicts of the Amphictyons were unjust. For though only an extremely small portion of the land had been cultivated, they had imposed a really huge penalty. Accordingly he advised them to set aside the penalties and declared that the Phocians had strong grounds for defying the Amphictyons, since in ancient times they had held both the control and the guardianship of the oracle. As witness thereto, he offered Homer, the most ancient and greatest of the poets, who says:

> But Schedius and Epistrophus led the Phocians, who inhabited
> Cyparissus and rocky Pytho.

6 Therefore he said that they should lay claim to the guardianship of the oracle on the grounds that it belonged to them from the time of their ancestors and he promised that, if they made him general with full powers and complete authority for the entire enterprise, he would bring matters to a successful conclusion.

24.1 When the Phocians, in alarm at the condemnations, elected him general with full powers, he proceeded vigorously to implement his promise. First of all he went to Sparta, and held secret talks with Archidamus the Spartan king, in the course of which he maintained that Archidamus had as much of an interest as himself in invalidating the Amphictyonic judgments. For there were grave and unjust verdicts against the Spartans also. He also disclosed his determination to seize Delphi and to cancel the decisions of the Amphictyons, should he succeed in securing the guardianship of the sanctuary. 2 Though Archidamus gave his assent to all that had been discussed, he declined assistance for the time being, but said that he would cooperate in secret and supply both funds and mercenaries. Having received fifteen talents from Archidamus and added no less than this from his own resources, Philomelus hired mercenaries and selected one thousand Phocians whom he called peltasts. 3 When he had assembled a large number of soldiers, he seized the oracle, slaughtering those of the Delphians called Thracidae who were opposed to him and confiscating their property. Seeing that the others were panic-stricken, he urged them to be confident since they would not be endangered. 4 When reports reached them of the seizure of the oracle, the neighbouring Locrians immediately marched against Phocis, but in the ensuing battle fought in the vicinity of Delphi the Locrians were vanquished and, losing many of their troops, they fled to their own country. Since Philomelus was buoyed up by his victory, he chiselled the Amphictyonic decisions out of their slabs and obliterated the letters which recorded the condemnations. 5 In addition he personally disseminated a report that his intention was neither to loot the oracle nor to perpetrate any other illegal action, but that, in laying claim to the ancestral guardianship and because he was desirous of cancelling the unjust verdicts of the Amphictyons, he was maintaining the traditional laws of the Phocians.

25.1 The Boeotians, gathered together in assembly, voted to come to the assistance of the oracle and sent out troops forthwith. Meanwhile Philomelus surrounded the shrine with a wall and began to assemble large numbers of mercenaries whose wages he increased by half as much again. In addition, by picking out the best of the Phocians and registering their names, he quickly amassed a considerable army. For with no fewer than five thousand troops he took up his stance in front of Delphi, being by now an object of fear to those who wanted to go to war with him. **2** After this he marched into Locrian territory, and, having laid waste much of the enemy's land, he encamped near a river which flowed past a strongly fortified place. However, being unable to capture it after several assaults, he abandoned the siege, and engaged in a battle with the Locrians in which he lost twenty of his men. Since he was unable to gain possession of the bodies, he requested through the agency of a herald permission to recover them. To this the Locrians replied that they were refusing to allow the recovery in accordance with the universal practice of the Greeks which cast out temple robbers unburied. **3** Indignant at this development, Philomelus engaged the Locrians in battle and by dint of supreme effort slew some of the enemy. Having gained possession of their bodies, he obliged the Locrians to make an exchange of corpses. Now that he was in control of the open country he laid waste a large part of Locrian territory and, loading his troops with booty, returned to Delphi. After doing this, out of a desire to consult the oracle about the war, he forced the Pythia to mount the tripod and give the oracle.

26.1 Now that I have mentioned the tripod, I think it not inappropriate to relate the traditional story handed down about it from ancient times. For in the distant past the site of the oracle is said to have been discovered by goats, and it is for this reason that the Delphians continue to this very day to make consultations with a goat in particular. **2** They say that the discovery came about in the following way. There is a chasm at this place which is the site of what is now known as the innermost sanctuary, and, as goats used to graze in the vicinity because Delphi was as yet uninhabited, it also happened that, whenever a goat approached the chasm and stared at it, it would begin to gambol about in an astonishing fashion and to utter a sound unlike the bleats which it was in the habit of uttering. **3** The goatherd who was in charge of the animals was amazed at the curious turn of events and, drawing near to the chasm and looking down into it, underwent the very same experience as had befallen the goats. For they behaved like creatures possessed, and he began to predict future events. After this, when news of the phenomenon reached those living nearby, more and more turned up at the place, and since all of them put it to the test because of the strangeness of the experience, those who approached invariably became possessed. It is for this reason that the site came to be regarded as miraculous and looked upon accordingly as the seat of the Earth Goddess.   4 For a time all those wishing to seek predictions would approach the chasm and prophesy for one another, but afterwards, when many were jumping down into the chasm under the influence of inspired frenzy and disappeared from sight, those who resided in the vicinity of the place decided that, to avoid endangering anyone, they should appoint one woman to serve as prophetess for all, and that the uttering of prophecies should be done through her agency. For her a device was constructed which she could mount in safety, and, becoming inspired, give oracles to those who wanted them.   5 Because this device has three supports, it is called a tripod, and all bronze tripods which are made to this day are, I should imagine, fashioned in imitation of this mechanism. I think that enough has been said of the manner of the discovery of the oracle and of the reasons for the construction of the tripod.   6 It is said that in ancient times prophecies were given by virgins because of their lack of any natural taint of defilement and because they share in the characteristics of Artemis. For virgins were believed to be particularly well qualified to keep safe the secrets of oracular prophecies. But it is said that in more modern times Echecrates the Thessalian, who arrived at the shrine and saw the maiden who gave the oracles, fell in love with her because of her beauty, then abducted and raped her. In the light of this incident the Delphians passed a law to the effect that in future no virgin should give oracles, but that prophecies should be delivered by an older woman of fifty who should be dressed in a maiden's outfit, in memory of the prophetess of former days. These are the stories which are related about the discovery of the oracle, and I shall now return to the deeds of Philomelus.

27.1 When this man took possession of the oracle, he instructed the Pythia to give her response from the tripod in the traditional manner, but in reply to her answer that this was not the traditional manner he threatened her and forced her to mount the tripod. But when she expressed her opinion in regard to Philomelus' overwhelming power and use of violence that he could act as he wished, he gladly accepted her remark, and declared that he had an oracle that was appropriate. Straightway he had the response engraved and, setting it up in public, made it manifest to everyone that the god was giving him permission to act as he pleased.   2 Summoning an assembly and revealing the oracle to the masses, he exhorted them to be confident and turned to warlike activities. He also obtained an omen in Apollo's temple. For an eagle which was flying over the god's temple swooped towards the earth in pursuit of the doves which were reared in the sanctuary and seized several of them from the very altars. Those skilled in matters of this kind claimed that the sign indicated to Philomelus and to the Phocians that they would secure control of the affairs of Delphi.   3 Buoyed up by this, Philomelus sent the most suitable of his friends on embassies, some to Athens, some to Sparta, others to Thebes, and in like manner he sent envoys to the other Greek states which were especially distinguished, to plead by way of defence that he had occupied Delphi not because he was aiming at the sacred treasures but to back his claim to the guardianship of the sanctuary; for it had been proclaimed in early times as belonging peculiarly to the Phocians. 4 He said that he would give an accounting of the monies to all the Greeks and was willing to pass on the weight and number of dedications to those desiring an examination. He also asked that, in the event of anyone going to war with the Phocians out of animosity or malice, they should preferably fight on his side, or at the very least, failing that, they should remain at peace. 5 When the delegates had performed the duty laid upon them, the Athenians, Spartans and some others made an alliance with them and undertook to support them, while the Boeotians, Locrians and some other states voted to do the exact opposite and went to war with the Phocians in defence of the god. Such were the activities carried out in this year.

The Events of the Archon Year 354/3

28.1 During the archonship at Athens of Diotimus, the Romans chose as consuls Gaius Marcius and Gnaeus Mallius. While these were in office Philomelus, who foresaw the extent of the war, began to collect large numbers of mercenaries and picked out for military service the most suitable of the Phocians. 2 Though the war required still more resources, he continued to abstain from the sacred dedications, but levied from those Phocians who were conspicuous for wealth and affluence a sum of money adequate to provide mercenaries' pay. Accordingly, having made ready a considerable army, he led it into open country and was clearly prepared to embark upon a struggle against anyone who was hostile to the Phocians. 3 When the Locrians marched against him, a battle was fought in the vicinity of the cliffs known as the Phaedriades, in which Philomelus was victorious, destroying in the process many of the enemy and capturing a good number alive. Yet others he compelled to throw themselves down from the rocks. After this battle, the spirits of the Phocians were buoyed up by their success, while the Locrians were chastened and sent envoys to Thebes to ask the Boeotians to come to the assistance both of themselves and of the god. 4 Because of their devotion to the god and because the implementation of the Amphictyonic judgments was to their advantage, the Boeotians sent an embassy to the Thessalians and to the other Amphictyons to request them to make common cause against the Phocians. When the Amphictyons voted for war with the Phocians, there was much turmoil and dissension throughout the whole of Greece. For some decided to come to the god's assistance and punish the Phocians as sacrilegious temple robbers, while others inclined towards helping the Phocians.

29.1 A split developed among the tribes and cities over the choice of alliance, for the Boeotians, Locrians, Thessalians, Perrhaebians, Dorians,

Dolopians, Athamanians, Achaeans of Phthia, Magnesians, Aenianians and some others resolved to come to the aid of the sanctuary, while the Athenians, Spartans and some other of the Peloponnesians were for fighting on the Phocian side. 2 The Spartans were most enthusiastic in their cooperation for the following reasons. In the Leuctric War the Thebans, having defeated the enemy, brought a charge against the Spartans before the Amphictyons, alleging that Phoebiadas the Spartiate had seized the Cadmea, and the Amphictyons assessed the offence at five hundred talents. Though judgment had been given against the Spartans, they did not pay the fine within the deadline set by the laws. The Thebans accordingly brought a charge against them and proposed a penalty of double the previous amount. 3 When the Amphictyons gave judgment against them for the sum of one thousand talents, the Spartans, because of the size of the fine, denounced the verdict just as the Phocians had done, claiming that they had been wrongly condemned. 4 Therefore though they now shared a common interest in the matter, the Spartans were reluctant to begin the war by themselves on account of their condemnation, considering it to be more appropriate to have the Amphictyonic verdicts invalidated through the person of the Phocians. For these reasons they were extremely willing to ally with the Phocians and helped them in their bid to secure the guardianship of the temple.

30.1 When it became obvious that the Boeotians would march against the Phocians with a large army, Philomelus decided to assemble a huge mercenary force, and when more money was needed for the war, he was obliged to lay his hands on the sacred dedications and to pillage the oracle, having fixed the wages of his mercenaries at one and a half times the previous amount. A large mercenary force was quickly collected, since the high rate of pay caused many to respond to the call to arms. 2 Whereas devotion to the gods ensured that not a single respectable individual had himself registered for the expedition, the most villainous sort, who despised the gods because of avarice, gathered round Philomelus with enthusiasm, and a strong force of men was quickly created who were hell bent on temple robbery. 3 Thanks to the extent of his resources, Philomelus speedily put together an army of some size. Then he immediately advanced into Locrian territory with cavalry and infantry amounting to more than ten thousand men. When the Locrians ranged themselves in opposition to him and the Boeotians came to help the Locrians, a cavalry battle took place in which the Phocians had the advantage. 4 After this the Thessalians with their allies from adjacent territories gathered to the number of six thousand and entered Locris. There they joined battle with the Phocians in the vicinity of a hill called Argolas and were defeated. But when the Boeotians appeared on the scene with thirteen thousand troops and the Achaeans from the Peloponnese came to help the Phocians with one thousand five hundred, the armies encamped opposite one another, both having gathered in one place.

31.1 After this the Boeotians, who had captured a considerable number of the mercenaries while foraging, brought them in front of the city and proclaimed that the Amphictyons were inflicting the death penalty on those men because they had campaigned with temple robbers. Action quickly followed on words, for they promptly shot them down with javelins. **2** The mercenaries who were in Philomelus' employment were so outraged by this that they demanded that Philomelus should deem the enemy to merit a similar punishment. Accordingly, by striving hard, they captured many of the enemy who were roaming over the countryside and took them back to Philomelus, who had all of them shot down. Because of this punishment they made the enemy abandon their arrogant and savage revenge. **3** After this, when the armies were invading another area and were passing through wooded and rough places, the two vanguards suddenly encountered one another. A close engagement was followed by a severe battle in which the Boeotians, who were far superior in numbers, defeated the Phocians. **4** As the flight took place over precipitous ground from which escape was difficult, many of the Phocians and mercenaries were cut down. Philomelus, having fought bravely and sustained many wounds, was forced into a precipitous area and shut in. Since there was no means of egress and because of a fear that he would be tortured after capture, he threw himself down from a rock and in this way paid the penalty to the god and terminated his life. **5** His fellow general Onomarchus succeeded to the command and, retreating with the survivors from the army, took with him those who returned from the flight. **6** While this was going on, Philip the king of the Macedonians captured Methone after a siege, sacked it and razed it to the ground. He then reduced Pagasae and compelled it to submit. In the Black Sea area Leucon king of the Bosporus died after a reign of forty years, and his son Spartacus, who succeeded to the throne, ruled for five years... .

The Events of the Archon Year 353/2

32.1 In the archonship at Athens of Thudemus, the Romans appointed to the consulship Marcus Poplius and Marcus Fabius. In their period of office the Boeotians, after defeating the Phocians, in the belief that the punishment by both gods and men of Philomelus, the man who bore the greatest degree of responsibility for the sacrilege, would discourage the others from similar wrongdoing, returned home. **2** But the Phocians, now free of the war for the present, went back to Delphi and, assembling the allies in a common gathering, debated about the war. The more reasonable people were inclined to peace, but the impious, who were notorious for their recklessness and greed, thought otherwise, and began to look around in search of someone who would speak up in support of their lawlessness. **3.** Onomarchus then made a carefully thought out speech in favour of keeping to the original policy, and diverted the multitude towards war, not so much out of regard for the common interest as in the belief that it would be advantageous for his own. For he had been condemned, just like the others, by many grave judgments of the Amphictyons and had not paid the fines which had been imposed. Therefore, since he saw that war was preferable to peace as far as he himself was concerned, he not unnaturally incited the Phocians and their allies to abide by the plans of Philomelus. 4 Having been elected as general with full powers, he began to gather a considerable number of mercenaries and, filling the ranks vacated by the dead and enlarging his forces with the multitude of mercenaries he had enrolled, he proceeded to make ready on a vast scale allies and whatever else might be of use for waging war.

33.1 He was elated in his planning by a dream which suggested to him the possibility of a great increase in his influence and reputation. For in his sleep he thought he was refashioning with his own hands the bronze statue which the Amphictyons had dedicated in Apollo's temple, in such a way as to increase its height and make it much bigger. He supposed this to be a sign from the god of the increasing glory accruing to him from his generalship, whereas in fact the truth was different, and the exact opposite was being indicated. For because the Amphictyons had dedicated the statue out of the fines which had been paid by the Phocians as a result of their sacrilegious behaviour in the shrine, the true meaning of the dream was that the fine imposed on the Phocians would be increased in consequence of the activities of Onomarchus, and this was indeed what happened. 2 When Onomarchus had been chosen as general with full powers, he made ready a huge quantity of weapons of bronze and iron, and, minting coins from the silver and gold, he proceeded to issue it to the allied cities and to distribute it in the form of bribes above all to the leaders of the cities. He even corrupted many of the enemy and persuaded some to ally with him while at the same time requiring others to keep the peace. 3 Everything he accomplished easily because of human greed, and he even induced by bribery the Thessalians, who enjoyed the highest reputation among the allies, to remain inactive. Those of the Phocians who were opposed to him he arrested, and, after putting them to death, confiscated their property. Then launching an invasion of enemy territory, he reduced by siege and enslaved the inhabitants of Thronium, and, by striking fear into the Amphissans, he forced them into submission. 4 Having pillaged the cities of the Dorians, he devastated their territory, and, in an incursion into Boeotia, he captured Orchomenus. However he was worsted by the Thebans in an attempt to storm Chaeronea and returned to his own land.

34.1 Simultaneously with these events, Artabazus, who was in revolt from the King, was engaged in fighting the satraps sent by the King to make war on him. Initially he opposed the satraps vigorously with the assistance of his ally Chares the Athenian, but when Chares departed, he was left alone. He persuaded the Thebans to send him forces and to fight on his side. They, selecting Pammenes as general and giving him five thousand troops, sent him to Asia. 2 Pammenes came to the assistance of Artabazus and, as a result of his defeat of the satraps in two major engagements, won great glory for himself and for the Boeotians. For it appeared astonishing that the Boeotians, at a time when they had been deserted by the Thessalians and when the war with the Phocians was involving them in great danger, were despatching forces across the sea to Asia and were on the whole prevailing in the battles in which they were involved. 3 At the same time as these events, war broke out between the Argives and the Spartans, and a battle was fought in the vicinity of the city of Orneae, in which the Spartans reduced Orneae by storm and returned home to Sparta. Chares the Athenian general sailed to the Hellespont, where he captured the city of Sestos, slaughtered those of military age and enslaved the remainder. 4 Cersobleptes the son of Cotys, because of his animosity towards Philip and his friendship for the Athenians, handed the cities of the Chersonese apart from Cardia over to the Athenians, and the people sent out settlers to the cities. Since Philip saw that the inhabitants of Methone were offering their city as a base for his enemies, he initiated a siege. 5 For some time the Methoneans endured the siege, but were eventually overcome and compelled to surrender their city to the king on condition that they should depart from Methone with one garment apiece. Philip rased the city to the ground and apportioned its territory among the Macedonians. In the course of the siege Philip happened to be struck in the eye with an arrow and was blinded in that eye as a result.

35.1 After this Philip was invited by the Thessalians and entered Thessaly with his troops, where at first he assisted the Thessalians and went to war with Lycophron the tyrant of Pherae. Subsequently, when Lycophron called in his Phocian allies, Phayllus, the brother of Onomarchus, was sent with seven thousand men. Philip defeated the Phocians and expelled them from Thessaly. 2 Onomarchus, taking with him his entire army in the belief that he would secure control of the whole of Thessaly, came with all speed to help Lycophron and his supporters. When Philip and the Thessalians ranged themselves against the Phocians, Onomarchus, who was superior in numbers, defeated him in two battles and destroyed many Macedonians. Philip was now in the midst of the greatest dangers and deserted by his despondent troops, but he encouraged the majority of them and with difficulty rendered them obedient. 3 After this Philip returned to Macedonia, while Onomarchus, marching into Boeotia, vanquished the Boeotians in battle and captured the city of Coronea. In Thessaly, Philip had just arrived from Macedonia with his troops and marched against Lycophron the tyrant of Pherae. **4** Since he was no match for him, Lycophron called upon his Phocian allies and promised to arrange things in Thessaly along with them. Therefore when Onomarchus came speedily to his assistance with twenty thousand infantry and five thousand cavalry, Philip, who had persuaded the Thessalians to wage the war in common, assembled all of them together. They amounted to twenty thousand foot and three hundred horse. **5** In the course of a fierce battle in which the Thessalian cavalry were superior both in numbers and in courage, Philip was victorious. Onomarchus and his men fled to the sea, where Chares the Athenian was by chance sailing past with many triremes. There a great slaughter of Phocians took place. For the fugitives, amongst whom was Onomarchus himself, casting off their armour, were attempting to reach the triremes by swimming. **6** In the end more than six thousand Phocians and mercenaries were killed, including their general, and no fewer than three thousand were captured alive. Philip hanged Onomarchus and drowned the remainder as despoilers of temples.

36.1 After the death of Onomarchus, his brother Phayllus succeeded to the military leadership of the Phocians. In a bid to remedy the disaster which had just taken place, he proceeded to assemble a huge number of mercenaries by doubling the normal rate of pay and called upon his allies for assistance. In addition he prepared a large amount of weapons and struck a currency of gold and silver. **2** About the same time Mausolus the ruler of Caria died after a reign of twenty four years and was succeeded as ruler by Artemisia, his sister and wife, who reigned for two years. **3** Clearchus the tyrant of Heracleia was assassinated as he was on his way to view the festival of Dionysus after a rule of twelve years, and his son Timotheus, succeeding to his position, ruled for fifteen years... .

The Events of the Archon Year 352/1

37.1 In the archonship of Aristodemus at Athens the Romans appointed as consuls Gaeus Sulpicius and Marcus Valerius, and the one hundred and seventh Olympiad was held at which Micrinas of Tarentum won the footrace. While these were in office Phayllus the Phocian general restored, after the defeat and death of his brother, the fortunes of the Phocians, which had been brought low by the defeat and destruction of their troops. **2** Because of his possession of a huge sum of money he collected many mercenaries and induced a considerable number of allies to participate in the war. For by the abundance of funds that was virtually beyond measure not only did he avail himself of the services of many private individuals as his willing accomplices but he also persuaded the most distinguished states to involve themselves in a concerted action. **3** For the Spartans sent him one thousand troops, the Achaeans two thousand and the Athenians five thousand infantry and four hundred cavalry, led by the general Nausicles. Lycophron and Peitholaus, the tyrants of Pherae, bereft of allies following the death of Onomarchus, handed Pherae over to Philip and, under the guarantee of a truce, gathered their two thousand mercenaries together and, taking refuge with Phayllus, ranged themselves on the side of the Phocians. **4** A fair number of the minor cities also sent assistance to the Phocians on account of the vast quantities of money that were being distributed. For gold, which stimulates the avarice of mankind, forced them to desert to that quarter most likely to secure for them the advantage which is derived from profit. **5** Phayllus then invaded Boeotia with his army but, worsted in the vicinity of the city of Orchomenus, he lost many of his troops. After this, in another battle which took place beside the river Cephisus, the Boeotians, victorious for a second time, destroyed more than five hundred of the enemy and captured no fewer than four hundred. **6** A few days later in a battle near Coronea, the Boeotians prevailed yet again, destroying fifty Phocians and capturing one hundred and thirty. Having thus narrated the events pertaining to the Boeotians and Phocians, we now return to Philip.

38.1 After he had defeated Onomarchus in a remarkable battle, Philip suppressed the tyranny at Pherae and restored freedom to the city. Then after arranging all the other affairs of Thessaly he advanced to Thermopylae with the aim of making war on the Phocians. **2** But since the Athenians prevented him from getting through the pass, he returned to Macedonia, now that he had expanded his kingdom as a result both of his own exploits and of his piety towards the god. **3** Phayllus, taking the field against those Locrians known as the Epicnemidians, took possession of all their cities apart from the one called Naryx, which he had indeed won through nocturnal treachery but from which he was subsequently driven out with the loss of no fewer than two hundred of his men. **4** After this when he was bivouacking in the neighbourhood of the city called Abae, the Boeotians, in a night attack on the Phocians, killed a considerable number of them. Buoyed up by their success, they passed into the territory of the Phocians, where they plundered a good part of it and collected a large amount of loot. **5** While they were on the way home and were aiding the besieged city of Naryx, Phayllus appeared suddenly and routed them. He then took the city by storm, sacked it and razed it to the ground. **6** Falling victim to a wasting illness and ailing for a long time, Phayllus suffered a painful death in a manner in keeping with his impiety. He left behind as general of the Phocians Phalaecus son of the Onomarchus who had kindled the Sacred War. As he was still little more than a youth, Phayllus appointed as his guardian and as general Mnaseas, one of his friends. **7** The Boeotians subsequently attacked the Phocians by night and killed the general Mnaseas and some two hundred of his men. Shortly afterwards another cavalry engagement was fought near Chaeronea, in which Phalaecus was defeated and lost a good many of his cavalry.

39.1 At the same time tumults and disturbances broke out in the Peloponnese for the following reasons. Since the Spartans had a quarrel with the Megalopolitans, they overran their territory under the command of Archidamus. The Megalopolitans accordingly were angry at what had happened, but as they were numerically inferior and no match for them by themselves, they called upon their allies for support. 2 The Argives, Sicyonians and Messenians came quickly to their aid in full force, and the Thebans, putting Cephesion in command, sent four thousand infantry and five hundred cavalry. 3 The Megalopolitans accordingly took the field along with their allies and encamped near the sources of the river Alpheus. The Spartans received three thousand foot from the Phocians and one hundred and fifty cavalry from Lycophron and Peitholaus, who had been expelled from their tyranny at Pherae. Having organised a formidable army, they encamped in the vicinity of Mantinea. 4 After this, on reaching the city of Orneae in Argive territory, they stormed it before the enemy could arrive, for it was allied with the Megalopolitans. When the Argives marched out against them, the Spartans joined battle and defeated them, killing more than two hundred of them in the process. 5 When the Thebans, twice as strong numerically but inferior in discipline, put in an appearance, a fierce engagement took place and, as the issue was in doubt, the Argives and their allies returned to their own cities, while the Spartans invaded Arcadia. There they stormed the city of Helissus and after pillaging it went back to Sparta. 6 Some time later the Thebans and their allies defeated the enemy in a battle near Telphousa, where they destroyed many and captured Anaxander their commander along with more than sixty others. Not long afterwards they were victorious in two other engagements and struck down a good number of the enemy. 7 Finally, when the Spartans prevailed in a battle of some significance, the armies of each side went back to their own cities. Then when the Spartans concluded a truce with the Megalopolitans, the Thebans returned to Boeotia. 8 While occupying himself in Boeotia, Phalaecus captured Chaeronea, but when the Thebans came to the assistance of the city, he was driven out. Then the Boeotians, taking the field against Phocis with a large army, laid waste the greater part of it and ravaged properties throughout the land. When they had also seized some of the small townships and amassed a large amount of booty, they returned to Boeotia.

The Events of the Archon Year 351/0

40.1 In the archonship of Theellus at Athens, the Romans elected as consuls Marcus Fabius and Titus Quintius. While they were in office, the Thebans, by now weary of the war with the Phocians and destitute of resources, sent envoys to the King of the Persians with an invitation to provide an abundant subsidy for the city. **2** Since Artaxerxes willingly heeded them, he gave them a gift of three hundred talents of silver. Meanwhile the Boeotians and the Phocians continued to skirmish and raid one another's territory, but no activities worthy of mention took place in the course of this year... .

44.1 Since in view of his earlier defeat he placed a high priority on the conquest of Egypt, the King sent ambassadors to the most important of the Greek cities with the request that they take part in the Egyptian expedition alongside the Persians. The Athenians and the Spartans declared that they were continuing to maintain their friendship with the Persians but declined to make a contribution to the allied force. **2** Choosing Lacrates as general, the Thebans sent him out with one thousand hoplites. The Argives dispatched three thousand troops without designating a general, but when the King asked for Nicostratus by name, they agreed. **3** Now this individual was skilled in both action and in deliberation, though his intelligence was tempered by irrationality. For, since he was outstanding in physical strength, he sought to imitate Heracles while on campaign by wearing a lion skin and carrying a war-club in battle. In like manner the Greeks who lived in the coastal areas of Asia Minor sent six thousand men, with the result that the Greek allies numbered in all ten thousand... .

45.7 A short time previously Artemisia the ruler of Caria died after a reign of two years, and her brother Idrieus, succeeding to the tyranny, ruled for seven years... .

The Events of the Archon Year 350/49

46.1 In the archonship at Athens of Apollodorus the Romans chose as consuls Marcus Valerius and Gaius Sulpicius... .

The Events of the Archon Year 349/8

52.1 In the archonship at Athens of Callimachus the Romans chose as consuls Gaius Marcius and Publius Valerius. While they were in office, Artaxerxes, seeing that his general Mentor had carried out great services for him in his war with the Egyptians, promoted him above any of his friends. **2** Rewarding the man for his sterling prowess, he honoured him with a gift of one hundred talents of silver and the choicest of the estates at his disposal. In addition he appointed him satrap of the coastal areas of Asia Minor and designated him supreme commander, entrusting him with the war currently being waged against those in revolt. **3** Since Mentor was related to Artabazus and Memnon, who had fought against Persia in the past and at this particular moment, after a flight from Asia, were living at Philip's court, he put in a request to the King and persuaded him to acquit the men of the accusations levelled against them. He summoned both of them forthwith into his presence with their entire kindred. **4** For Artabazus had begotten eleven sons and ten daughters by the sister of Mentor and Memnon. Attracted by the number of his children, Mentor advanced the young men and gave them the most notable military commands. **5** He first took the field against Hermias the tyrant of Atarneus, who was in revolt from the King and in control of a large number of strongholds and cities. **6** Having promised him that he would persuade the King to free him from the charges against him, he misled him by meeting him for a parley at which he had him arrested. Securing possession of his ring and writing to the cities that had been reconciled with the King through Mentor's agency, he sealed the letters with Hermias' ring and sent along with the letters men to take control of the places concerned. **7** Since those living in the cities believed what had been written, they accepted the peace gladly and handed over the strongholds and cities without exception. Mentor was accordingly held in high favour by the King for having taken over the rebel townships in record time and without risk, since he seemed to be able to carry out a general's functions most competently and efficiently. **8** In like manner he quickly overcame the other commanders who were alienated from the Persians, some by force and others by duplicity. Thus stood events in Asia. **9** In Europe Philip the king of the Macedonians marched against the Chalcidian cities and, having captured by storm the stronghold of Zereia, destroyed it. He filled some of the other towns with panic and forced them to submit. Then arriving at Pherae in Thessaly, he drove out Peitholaus the ruler of the city. **10** At the same time as these events were taking place, Spartacus the king of Pontus died after a reign of five years and his brother Paerisades who succeeded to the kingship ruled for thirty eight years.

The Events of the Archon Year 348/7

53.1 After the passage of this year Theophilus held the archonship at Athens, while at Rome Gaius Sulpicius and Gaius Quintius were elected to the consulship. The one hundred and eighth Olympiad was also held at which Polycles of Cyrene won the footrace. **2** While these men were in office, Philip was eager to subdue the cities on the Hellespont and gained control of Mecyberna and Torone by treachery, at no risk to himself. Then marching with a huge army against Olynthus, the largest of the cities of this area, he first defeated the Olynthians in two battles and, shutting them up inside, he instituted a siege. In the course of a constant series of assaults, he lost many of his troops in the battle for the walls, but eventually he bribed Euthycrates and Lasthenes, two of the Olynthian commanders through whose agency he took the city by treachery. **3** Having plundered the city and enslaved the inhabitants, he put the spoils up for sale. As a result of this action he secured an abundance of money for waging war and alarmed the other cities which were at war with him. He honoured those of the soldiers who had distinguished themselves in battle with such rewards as were appropriate and distributed a large sum of money among influential men in the cities. In this way he secured the services of many men willing to betray their city. He himself was in the habit of asserting that he had increased his kingdom far more by gold than by force of arms.

54.1 Looking with suspicion on the increase of Philip's power, the Athenians would come to the aid of whoever was currently the object of Philip's aggression. They also sent to the cities ambassadors who would call upon them both to preserve their freedom and to punish with death those who were treasonably inclined. In addition they undertook to fight alongside all of them, and, by openly proclaiming themselves the king's enemies, they committed themselves to unremitting warfare with Philip. **2** They were urged on to the leadership of Greece above all by Demosthenes the orator, who was the most silver tongued of the Greeks of his day. Yet so great was what might be called the crop of traitors which had been sown at that time all over Greece that not even his city was able to curb the impulse of its citizens to treachery. **3** Wherefore it is said that when Philip wanted to capture some city which was conspicuous for its strong position and which one of the locals pronounced to be impregnable because of its strength, he asked whether its walls could not be scaled even by gold. **4** For experience had taught him that it was easy to subdue with gold what it was impossible to master by force of arms. Accordingly by employing bribery and calling those who accepted his gold 'guests' and 'friends', he built up a group of traitors in the cities and so by the wickedness of his company he corrupted men's character.

55.1 After the capture of Olynthus he held the Olympia and carried out lavish sacrifices to the gods in celebration of his victory. He arranged a great festal assembly and held splendid contests, after which he invited to the banquet many non-Macedonians who had come to visit the country. **2** In the midst of the revelry he engaged a large number of them in conversation and gave drinking goblets to many of them as he toasted their health. Because of the gifts he distributed to a large number of them and the extravagance of the promises he obligingly made to all, he acquired many adherents eager to cultivate his friendship. **3** On one occasion in the course of the drinking party, observing that Satyrus the actor appeared downcast, he asked him why he alone chose not to share in the acts of generosity he was performing. When Satyrus replied that there was a boon he wished to obtain from him, but that he was afraid that he would be denied the petition he had determined upon were he to divulge it, the king, thoroughly delighted, affirmed that he granted everything he requested. Satyrus then answered that there were among the female captives two maiden daughters of a friend of his who were of an age for marriage: these he desired to obtain, not in order to make a profit were he to succeed in receiving them as a gift, but in order to provide them both with a dowry and arrange marriages for them, so as not to see them suffer in a way inappropriate to their tender years. **4** Philip thereupon gladly granted the request and straightway presented the girls to Satyrus. By dispensing many other kindnesses and gifts of all sorts, he gained rewards many times more valuable than the cost of the favours he had granted. For many men who were spurred on by hopes of benefactions sought to be the first to deliver themselves and to hand over their countries to Philip.

The Events of the Archon Year 347/6

56.1 In the archonship at Athens of Themistocles, Gaius Cornelius and Marcus Popilius succeeded to the consulship at Rome. During their period of office the Boeotians, after plundering a large part of Phocis, defeated the enemy near the city called Hya and killed about seventy of them. **2** After this the Boeotians, engaging in battle with the Phocians near Coronea, were defeated and lost a large number of men. Then when the Phocians seized several sizeable cities in Boeotia, the Boeotians marched out on campaign and destroyed the grain in enemy territory, but on the way home suffered a defeat. **3** At the same time Phalaecus the Phocian commander was charged with the theft of many sacred properties and relieved of his post. In his place three commanders were chosen, Deinocrates, Callias and Sophanes. In the course of an enquiry which was held into the matter of the sacred property, the Phocians demanded an accounting from those who had managed it. The administrator of most of it was Philon. **4** Since this man was unable to render an account, judgment was given against him. When he had been stretched out on the rack by the generals, he disclosed the names of those who had been involved in the embezzlement, and he himself, succumbing to the most extreme tortures, ended his life in a manner fully in keeping with his impiety. **5** Those who had appropriated the funds gave back whatever of the stolen money remained intact, and were themselves put to death for the sacrilege. Of the generals who had previously held the command, the first, Philomelus, abstained from the dedications, but the second, a brother of Philomelus named Onomarchus, spent a large part of the god's funds, while the third, Phayllus the brother of Onomarchus, on becoming general converted a good part of the dedications into currency in order to provide wages for his mercenaries. **6** For he melted down into coinage the one hundred and twenty gold bricks weighing two talents each which had been dedicated by Croesus king of the Lydians, as well as three hundred and sixty gold drinking bowls weighing two minae each, along with a lion and a woman of gold, which weighed thirty talents. Consequently the total amount of gold turned into coinage, when converted into its equivalent in silver, is found to be four thousand talents. Of the offerings in silver presented by Croesus and all other dedicants, the generals had collectively spent more than six thousand talents, and when the value of the gold dedications is added, the sum total exceeded ten thousand talents. 7 Some historians state that the amount of looted property was no less than the sums acquired by Alexander in the treasuries of the Persians. Phalaecus' supporters on the board of generals even attempted to uproot the temple, because of a rumour that it contained a treasure room holding a large sum of silver and gold and they proceeded enthusiastically to dig up the area around the hearth and the tripod. The instigator of the report concerning the treasure cited as evidence the lines of the most celebrated and the most ancient of poets, Homer, where he says:

> Not even the wealth enclosed within by the stone threshold of
> Phoebus Apollo the Archer in rocky Pytho.

8 While the soldiers were trying to dig up the area around the tripod, great earthquakes took place which instilled fear in the Phocians, and, since the gods were manifestly indicating the punishment about to be visited upon the sacrilegious, they abandoned the work. Philo, the instigator of this illegality, whom I have mentioned above, speedily paid the appropriate penalty to the god.

57.1 The Phocians came to be saddled with the entire responsibility for the loss of the sacred property, although the Athenians and the Spartans, who had fought as allies of the Phocians and received payments that were excessive in relation to the number of soldiers being sent out, were also involved in its seizure. **2** The Athenians were at this period so disposed to sin against the divine that a little before the Delphic crisis, when Iphicrates was occupied in the vicinity of Corcyra with a naval force, they fell in with ships transporting statues fashioned from gold and ivory which Dionysius the ruler of Syracuse was sending to Olympia and to Delphi. Iphicrates, having secured possession of them, sent to the people of Athens to ask what he should do. The Athenians ordered him not to enquire too closely into what concerned the gods but to ensure that his soldiers were properly fed. **3** In obedience to the decree of his country Iphicrates put up for sale the spoils which consisted of the *objects d'art* belonging to the gods. The tyrant was enraged with the Athenians and wrote to them a letter along the following lines:

> Dionysius to the Council and People of Athens. It would be
> unseemly to wish you well for you are guilty of sacrilegious
> behaviour towards the gods by land and sea. Since you have
> purloined the statues which we had sent as dedications to the

gods and melted them down for use as currency, you have sinned against the greatest of the gods, Apollo who resides at Delphi and Olympian Zeus.

4 The Athenians were guilty of such behaviour towards the gods, even though they claimed that Apollo was their patron deity and forefather. The Spartans, even though they had consulted the oracle at Delphi and through it had acquired their universally admired constitution, as well as enquiring of the god concerning issues of the greatest significance, yet had the brazenness to participate in sacrilege along with those who had plundered the sanctuary.

58.1 In Boeotia, the Phocians, who held three strongly defended cities, Orchomenus, Coronea and Corsiae, used these as bases for their campaigns against the Boeotians. With an abundance of mercenaries they proceeded to lay waste the countryside and in their attacks and engagements they got the better of the locals. **2** Accordingly the Boeotians, who were under pressure in the war and suffering from the loss of many troops and from the lack of financial resources, sent envoys to Philip with a request for aid. **3** The king, delighted to witness their humiliation and eager to deflate their Leuctric arrogance, sent only a few troops, for he took pains to avoid being seen by public opinion as one who looked on impassively at the plundering of the oracle. **4** While the Phocians were constructing a fort at the place called Abae, where there is a shrine sacred to Apollo, the Boeotians marched out against them. Some of the Phocians immediately fled to the nearest cities and dispersed, while some five hundred others sought shelter in the temple of Apollo, only to perish. **5** Among the many divine manifestations to fall upon the Phocians in this period was the following, which I am about to describe. The men who had fled to the temple believed that they would be saved by divine assistance, whereas in fact the very opposite happened, and through the operation of what might be regarded as divine providence they met with a punishment that was fitting for temple robbers. **6** Now there was a large amount of straw scattered about the area of the temple, and when the fugitives left a fire behind in their tents, the straw caught fire and miraculously sparked off so great a conflagration that the temple was destroyed and the Phocians who had sought refuge there were burned alive. For the divinity was believed to have refused to the sacrilegious the salvation that is customarily granted to the petitions of suppliants.

The Events of the Archon Year 346/5

59.1 In the archonship of Archias at Athens, the Romans elected to the consulship Marcus Aemilius and Titus Quintius. During their period in office the Phocian War, which had lasted for ten years, was brought to an end in the following way. Since both the Boeotians and the Phocians had been humbled by the length of the war, the latter, in an attempt to obtain assistance, sent ambassadors to the Spartans, who dispatched one thousand hoplites under the command of their king, Archidamus. 2 In like manner the Boeotians sent envoys concerning an alliance to Philip, who picked up the Thessalians en route and arrived in Locris with a large force. Then, having caught up with Phalaecus, who had once again been deemed worthy of the generalship and who had the lion's share of the mercenaries, he made ready to determine the outcome of the war in pitched battle. But Phalaecus, who was lingering at Nicaea and saw that his numbers were unequal to the task of taking on Philip, entered into negotiations with the king with a view to concluding an armistice. 3 An agreement was made permitting Phalaecus to depart with his troops wherever he wished, and he retired to the Peloponnese with his mercenaries, who were around eight thousand in number. The Phocians, their hopes now completely shattered, surrendered to Philip. 4 The king, who had unexpectedly brought the Sacred War to an end without a battle, met in deliberation with the Boeotians and the Thessalians. Whereupon he determined to summon a meeting of the delegates of the Amphictyonic League and to entrust to this body the resolution of the whole issue.

60.1 The delegates accordingly decreed that Philip and his descendants should be members of the League and should have the two votes which had formerly belonged to the vanquished Phocians. In addition they decreed that the walls of the three cities which were controlled by the Phocians should be demolished and that the Phocians should have no share in the shrine or in the Amphictyonic Council. Moreover they were to be denied the use of horses and weapons until such time as they paid back to the god the money which had been embezzled, while the Phocians who had fled into exile and any others who had been implicated in the sacrilege should be declared accursed and liable to seizure from wherever they happened to be. 2 The Amphictyons also resolved to destroy all the Phocian cities and to split them up into villages which should be separate from one another by not less than one stade and each of which should contain no more than fifty houses; the Phocians were to possess their land and to pay every year to the god an indemnity of sixty talents until they had repaid the amount which had been entered in the inventories at the time of the sacrilege; Philip was henceforth to celebrate the Pythian festival along with the Boeotians and the Thessalians, because of Corinthian involvement with the Phocians in the illegal transactions against the divinity.
3 The Amphictyons and Philip were to dash the weapons of the Phocians and those of their mercenaries against the cliffs and incinerate what remained of them, and to sell their horses. In like manner the Amphictyons made arrangements for the guardianship of the oracle and all matters pertaining to reverence for the gods and to concord among the Greeks. 4 After this,

when Philip had assisted the Amphictyons in implementing the resolution and had dealt generously with everyone, he returned to Macedonia. For he had not only made a name for himself for his piety and talented generalship but had also built a sure foundation for the future increase in his power. 5 For he was eager to be nominated commander-in-chief of the Greeks with full powers and to conduct the war with the Persians, an event which actually did take place. But we shall relate the events severally, each under its appropriate date, and for the present we shall revert to the continuity of our narrative.

61.1 We think it right first of all to put on record the punishment which the god inflicted on those who had sinned against the oracle. For the implacable vengeance of the gods pursued not only the actual perpetrators of the sacrilege but everyone who was even minimally involved in the transgression. 2 For Philomelus the instigator of the seizure of the sanctuary, when faced with an extreme situation in the course of the war, threw himself from a rock, while his brother Onomarchus, who succeeded to the generalship of his desperate people, was cut down in Thessaly along with the Phocians and mercenaries under his command, and crucified. 3 Phayllus, the third commander, who had converted the bulk of the dedications into currency, fell victim to a lingering illness and was unable to achieve a quick release from his punishment. Phalaecus the successor of all of these, who gathered together what was left over from the sacrilege, lived on for a considerable time amid great fears and dangers, leading the life of a wanderer, not so that he would be happier than his accomplices in the act of sacrilege, but so that he might suffer torment longer, and, by becoming conspicuous in the eyes of many for his misfortunes, might meet with an end that was to be a matter of widespread public knowledge. 4 For after the conclusion of the compact he had made, this man went into exile with his mercenaries and at first spent some time in the Peloponnese, where he maintained his troops on what remained of the proceeds of the acts of sacrilege. Subsequently however he hired a number of large cargo ships at Corinth and with four light vessels began preparations for a voyage to Italy and Sicily, in the belief that he would either capture some city or other in those regions or at least find paid military employment. For it so happened that a war was currently being fought between the Lucanians and the Tarentines. He told his fellow voyagers that he was sailing because he had been sent for by the Italiots and Siceliots.

62.1 In the course of the voyage while he was in the open sea, some of the soldiers on the largest vessel, on which Phalaecus himself was sailing, held discussions with one another because of a suspicion that noone had summoned them. For they could see not see on board any commanders from the states that had summoned them, and moreover the voyage was not only far from short but was in fact quite protracted and difficult. 2 Accordingly because they distrusted what they had been told and were afraid of an expedition across the sea, they formed a conspiracy, the ringleaders being the commanders of the mercenary force. At length they drew their swords, and by intimidating both Phalaecus and the helmsman they compelled them to turn around. When those being transported on the other vessels did the same, they sailed back to the Peloponnese. 3 There they assembled at Cape Malea in Laconia, where they found representatives from Cnossus who had sailed from Crete to gather mercenaries. After negotiating with Phalaecus and the commanders and offering them wages that were well above the average, they all sailed away together. Putting in at Cnossus in Crete, they forthwith assaulted and captured the city called Lyctus. 4 But the Lyctians who were expelled from their city obtained assistance that was both sudden and unforeseen. For at about the same time the Tarentines, who were at war with the Lucanians, sent an embassy to beg assistance from the Spartans, and the latter, since they were the founders of their race, were ready and eager to fight by their side. They accordingly got together an infantry force and a fleet, and were on the point of departing for Italy when the Lyctians requested them to come to their aid first. The Spartans were persuaded, and, sailing to Crete, defeated the mercenaries and returned the Lyctians safe to their native land.

63.1 After this Archidamus sailed for Italy, where he allied with the Tarentines, only to meet an illustrious death in battle. He was a man who won praise for his generalship and for the whole course of his life, though the alliance which he concluded with the Phocians brought him reproach as one especially responsible for the seizure of Delphi. 2 Archidamus was king of Sparta for twenty-three years and was succeeded by his son Agis, who ruled for fifteen years. Archidamus' mercenaries, who had shared in the pillaging of the shrine, were subsequently shot down by the Lucanians, while Phalaecus, following upon his expulsion from Lyctus, attempted to besiege Cydonia. 3 When he had constructed siege-engines and was bringing them up against the city, they were struck by lightning and consumed by the heaven-sent fire. In the course of trying to save the engines many of the mercenaries too were destroyed in the flames, Phalaecus the general included. 4 However it is maintained by some that he was killed by one of the mercenaries to whom he had given offence. The surviving mercenaries were hired by exiles from Elis and conveyed to the Peloponnese, where they went on to wage war along with the exiles against the Eleans. 5 When the Arcadians fought alongside the Eleans in the war and defeated the exiles in battle, many of the mercenaries were killed, and the survivors, some four thousand in number, were taken alive. Following a division of the spoils between the Arcadians and the Eleans, the Arcadians put those in their share of the allocation up for sale, while the Eleans put theirs to death because of the impious acts which they had perpetrated against the oracle.

64.1 Such was the punishment inflicted by the divinity upon those who had been implicated in the sacrilege. The most famous cities which had been involved in the lawless behaviour were later vanquished by Antipater and lost simultaneously their leadership and their autonomy. **2** The wives of the Phocian leaders who had placed around their necks the necklaces taken from Delphi likewise met with a punishment appropriate to their impiety. For the woman who had worn the one which had belonged to Helen was reduced to the degradation of prostitution, while the wearer of Eriphyle's was burned alive when her house was consumed in an act of arson committed by her eldest son in a fit of madness. And so those who had dared to show contempt for the god had punishment visited upon them by the gods in the manner I have related. **3** Philip on the other hand, who had come to the assistance of the oracle, continued to have his strength built up from that time until in the end, because of his piety towards the gods, he was designated commander-in-chief of the whole of Greece and won for himself the greatest of all the kingdoms of Europe. Having given a sufficiently detailed account of the Sacred War, we shall return to a different kind of event.

65.1 In Sicily, since the Syracusans were at variance with one another and were constrained to be slaves to many diverse types of tyranny, they sent envoys to Corinth to request that the Corinthians send them someone to take charge of their city and to put an end to the aggressive behaviour of those who were aspiring to tyranny. **2** Once they made up their minds that it was right to help those descended from themselves, the Corinthians voted to send as commander Timoleon son of Timaenetus, who was foremost among the citizens for valour and military talent, and was in short endowed with every conceivable virtue. A curious happening had befallen this man, which contributed to his selection as general. **3** His brother Timophanes, a man who surpassed the Corinthians in wealth and daring, had for a long time clearly been aspiring to tyrannical rule, and at the moment in question was recruiting the poor and accumulating complete sets of hoplite armour. He also made a habit of going around the market place in the company of the most worthless element among the lower classes. His behaviour in fact was very much like that of a tyrant, while he kept up the pretence that he was not one. **4** Timoleon, who was hostile to the whole idea of autocratic rule, endeavoured initially to persuade his brother to abandon his schemes, but, when he paid no attention and grew even more devoted to his reckless behaviour, Timoleon found it impossible to reform him by argument and slew him as he was walking about in the market place. **5** Uproar arose when the citizens rushed up, and, because of the unusual and horrific nature of the deed, discord ensued. For one faction maintained that, since Timoleon had committed the murder of a kinsman, he merited the full legal penalty, while those of the opposite viewpoint declared that they should be praising him as a tyrannicide. **6** When the council of elders met in the council chamber and the controversy about the deed was referred to the meeting, Timoleon's enemies denounced him, while those who were sympathetically inclined spoke up in his defence and recommended that his life be spared. **7** While the issue was still undecided, envoys from Syracuse sailed in and, disclosing their instructions to the Council, requested it to send them the general whom they were seeking. **8** The councillors accordingly resolved to send Timoleon and, with a view to bringing the matter to a successful conclusion, they laid before him alternatives which were both novel and unbelievable. For they asserted that if he ruled the Syracusans justly they judged him to be a tyrannicide, but if he put his own interests first, they deemed him to be a fratricide. **9** Timoleon directed the affairs of Sicily both justly and profitably not so much through fear of the Council's menaces which loomed over him as through his own ability. For he defeated the Carthaginians, re-established in their original state the Greek cities which had been demolished by the barbarians and liberated the whole of Sicily. In short he found Syracuse and the other Greek cities desolate and made them outstanding for the sheer size of their populations. But we shall soon be relating these matters each in order under its proper date, and for the moment we shall change direction and proceed with the continuity of our narrative.

The Events of the Archon Year 345/4

66.1 In the archonship of Eubulus at Athens, the Romans appointed as consuls Marcus Fabius and Servius Sulpicius. During their period in office Timoleon the Corinthian, who had been elected by the citizens as general at Syracuse, made preparations for the voyage to Sicily. **2** He had seven hundred mercenaries and, manning four triremes and three fast sailing ships with his troops, he sailed out from Corinth. In the course of his voyage along the coast, he received an additional three ships from the Leucadians and Corcyreans, and with ten ships he crossed what is known as the Ionian Gulf... .

The Events of the Archon Year 344/3

69.1 In the archonship at Athens of Lyciscus, the Romans chose as consuls Marcus Valerius and Marcus Poplius and the one hundred and ninth Olympiad was celebrated in which Aristolochus of Athens won the footrace. During this year the first treaty was made between the Romans and the Carthaginians. **2** In Caria Idrieus the ruler of Caria died after a rule of seven years and Ada, who was his sister and wife, succeeded to the rule and reigned for four years... .
7 In Macedonia Philip, who had inherited an ancestral enmity with the Illyrians and found the quarrel to be irreconcilable, invaded Illyria with a large army. After pillaging the land and securing many of the townships he returned to Macedonia with large quantities of booty. **8** After this he

passed through Thessaly where he expelled the tyrants from the cities and won the devotion of the Thessalians through gratitude. For he hoped that, if he had them as allies, he would easily secure the goodwill of the Greeks as well, a hope that was indeed fulfilled. For the adjacent Greeks immediately assented to the decision of the Thessalians and eagerly concluded an alliance with him.

The Events of the Archon Year 343/2

70.1 In the archonship at Athens of Pythodorus, the Romans elected as consuls Gaeus Plautius and Titus Manlius... .

71.1 In Macedonia Philip launched an expedition against Thrace with the aim of securing the goodwill of the Greek cities on the Thracian coastline. For Cersobleptes the king of the Thracians was engaged in a campaign to subdue the cities on the Hellespont that were adjacent to Thrace and was laying their territories waste. **2** Wishing therefore to terminate the barbarian attacks, he marched out against them with a large army. Defeating the Thracians in several engagements, he ordered the subjugated barbarians to pay tithes to the Macedonians, while he himself, by founding significant cities in advantageous localities, put an end to Thracian insolence. **3** Among the historians, Theopompus of Chios included in his *Histories of Philip* three books covering events in Sicily. Beginning with the tyranny of the elder Dionysius, he included a period of fifty years and ended with the expulsion of Dionysius the Younger. The three books in question are the forty first to the forty third.

The Events of the Archon Year 342/1

72.1 In the archonship of Sosigenes at Athens, the Romans chose as consuls Marcus Valerius and Marcus Poplius. While they were in office, Arymbas the king of the Molossians died after a reign of ten years, leaving a son Aeacides the father of Pyrrhus. However he was succeeded by Alexander the brother of Olympias thanks to the involvement of Philip of Macedon... .

The Events of the Archon Year 341/0

74.1 In the archonship of Nicomachus at Athens, the Romans elected to the consulship Gaius Marcius and Titus Manlius Torquatus. During their year in office Phocion the Athenian defeated Cleitarchus the tyrant of Eretria who had been raised to power by Philip. **2** In Caria Ada was driven from the throne by her younger brother Pizodarus, who ruled for five years till Alexander's crossing into Asia. Philip, whose power was waxing to an ever increasing degree, marched against Perinthus which was opposed to him and which inclined to the Athenians. Having instituted a siege, he applied engines to the city and assaulted the walls each day in relays. **3** Having constructed towers eighty cubits in height which rose far above the towers of Perinthus, he contrived from the commanding heights of these machines to reduce the besieged. In like manner his battering rams shook the walls, and his mining operations which dug underneath them threw down a large portion of the wall. But when the Perinthians fought back vigorously and quickly erected another wall against him, some unbelievable contests took place in the course of the fighting for the wall. **4** The rivalry was intense on both sides: on the one hand the king had large quantities of artillery of different types and sought to use it to destroy those who were fighting from the parapets, and on the other the Perinthians, though sustaining heavy losses each day, received from their allies the Byzantines reinforcements, weapons and catapults. **5** Accordingly when they were once more equal in number to the enemy, they regained their confidence and resolutely endured hazards on behalf of their country. Nor was the king any less determined, but, dividing his forces into several parts he maintained unremittingly his attack on the walls in relays by day and night. He had thirty thousand soldiers and a store of missiles and siege engines as well as a quantity of machines of other kinds that could not be bettered, and sought to wear down the besieged.

75.1 The siege proved to be a protracted affair that resulted in the death of many and the wounding of a considerable number of those within the city, and, when provisions began to run out, it looked likely that the city would fall. Nor did fortune neglect the salvation of those in peril but provided them with assistance that was unexpected. For since news of the king's increase in power had reached Asia, the Great King, who regarded Philip's power with suspicion, wrote to the satraps on the coast with instructions to help the Perinthians to the best of their ability. **2** Consequently after deliberation the satraps sent to Perinthus a force of mercenaries, abundant supplies of money and adequate stocks of missiles and of everything else that would be of use in the war. Similarly the Byzantines dispatched the best of the commanders and soldiers they had at their disposal. Now that the armies were a match for one another, the battle was renewed and the siege came to be characterised by an unprecedented degree of rivalry between besiegers and besieged. **3** For Philip, by launching constant strikes against the walls with his battering rams, kept trying to knock them down. Moreover by thrusting back the enemy on the battlements, he sought simultaneously to force his way in with his troops in compact formation through breaches in the walls and to use ladders to climb over the parts of the wall that were denuded of defenders. Accordingly a hand to hand struggle took place in which some were killed and others fell only after succumbing to many wounds. The rewards of victory proved a challenge to the valour of the combatants. **4** For the Macedonians, who were hoping to plunder a city that was opulent and to be honoured by Philip with gifts, remained firm in the face of danger because of their expectation of profit, while the besieged had before their eyes a vision of the horrors of capture and courageously stood firm in the fight for their salvation.

76.1 The nature of the city greatly assisted the besieged in winning total victory. For Perinthus lies by the sea on what might be called the neck of a high peninsula which is a stade in breadth. The city also has houses which are densely packed together and conspicuous for their height. 2 These houses are constructed in such a way that they invariably project above one another along the slope of the hill and endow the entire city with the appearance of a tiered theatre. Accordingly though the walls were being constantly knocked down, the besieged were in no way disadvantaged, because they kept barricading the alleys, making use of the lowest tier of houses on each occasion as a substitute for strong walls. 3 When he had under these circumstances taken possession of the wall at the cost of much effort and risk, Philip discovered that the makeshift wall constructed from the housing was naturally even stronger. In addition, since everything suitable for the war was readily supplied from Byzantium, he divided his troops into two parts and, putting half under his best commanders, left them behind to prosecute the siege, while he himself suddenly made an assault with the remainder on Byzantium and instituted a close siege. 4 Since the Perinthians already had the Byzantian troops, missiles and other implements of weaponry within their city, the people of Byzantium found themselves in severe difficulty. Such was the course of events involving the Perinthians and Byzantians. 5 Among the historians Ephorus of Cyme concluded his work at this point with the siege of Perinthus. He included in his History the deeds of both Greeks and barbarians, beginning with the return of the descendants of Heracles. He covered a period of nearly seven hundred and fifty years and wrote thirty books, introducing each of them with a preface. Diyllus the Athenian commenced the second portion of his work at the end of Ephorus' History and compiled a connected account of the deeds of Greeks and barbarians that happened in sequence down to the death of Philip.

The Events of the Archon Year 340/339

77.1 In the archonship of Theophrastus at Athens, the Romans appointed Marcus Valerius and Aulus Cornelius to the consulship and the one hundred and tenth Olympiad was celebrated at which Anticles the Athenian won the footrace. 2 While these men were in office, the Athenians resolved, now that Philip was besieging Byzantium, that he had broken the peace which he had made with them and immediately sent a naval force of considerable size to assist the Byzantians. Similarly the Chians, Coans, Rhodians and some other Greek states dispatched reinforcements as well. 3 Consequently in alarm at the coalition of the Greeks, Philip abandoned the siege of the cities

51

and concluded peace with the Athenians and the other Greeks who were opposed to him... .

The Events of the Archon Year 339/8

82.1 After the end of this year Lysimachus was archon at Athens, and at Rome Quintus Servilius and Marcus Rutilius were appointed to the consulship... .

The Events of the Archon Year 338/7

84.1 In the archonship of Chaerondas at Athens, Lucius Aemilius and Gaius Plotius succeeded to the consulship at Rome. During their period in office king Philip, having persuaded most of the Greeks to be his friends, was keen to intimidate the Athenians and to win the undisputed hegemony of Greece. He accordingly suddenly occupied the city of Elataea and, gathering his forces in this place, resolved to make war on the Athenians. **2** Since they were unprepared because of the peace which they had concluded with him, he expected that he would overcome them with ease, an expectation which in fact came to fruition. For when Elataea had been captured, certain individuals arrived by night and announced both the capture of the city and the imminent arrival of Philip in Attica with his army. **3** Terrified by the unexpected nature of the event, the Athenian generals sent for the trumpeters and instructed them to continue signalling the alert all night long. When the news had been disseminated in every household, the city was rigid with fear and the people rushed to the theatre at dawn, even before the customary summons from the magistrates. **4** When the generals arrived, the informant was brought forward and addressed them. A silent panic had seized the theatre, and none of the regular orators ventured to give advice. Though the herald repeatedly called upon someone to speak on the subject of the salvation of the community, not a single adviser came forward. **5** In the grip of the most extreme fear and helplessness, the people kept looking towards Demosthenes, who eventually stepped down and, urging them to be of good cheer, expressed the opinion that they should send ambassadors to Thebes immediately and call upon the Boeotians in common with themselves to embark on a struggle for freedom. For time did not permit the dispatch of envoys to the other allies with a view to the implementation of the terms of their alliance. Since the king was expected to arrive in Attica and his march led through Boeotia, only an alliance with the Boeotians remained for them, even though Philip, who was a friend and ally of the Boeotians, would be sure to make an attempt to take them with him en route for his war with the Athenians.

85.1 When the people had assented to the proposal and Demosthenes had proposed the decree concerning the embassy, the people began to look for the man most well versed in public speaking. Demosthenes wholeheartedly complied with their wishes in their hour of need. Having set off quickly on the embassy, he persuaded the Thebans and returned to Athens. Having thus doubled the strength of the existing alliance, the people were elated with hope once more. **2** They forthwith appointed Chares and Lysicles as generals and sent out their entire force under arms to Boeotia. Because all the young men embarked upon the conflict with enthusiasm, the Athenians marched with all speed and arrived at Chaeronea in Boeotia. Amazed as they were at the speed of the Athenian arrival, the Boeotians were themselves no less prompt and went to meet them under arms. Encamping together, they awaited the approach of the enemy. **3** Initially Philip sent envoys to the Boeotian League, of whom the most prominent was Pytho. This man was famous for his oratorical skills, but, when he was contrasted with Demosthenes, in the eyes of the Boeotians in the debate to secure their alliance he excelled all others but was manifestly inferior to this man. **4** And Demosthenes himself takes pride on having accomplished a deed of the greatest magnitude in his debate with this orator when he says in his published speeches:

> I did not shrink before Pytho for all his confidence despite the
> spate of words he used against you.

5 Despite his failure to secure the adherence of the Boeotians, Philip resolved to take on both peoples. Therefore after waiting for the arrival of those of his allies who had lagged behind, he proceeded into Boeotia with more than thirty thousand infantry and no less than two thousand cavalry. **6** Since the spirits of both sides were high, they were both ready and keen for battle. In valour they were equally matched, but in the number of his troops and in generalship the king was superior. **7** For since he had contended in numerous pitched battles of the most heterogeneous kinds and had emerged victorious in most of them, he had great experience in the deeds of war, whereas among the Athenians the best of their generals, Iphicrates and Chabrias as well as Timotheus, were dead, and Chares, the best one among those who remained, was in no way superior to the average private soldier in the formulation and implementation of the tactics required of a general.

86.1 The battle lines were drawn up at daybreak. On one wing the king posted his son Alexander, in age a mere youth but conspicuous for his bravery and swiftness in action. He stationed alongside him the most important of his commanders, while he himself, keeping his specially selected men by his side, had charge of the other wing. He also placed the individual units wherever the circumstances required them. **2** The Athenians divided up their line by nationality, assigning one wing to the Boeotians while they themselves commanded the other. When battle was joined, there was a bitter struggle for a long time, and many fell on both sides so long as the prospects for victory offered by the contest remained uncertain. **3** But later, Alexander, who was eager to give his father proof of his own valour and allowed no other to surpass him in determination, first opened up a gap in the enemy line with the support of the many brave men contending by his side. He broke through and by slaying many wore down the resistance of those ranged against him. **4** After his comrades achieved the same result, the compact formation of the enemy line underwent a steady process of dissolution. When large numbers of corpses began to accumulate, Alexander and his men were the first to force their way through those arrayed against them and put them to flight. Then the king himself, who, since he was bearing the brunt of the fighting, was unwilling to yield the credit for the victory even to Alexander, forcibly thrust back the troops opposite him and, by compelling them to turn tail, became himself the architect of the victory. **5** Of the Athenians more than one thousand fell in the battle and no fewer than two thousand were taken prisoner. **6** Many of the Boeotians too were killed and a considerable number captured. After the battle Philip erected a trophy, gave back the dead for burial, sacrificed to the gods in celebration of the victory and rewarded according to merit those who had been outstanding for gallantry on the field.

87.1 It is alleged by some authorities that in the course of the carousal he drank his fill of large quantities of unmixed wine and, leading the revel in celebration of the victory in the company of his friends, made his way through the middle of the prisoners of war while verbally taunting the wretches with their misfortune. The story is told that Demades the orator, who was at that time among the captives, spoke frankly and uttered a remark that acted as a restraint on the king's outrageous behaviour. **2** For he is reported to have said:

> Your majesty, now that fortune has bestowed upon you the part
> of Agamemnon, aren't you ashamed to be playing the role of
> Thersites?

Under the influence of such well directed censure, Philip is said to have changed his whole attitude to such an extent that, throwing off his garlands and repudiating the tokens of arrogance that are associated with the revel, he marvelled at the man who had used such frankness of speech and, freeing him from captivity, admitted him with all honour to his own circle. **3** In the end, having been won over, it is said, by the Attic charm of Demades, he released all the prisoners without ransom and, completely laying aside the insolence brought about by the victory, sent envoys to the Athenian people and concluded with them both peace and alliance. In the case of the Boeotians he installed a garrison in Thebes and granted them peace.

88.1 After the defeat the Athenians condemned to death Lysicles the general when he was prosecuted by Lycurgus. For this man enjoyed the greatest reputation of all the orators of the day and, though he administered the revenues of the city in a most commendable manner for twelve years and led a life that was exemplary for its probity, as an accuser he was exceedingly harsh. **2** It is possible to judge his reputation and his harshness from the speech with which he prosecuted Lysicles, in which he says,

> You were general, Lysicles. One thousand citizens have fallen and two thousand have been taken prisoner. A trophy has been erected over the city, and the whole of Greece is enslaved. Though all of this has occurred under your leadership and generalship, you nevertheless have the effrontery to live on and behold the light of the sun and to obtrude yourself into the market place, a living memorial to the shame and disgrace of your country.

3 A peculiar coincidence occurred in the period with which we are dealing. For simultaneously with the battle of Chaeronea another battle took place in Italy on the same day and at the same time. The Tarentines, with their ally Archidamus the king of Sparta, were fighting the Lucanians, when it so happened that Archidamus himself was killed. **4** This man was king of Sparta for twenty three years, and his son Agis who succeeded him reigned for nine years. **5** At the same time Timotheus the tyrant of Heraclea on the Black Sea died after a reign of fifteen years. His brother Dionysius succeeded to the tyranny and ruled for thirty two years.

The Events of the Archon Year 337/6

89.1 In the archonship of Phrynichus at Athens, the Romans appointed as consuls Titus Mallius Torquatus and Publius Decius. During their period in office, since he prided himself on his victory at Chaeronea and had intimidated the most celebrated cities, king Philip was ambitious to become the leader of the whole of Greece. **2** Letting it be generally known that he wanted to go to war with the Persians on behalf of the Greeks and to inflict punishment on them for the acts of sacrilege they had committed against their sanctuaries, he won the Greeks over to his cause by his acts of goodwill. Dealing kindly with everyone both in private and in public, he declared to the cities his desire to hold talks with them on matters to their advantage. **3** Therefore a common council was held in Corinth at which he addressed the delegates on the issue of the war with Persia and, by holding out high hopes, he urged them on to war. In the end when the Greeks had elected him as general of Greece with full powers, he began to make preparations on a vast scale for the expedition against Persia. Having worked out for each city the number of troops to be contributed to the alliance, he returned to Macedonia. Such was the situation as regards Philip.

90...

2 At about the same time Ariobarzanes died after a reign of twenty six years and Mithridates, who succeeded to the throne, ruled for thirty five.... .

The Events of the Archon Year 336/5

91.1 In the archonship at Athens of Pythodorus the Romans elected to the consulship Quintus Publius and Tiberius Aemilius Mamercus. While they were in office, the one hundred and eleventh Olympiad was held at which Cleomantis of Cleitor won the footrace. **2** During their period in office king Philip, once appointed as leader by the Greeks, inaugurated the war against Persia by sending to Asia Attalus and Parmenio, to whom he assigned part of his army with instructions to free the Greek cities. He himself, eager to embark upon the war with the approval of the gods, enquired of the Pythian priestess if he would be victorious over the King of Persia. She gave him the following response:

> The bull is garlanded, he comes to an end, the one who will strike
> him is at hand.

3 Though the oracle was in fact ambiguous, Philip accepted it as being in his own interest, supposing that the response predicted the striking down of the Persian like a beast for sacrifice. But in actual fact the event turned out otherwise, and the oracle portended quite the contrary, namely that Philip would be slaughtered like the garlanded bull at a festival amid sacrifices to the gods. **4** However in the belief that the gods were on his side, he rejoiced exceedingly at the prospect of Asia being made captive at the hands of the Macedonians. Accordingly he proceeded to perform sacrifices of the utmost magnificence to the gods and to celebrate the wedding of Cleopatra, his daughter by Olympias. For he gave her in marriage to Alexander the king of the Epirots, who was the full brother of Olympias. **5** Wishing as many Greeks as possible to participate in the festivities, he arranged as accompaniments to the ceremonies in honour of the gods musical competitions and sumptuous feasts for those bound to him by the ties of guest friendship. **6** When he had accordingly invited his personal guest friends from all over Greece, he instructed his own friends to bring from abroad as many of their acquaintances as they could. For he was extremely keen to demonstrate his affability to the Greeks and to offer fitting hospitality in return for the honours bestowed on him when he was given the supreme command.

92.1 At length, when many people flocked together form all quarters to the festival and to the contests, the wedding was held at Aegae in Macedonia. Not only was Philip awarded crowns of gold by individuals of importance but most of the prominent cities crowned him as well, including Athens. **2** When the herald was announcing the crown, he ended up by proclaiming that if anyone who plotted against the king should seek refuge in Athens, he was to be handed over. By means of this phrase so casually uttered as if by divine providence, the divinity was indicating the plot against Philip soon to be implemented. **3** In keeping with this there were similar inspired utterances which foretold the king's demise. For at the royal drinking party, Neoptolemus the tragic actor, who was preeminent both in reputation and for the resonance of his voice, was ordered by Philip to declaim some popular passages, and in particular ones that had some bearing on the expedition against the Persians. The artist, in the belief that the passage would be considered appropriate to Philip's crossing, and out of a desire simultaneously to criticise the notoriously immense riches of the Persian King and to imply that fortune might one day change them for the worse, proceeded to speak the following passage:

> Your thoughts now go higher than the air, you contemplate immense plains becoming cultivated fields, you think of houses, making them greater than the houses of men, in your folly regulating your life at a distance. But Hades, who brings much distress upon mortals, encompasses those who are swift of foot, and, advancing along a path that is dark, suddenly and imperceptibly draws nigh and wrests from us our fondest hopes.

He went on to piece together the remainder of the passage, all of it in the same vein. **4** Delighted with the message that was being conveyed, Philip was totally occupied with thoughts of the overthrow of the Persian King, while at the same time taking into account the oracle delivered by the Pythia which had the same meaning as the words uttered by the actor. **5** Finally, once the drinking party was ended and the beginning of the competitions fixed for the next day, the crowds rushed to the theatre while it was still dark, and at daybreak the procession was drawn up. Among the splendid accompaniments he paraded statues of the twelve gods extravagantly fashioned with the most magnificent workmanship and wondrously adorned with the gleam of precious metal. Along with these a thirteenth was carried in procession, a statue fit for a god, one of Philip in person, who was displaying himself as enthroned with the twelve gods.

93.1 Once the theatre had been filled, Philip himself entered, wearing a white cloak. He had ordered his bodyguards to follow, removed at some distance from him, as an indication to everyone that he had no need of the protection of guards. 2 Such was the degree of preeminence that he had attained. But amid the encomia of everyone as they were congratulating him, an unbelievable and totally unexpected plot against the king came to light that was to bring about his death. 3 In order that our account of this matter may be clear, we shall first explain the causes of the plot. There was a Macedonian named Pausanias who originated in the canton known as Orestis. He was a bodyguard of the king who was loved by Philip for his good looks. 4 On observing that another man of the same name as himself was becoming the object of the king's affections, he abused this second Pausanias by calling him an effeminate who was willing to submit to the erotic advances of anyone who desired to initiate them. 5 This second Pausanias, unable to tolerate the insult, for a time kept his mouth shut, but eventually informed Attalus, who was a friend of his, of his intentions. Of his own free will he encompassed his own death in the following unexpected way. 6 A few days later, when Philip was involved in a battle with Pleurias the king of the Illyrians, he positioned himself in front of the king and, submitting his own body to all the blows aimed at the king, he perished. 7 When the incident became widely known, Attalus, who was a courtier and exercised a good deal of influence with the king, invited Pausanias to dinner, and, filling him with vast quantities of unmixed wine, handed his body over to his stablemen to abuse sexually in drunken rape. 8 On sobering up from his intoxication, he was extremely bitter about the physical abuse he had suffered and accused Attalus before the king. Philip, though incensed at the enormity of Attalus' transgression, was nevertheless unwilling to show his abhorrence because of his kinship with him and his present need of his services. For Attalus was the nephew of Cleopatra, Philip's latest wife, and, since he was courageous in military engagements, he had been chosen as commander of the advance force dispatched to Asia. Accordingly the king, wishing to appease Pausanias' justified anger at what had been done to him, conferred on him valuable gifts and promoted him to a more honourable position among the bodyguards.

94.1 Pausanias however implacably kept up his resentment, and was eager not only to exact vengeance from the perpetrator of his injury but also from the one who had declined to avenge him. This resolution of his was strengthened by the arguments of the sophist Hermocrates. For when Pausanias, who was a student of his, asked him in the course of his studies how one could achieve the greatest fame, the sophist answered that he would do so if he killed the one who had performed the greatest deeds, for the killer of this man would be remembered no less than the victim. 2 Applying the response to his own personal anger and brooking no delay to his plan because of his wrath, he set his plan in motion at the current festival in the following manner. 3 Having stationed horses at the gates, he presented himself at the entrance to the theatre with a Celtic dagger concealed about his person. When Philip instructed the friends who were escorting him to enter the theatre in front of him and the bodyguards were standing somewhat apart, Pausanias, seeing that the king was alone, rushed forward and, driving the blow right through the ribs, laid him out prostrate and lifeless. Then he sprinted for the gates and the horses he had made ready for his escape. 4 Some of the bodyguards immediately rushed to the king's corpse while others, including Leonnatus, Perdiccas and Attalus, streamed out in pursuit of the killer. Pausanias had a head start in the pursuit, and would have succeeded in mounting his horse before they could stop him, had he not entangled his sandal in a vine and fallen. As he was getting up from the ground, Perdiccas and those with him seized him, ran him through and killed him.

95.1 Such was the end of Philip who, in the course of a reign of twenty four years, had been the greatest of the kings of Europe of his day and, because of the size of the empire he ruled, regarded himself as one enthroned alongside the twelve gods. 2 This king is believed to have deployed the most meagre resources to attaining his rule, but to have acquired the greatest kingdom among the Greeks: moreover he enlarged his position not so much by the bravery of his deeds on the battlefield as by the diplomatic skill and affability which he brought to bear while engaged in negotiations. 3 Philip is said to have prided himself more on the shrewdness of his leadership and on his negotiating abilities than on his prowess in battle. 4 Moreover it is related that, whereas all his troops made a contribution to his military victories, he alone won credit for his successes in the field of diplomacy. 5 Now that we have reached the death of Philip, we shall set a limit to this book just as we stated at the beginning. We shall commence the following book with the succession of Alexander to the kingship and attempt to cover all his exploits in one book.

Commentary

1.1 THE PREFACE: In contrast to the long established view that Diodorus simply took over and adapted the comments he found at the beginning of the relevant book of his source, modern scholarship grants him a much greater degree of originality (see Sacks, pp. 9-22).

Actions that are self-contained from beginning to end: Diodorus means that a book should have well defined beginning and end points, in this case the accession and death of Philip. Since a fair amount of space is given to events in Italy, Sicily and Egypt in which Philip was in no way involved, he is not restricting himself to the personal exploits of Philip, but seems to accept that events contemporary with Philip's activities can be included within the scope of his self-contained actions.

1.2 Events that are only half complete: Diodorus is here contrasting, not without some irritation, his work with that of his principal source Ephorus, whose thematic treatment of events led him to leave his account of Philip's reign incomplete and obliged Diodorus to change source more frequently than usual (see Introduction, pp.11-14).

1.3 Twenty four years: he ascended the throne in 359 and died in 336.

Slave to the Illyrians: a reference to the defeat and death of Philip's brother Perdiccas III at the hands of Bardylis in 359.

Ruler of many tribes, including the Illyrians, Paeonians, Thracians and Scythians mentioned in section 5 below.

And cities, such as Amphipolis (ch. 8.2), Pydna (ch. 8.3) and the Chalcidian cities (ch. 53).

1.4 The hegemony of the whole of Greece: a reference to the creation of the League of Corinth, with himself as *hegemon*, in 338/7, taken out of chronological order.

Willingly submitted: there is some exaggeration here, as most were coerced into membership after the battle of Chaeronea, though the archonship of

Thessaly was bestowed on him unasked in 353/2 (Justin 8.2.11, cf. 11.3.2 and Diodorus 17.4.1.).

Those who sacked the sanctuary at Delphi: the Phocians, vanquished in the Sacred War which ended in 346 (ch. 59-60).

Member of the Council of the Amphictyons: in 346 (ch. 60.1). The Delphic Amphictyony was a religious league of states in northern Greece which met originally to administer the temple of Demeter at Anthela near Thermopylae, but which came in the course of time to acquire supervisory duties over the cult of Delphic Apollo and the Pythian Games celebrated in the neighbourhood.

Piety: cf. ch. 60.4.

The votes of the Phocians: the two Phocian votes were transferred to Philip in 346 as a reward for his services on Apollo's behalf (see 60.1 below and Speusippus' *Letter to Philip* 4).

1.5 He subdued the Illyrians, Paeonians, Thracians and Scythians: the Illyrians and Paeonians were defeated in 358 (ch. 4 below), and the Thracians in a series of campaigns which continued till the overthrow of Cersobleptes and Teres in 342 (ch. 71). Among the Scythian rulers who became his subjects were Cothelas, king of the Getae, who became his sixth father-in-law in 342 or 339 (Satyrus, *Life of Philip*, Frag. 5), and Ateas ruler of the area now known as the Dobruja, whom Philip defeated and killed in 339 (Justin 9.2.16). It is curious that despite this reference Diodorus should ignore Philip's Scythian campaigns in his narrative.

Conveyed forces across to Asia, in 337, after the declaration of war on Persia by the Corinthian League, when Philip sent Parmenio, Attalus and Amyntas with an advance force to Asia Minor to prepare the way for the forthcoming invasion (ch. 93 below and Book 17.2.4, 17.4, 17.5; Justin 9.5.8-9).

Cut off by Fate: a reference to his murder by Pausanias (ch. 94).

1.6 Through the indulgence of his fortune: the question whether great deeds should be ascribed to a man's innate ability (*arete*) or to the indulgence of fortune (*tyche*) was frequently debated in antiquity. Cf. the treatise in Plutarch's *Moralia* (326d-345b) entitled *On the Fortune or Virtue of Alexander*

Shrewdness of leadership: cf. 60.4, 95.3.

2.1 The 105th Olympiad: the first year of the 105th Olympiad (360/59-357/6) reckoning forwards from the traditional date for the foundation of the Games in 776.

Footrace: the winner of the *stadion* or footrace comprising one length of the track and corresponding roughly to our 200 metres, traditionally gave his name to the Olympiad in which he was victorious, because the stadion was the only athletic event in the games till the introduction of the *diaulos* (two lengths of the track) in 724.

Cn. Genucius and L. Aemilius: Cn. Genucius Aventinensis and L. Aemilius Mamercinus were consuls for the year 363.

2.2 Vanquished by the Illyrians: in 383/2 (Isocrates 6.46, Diod. 15.19.2).

The Illyrians took Philip hostage: so too Justin 7.5.1, though the story as told by Diodorus is improbable. There is no known link between the Illyrians and the Thebans which might explain the transfer, and the Boeotians were not in any way involved in either Illyrian or Macedonian affairs at this time. Moreover in 382 Philip was a mere infant, a few months old at most. It is possible that he did live for a time as a hostage in Illyria in his boyhood but, if so, it must have been later than the date given by Diodorus, and did not result in his subsequent transportation to Thebes.

Entrusted to the Thebans: the date of Philip's residence in Thebes is far from clear. Diodorus' date given here is to be rejected, since it is both intrinsically implausible and is contradicted by his account at 15.67.4, where Philip is said to have been handed over by his brother Alexander II (369-8) in response to a demand from Pelopidas. Since this is also the version of Plutarch (*Pelopidas* 26.4), it might be accepted without hesitation were it not for a passage in Aeschines (2.28) where he tells a jury how the queen mother Eurydice set the young Philip on the knees of the Athenian general Iphicrates in the course of an appeal for his aid against the pretender Pausanias, an event dated to 368. Some scholars therefore ascribe Pelopidas' demand for Philip as a hostage to his second intervention in Macedonia (late 368 or 367), when, according to Plutarch (*Pelopidas* 27.4) he demanded the surrender of Philoxenus son of the new ruler, Ptolemy. Either Plutarch has confused the two interventions of Pelopidas or Aeschines is guilty of imaginative reconstruction in his recreation of Iphicrates' visit to Macedonia: at all events Philip's detention at Thebes (of three years' duration, Justin 6.9.7, 7.9.3) should be dated to 368-5 or 367-4.

The father of Epaminondas: Polymnis (Nepos, *Epaminondas* 1, Plutarch, *Moralia* 579d). According to Plutarch (*Pelopidas* 26.5), Philip was placed in the house of the general Pammenes, though he did meet and come to admire Epaminondas while in residence there.

2.3 Pythagorean philosopher: Epaminondas' tutor was the Pythagorean Lysis of Tarentum (Nepos, *Epam.* 2.2, Plutarch, *Moralia* 579e), who was already an old man at the time and was dead by 379, the dramatic date of Plutarch's dialogue *On the Divine Sign of Socrates* (Plut. *Mor.* 579e, 585e,

586a), some eleven years before Philip's arrival there.

Philip was reared along with him: this story presupposes that Epaminondas and Philip were approximately the same age, whereas the former, who came into prominence in the 370s and had allegedly spent his first forty years as a private citizen (Plut. *Moralia* 1129c), must have been older by about a generation and, as such, completed his education long before Philip's arrival. The story is a clear fabrication, designed to bring two of the great men of the day into a closer relationship with one another than the facts strictly allowed.

Pythagorean philosophy: Plutarch (*Pelopidas* 26.5) writes that what Philip learned from Epaminondas was not philosophy but military science. Moreover modern scholarship tends to the view that the Pythagorean influence on Epaminondas was negligible (see, e.g. J.Buckler, *Epaminondas and Pythagoreanism*, Historia 42, 1993, pp. 104-8). The comparision between Philip and Epaminondas in Plutarch is far less favourable to the former, in that he denies to Philip any share of Epaminondas' self-restraint, justice, magnanimity and humanity.

2.4 After the death of Amyntas: in 370/69 (Book 15.60.3).

Alexander: i.e. Alexander II, Philip's eldest brother, who ruled for one year (Diod. loc. cit.).

Ptolemy of Alorus, a member of the royal family (perhaps a son of Amyntas II, Hammond and Griffith p. 182), who was married to Alexander's sister Eurynoe and reputedly the lover of the queen mother Eurydice (Diod. 15.71.1, where he is wrongly said to be Alexander's brother). Alexander was assassinated at a festival in 368/7 (Marsyas of Pella, Frag. 3, Jacoby; cf. Demosthenes 19.195 and Justin 7.5, who implies that Eurydice as well as Ptolemy was implicated). At 15.71.1 and 77.5 Diodorus gives Ptolemy the royal title after Alexander's death, whereas Aeschines (2.29) and Plutarch (*Pelopidas* 27.3) call him regent for Alexander's young brother Perdiccas. Alorus, where Ptolemy's estates were situated, was a Macedonian city on the lower reaches of the Haliacmon.

Removed by Perdiccas: in 365, after a reign of three years (Diod. 71.1 and 77.5).

Worsted by the Illyrians: see ch. 1.3, above.

Who had fled from detention: in 365 or 364 (see note on 2.4, above). He was at all events back in Macedonia in time for Perdiccas to assign him a portion of territory to govern, allegedly at the request of Plato (Athenaeus 11.506e; cf. Speusippus, *Letter to Philip* 6).

2.6 Paeonians: a barbarian people living to the north of Macedonia, in the upper reaches of the Axius and Strymon. Some Paeonian tribes were under Thracian rule, others were independent and currently ruled by Agis from his capital at Astibos (the modern Stip).

The Illyrians began to assemble large armies: nothing resulted from this mobilisation, and their failure to follow up their victory of the previous year is left unexplained. It is possible that they were distracted by some domestic problem or by some unrest on their northern frontier of which we know nothing, but equally Philip may have patched up a temporary truce to buy himself time. It may have been on this occasion that he took as his first wife Audata, an Illyrian princess who was doubtless related in some way to Bardylis the Illyrian king (Satyrus, Frag. 5). On this interpretation the marriage will have been imposed upon him by the Illyrians as a guarantee of his future good behaviour.

Pausanias: a member of the royal family, perhaps a son of Archelaus (Hammond and Griffith, p. 184), who had already unsuccessfully claimed the throne in 368/7 (Aeschines 2.27).

The Thracian king: perhaps Cotys I, who was still alive at the time of Philip's accession (Theopompus, Frag. 31). After his assassination in 359, the Odrysian kingdom was divided between Cersobleptes in the east, Amadocus in the centre and Berisades in the west (Tod 151, Harding 64). Since only Berisades shared a border with Macedonia, he will have been the king who promoted Pausanias' candidature after Cotys' death.

Argaeus, a member of the royal family, perhaps a son of Archelaus (Hammond and Griffith, pp. 175-6), who had ruled as Argaeus II with Illyrian backing in 393/2-392/1 (Diod. 14.92.4), and who in all probability now recognised the Athenian claim to Amphipolis as the price of their support (see 3.3, below).

Mantias, the son of Mantitheus of Thoricus (J.K.Davies, *Athenian Propertied Families*, Oxford, 1971, no. 9667), who is best known for his complicated matrimonial life, which led subsequently to the dispute between the sons of his two wives that forms the subject of speeches 39 and 40 in the Demosthenic corpus.

3.1 Reformed the military formations: a vague phrase of uncertain meaning. There is no reason to suppose that he introduced the basic infantry units (the *taxis* or brigade and the *lochos* or company) that existed in Alexander's time, though he did increase the size of the army as time went on. Hammond and Griffith (pp. 419-20) may be correct in believing that he increased the size of the smallest infantry unit, the decad, from its original ten to the sixteen it seems to have comprised in the reign of Alexander. The only certain reference we have to a reform introduced by Philip in the first year of his reign, which Diodorus may have found in his source but omitted in his condensed version, is the following statement of Frontinus (*Strat.*

4.1.6): 'When Philip was organising his first army, he banned the use of carriages. The cavalry were allowed one attendant each, the infantry one attendant for every ten men, and this servant was instructed to carry the handmills. When the troops marched out to summer quarters, each man was ordered to carry on his shoulders sufficient flour for thirty days'.

Provided the troops with appropriate weapons of war: scholars disagree on the meaning of this phrase. At face value, it should mean that Philip himself paid for the weapons which were issued to his men. However with few exceptions, such as the Athenian ephebes, who were provided with weapons at state expense after the reform of the ephebate in 336/5 ([Aristotle], *Ath.Pol.* 42.4), the normal practice was for soldiers to equip themselves. It has been argued by Paul McKechnie, *Outsiders in the Greek Cities in the Fourth Century BC*, London, 1989, pp. 80-85) that in the fourth century mercenaries were provided with weapons by their employers 'often, perhaps even usually'. McKechnie's view has however been challenged by David Whitehead in his article, *Who Equipped Mercenary Troops in Classical Greece?* (Historia 40, 1991, pp.105-112). Certainly Athenian ephebes were very different from Macedonian infantrymen, unless it was Philip's example that led Athens so to arm her ephebes. The principal difficulty in accepting Diodorus' statement at face value lies in the bankrupt state of Philip's treasury in the first year of his reign: money was in short supply with Paeonians, Illyrians and Thracians to be bought off, and he simply did not have the funds to arm his troops on anything like the scale that Diodorus would have us believe. Either Diodorus is telescoping by listing under the first year of his reign a series of reforms which were implemented piecemeal over several years as funds became available or he errs in making him provide the weapons at his own expense, if indeed this is what he is trying to say. Perhaps Hammond and Griffith are correct in believing (p. 421) Diodorus to mean no more than that Philip insisted on his troops acquiring the weapons that he deemed acceptable, above all the *sarissa* (see note on 3.2, below).

Manoeuvres under arms (exoplasia): perhaps the exercise described by Polyaenus (4.2.10): 'Philip was in the habit of training the Macedonians before the approach of danger to take up arms and to march for 300 stades carrying with them their helmets, shields, greaves and spears, and, in addition to their arms, food and utensils for daily use'.

Competitive exercises: presumably competitions with graded financial rewards for the best performers, the sort of incentive employed later by Alexander in the field, e.g. the award of a series of graded prizes to those who scaled the Sogdian Rock (Arrian, *Anabasis* 4.18.7, Curtius 7.11.12).

3.2 The close array of the phalanx and its equipment: Philip's greatest innovation in infantry tactics was the introduction of the long pike or thrusting spear (*sarissa*), some sixteen to eighteen feet in length which because of its weight was wielded in both hands and on the march projected outwards some thirteen to fifteen feet. By way of contrast the spear carried by a Greek hoplite was a throwing spear normally some seven feet long, which could be wielded in one hand, thus freeing the other hand to bear the shield. His Macedonian opposite number, who needed both hands free to wield the *sarissa*, had to be content with a very small shield hung over his left shoulder and, in the absence of a breastplate, would be obliged to rely for protection on archers or other lightly armed troops. In combat the pike rendered the phalanx virtually unstoppable and the enemy extremely vulnerable, since the spears of the first four or even five ranks would all project beyond the first row of troops and create havoc among the enemy before it had much of an opportunity for striking back. Moreover the absence of a large shield enabled the phalanx to operate in a more densely packed formation than the opposing hoplites and facilitated the opening up of a gap in the enemy line. For a general discussion of the Macedonian phalanx, see Polybius 18.29-30 and W.K.Pritchett, *The Greek State at War*, Part I, Berkeley and Los Angeles, 1971, pp. 134-54. There are good diagrams of the phalanx in action in N.G.L.Hammond, *The Macedonian State*, London and New York, 1991, p. 60, and Hatzopoulos and Loukopoulos, pp. 68-9.

The close formation of the heroes at Troy: a reference to the description of the Achaeans at *Iliad* 13.130-5 as they await the onset of the Trojans:

> For those who were judged the best awaited the Trojans and godlike Hector, linking spear close with spear and shield with shield, one upon the other. Buckler pressed on buckler, helmet on helmet, man on man. The crested helmets touched with their shining plates when the men nodded, so closely packed did they stand over one another; the spears in strong hands overlapped as they were brandished.

The passage is also cited by Polybius in his description of the phalanx at 18.29.6.

3.3 In conversation he was gracious: Philip's courtesy and the charm of his conversation are also attested at 60.4, 91.6 and 95.2 below.

Gifts and promises: Philip was generous by nature, even to a fault, but the distinction between gifts and bribes (the same Greek word is used for both) was very thin and at times distinctly blurred. Demosthenes in particular tends to see the bribes of Philip as a motivating factor for practically all pro-Macedonian political activity (e.g. 18.41, 48, 295; 19.137, 145, 167, 265, 306), but since such stories are attested in a wide variety of authors from

Theopompus (Frag. 27J) to Cicero (*Ad Att. 1.67*), *from Hyperides (4.29) to Horace (Odes* 3.16.13), from Valerius Maximus (7.2.10) to Pausanias (7.10.3), by way of Plutarch (*Demosthenes* 14.2, *Aemilius* 12.5, *Moralia* 178b), they are unlikely to be totally without foundation. Even Diodorus is far less charitable in his references to Philip's gifts at 8.7, 53.3 and 54.3-4 below.

Amphipolis: an Athenian colony on the Strymon in Thrace, founded in 437/6 (Thucydides 4.102.3; Diod. 12.32.3 and 68.2) but lost to Brasidas in 424 (Thuc. 4.106; Diod. 12.68.3). Because of its strategic importance and the proximity of a silver mining area, the Athenians never recognised its loss and made its recovery paramount in determining issues of foreign policy.

Argaeus: see note on 2.6 above.

Withdrew from the city: the date of the installation of the Macedonian garrison is uncertain. Given Philip's critical, even desperate position at the time of his accession, it is unlikely that he was involved in the occupation of the city, and a more plausible candidate should be sought in Perdiccas III, who was, according to Aeschines (2.29), assisting Amphipolis against Athens in the late 360s. Philip's unilateral withdrawal of the garrison will have been intended as a friendly gesture towards Athens, and a signal of his desire to avoid any entanglement in the fighting that would result from any Athenian attempt to regain possession.

3.4 The king who was intending to restore Pausanias: see note on 2.6, above.

3.5 Methone: a city on the west coast of the Thermaic Gulf and an Athenian possession since its capture by Timotheus in 363 or 362 (Deinarchus 1.14; 3.17). Mantias' failure to accompany Argaeus or even to send him citizen troops suggests that the Athenians were sufficiently convinced by Philip's gestures to whittle down their support for Argaeus to the bare minimum.

Aegae: modern Vergina, the burial place of the Macedonian kings and the old capital before the move to Pella by Archelaus.

3.6 He let go under truce: among these were the few Athenians who had accompanied the expedition voluntarily (Demosthenes 23.121).

Received the exiles: since Argaeus is not heard of again, it is likely that he was one of those handed over and, presumably, put to death.

3.7 Crenides: a Thasian foundation inland from Neapolis, on the site of an existing Thracian village, which was the centre of a silver and gold mining district to the north west of the mines of Mount Pangaeus. This is the first known Thasian activity in the *peraea* since its loss to Athens in 463 (Thuc. 1.101.3; Diod. 11.70.1), and was taken on the initiative of the exiled Athenian politician Callistratus (Isocrates 8.24; Zenobius 4.24), formerly economic adviser to Perdiccas III and now working freelance.

Philippi: the change of name followed its seizure by Philip in 356 (see 8.6-7 below).

Theopompus: the contemporary historian and author of the *Philippica*, the definitive account of the reign of Philip. The surviving fragments have been collected by F. Jacoby in *Die Fragmente der griechischen Historiker* IIB, no.115 and translated by G. Shrimpton, *Theopompus the Historian* (Montreal and Kingston, 1991). He had previously written a *Hellenica* or *History of Greece* covering the period 411-394.

Five have perished: according to the ninth century A.D. excerptor Photius (*Bibl.* 176, p.120a 14, Test.18 Jacoby), 53 Books of the *Philippica* were still extant in his day and Books 6, 7, 29 and 30 were lost. Since Photius' arithmetic does not add up, it is probable that another missing book number has fallen out of his text. It is tempting to identify the five missing in Diodorus' day with the five unknown to Photius, but in fact fragments of Books 6 and 30 are quoted by writers who are later than Diodorus, and Photius himself tells us that the grammarian Menophanes was unable to find a text of Book 12, which Photius proceeds to summarise in order to prove Menophanes wrong. It is possible that in Diodorus' time major libraries still possessed a complete edition of Theopompus, but that in smaller ones, including that at Agyrium, the complete text of such a voluminous work was unobtainable. If so, the loss of the books enumerated by Photius will have happened at some unknown date somewhere between the time of Diodorus and his own.

4.1 Q.Servilius and Q.Genucius: Q.Servilius Ahala and L.Genucius Aventinensis were the consuls for the year 362.

Now that he was no longer laying claim to Amphipolis: as indicated by the removal of the Macedonian garrison stationed there (see 3.3, above). G.E.M.de Ste.Croix in his article *The Alleged Secret Pact between Athens and Philip II concerning Amphipolis and Pydna* (CQ 13, 1963, pp. 110-9) doubts that Philip abandoned his claim to Amphipolis, but Hammond and Griffith rightly point out (p.236, note 4) that, as the weaker party in 359, Philip was desperate to avoid becoming embroiled with Athens when the Illyrians and Paeonians were so formidable, and might well have made concessions at this time, only to repudiate them when it was safe to do so. They also argue for an alliance as well as a peace between Philip and Athens in 359 on the grounds that, since Demosthenes (2.7, 7.10) describes Philip as an ally of Potidaea, a city which was an Athenian possession with resident Athenian cleruchs, he can hardly have done so unless he was himself an ally of Athens at the time.

4.2 Agis: Philip may have hoped that the death of the Paeonian king would lead to a disputed succession, or, at very least to the accession of a new and untried ruler who could be attacked before he could consolidate his rule. Agis' successor was the Lyppeius or Lycceius who subsequently joined an anti-Macedonian coalition (Tod 157, Harding 70).

4.3 Illyrians: the Illyrians were not a politically united people. Those attacked by Philip were probably the Dardanians (N.G.L. Hammond, *The Kingdoms in Illyria circa 400-167 BC*, ABSA 61, 1966, pp. 239-53), a powerful tribe based on what is now the Kosovo area of Serbia.

4.4 Bardylis: the Dardanian king. According to Theopompus (Frag. 286J) he was originally a brigand, and is said by [Lucian] 12.10 to have fought in person on horseback in this battle at the age of ninety.
Previous victories: those over Amyntas III in 393/2 (Diod. 14.92.3) and 383/2 (Diod. 15.19.2) and over Perdiccas in 359 (Ch. 2.4-5 above, cf. Polyaenus 4.10.1). Diodorus may also have in mind Bardylis' victories over the Molossians in 385/4 (Diod. 15.13.2-3) and again over Arybbas (Frontinus, *Strat.* 2.15.9) shortly before Philip's accession.

4.5 The pick of the Macedonians: probably what in Alexander's day was called the *agema* of the hypaspists.

4.6 Formed themselves into a square: a curiously defensive tactic, suggesting that the Illyrians had received intelligence of Philip's military reforms and that despite their confidence they still felt some uncertainty about the best method of dealing with them.

4.7 Withdrew from all Macedonian cities: i.e. those they had occupied as a result of their victory over Perdiccas, the return of which Philip had demanded as the price of peace (sections 2-3 above). In addition we hear of Philip's acquisition of territory as far as Lake Lychnitis (ch. 8.1 below). It is also possible that it was now rather than in the previous year that Philip married Audata: in this event the initiative will have come from Philip with the aim of guaranteeing the future good behaviour of the Illyrians. Satyrus (Frag. 5) prefaces his list of Philip' wives with the comment that he always married *kata polemon*, 'in the course of each campaign', or possibly 'with war in mind', i.e. what we would call a diplomatic marriage or marriage of policy.

6.1 C.Licinius and C.Sulpicius: the consuls for 361 were C.Licinius Calvus (according to the *Fasti Capitolini*, his cognomen was Stolo) and C.Sulpicius Peticus.

7.2 Simultaneously with these events: i.e. the preparations for Dion's bid to overthrow the tyranny of the Younger Dionysius and the refoundation of Tauromenium by Andromachus, as related in chapters 5 and 6.

Euboea: all four of the major Euboean cities, Chalcis, Eretria, Carystus and Hestiaea had been members of the Second Athenian Confederacy, but had seceded in 370/69 in order to join the Boeotian alliance (Xenophon, *Hellenica* 6.5.23, 7.5.4, *Agesilaus* 2.24; cf. Diod. 15.85.2 and 87.3), but by now Theban hegemony was proving no less irksome.

Some called in the Boeotians and others the Athenians: two of those who called in the Athenians were Mnesarchus of Chalcis and Themison of Eretria, whom Athens assisted in the ensuing campaign despite their previous pro-Boeotian stance (Demosthenes 18.99, Aeschines 3.85). Epigraphical evidence (Tod 154, Harding 66) confirms the pro-Athenian attitude of Eretria at this time.

No major pitched battle: Diodorus condenses drastically at this point, but his account can be supplemented with references in the orators: Demosthenes informs us that it was Timotheus who persuaded the Athenians to become involved in the war (8.74) and that Chares (23.173) and Diocles (21.174) were two of the generals on this campaign. We owe to Aeschines (3.85) the information that the Thebans were expelled within thirty days.

Made peace: separate treaties appear to have been concluded with the individual cities (that made with Carystus survives in part, Tod 153, Harding 65), and all were readmitted into the Athenian Confederacy. The Athenians also passed, on the motion of Hegesippus, a decree punishing the invaders of Eretrian territory and threatening any future aggressor with a similar penalty (Tod 154, Harding 66, too fragmentary for certain restoration). Since this inscription is dated 357/6 and includes among the generals of the year the Diocles who was general in the Euboean campaign (see previous note), either Diodorus is inaccurate in his date for the fighting in Euboea or Diocles was general for two successive years and work on the settlement spilled over into the following archon year.

7.3 The Chians, Rhodians, Coans and Byzantians: Chios, Rhodes and Byzantium were founder members of the Second Athenian Confederacy but had already been encouraged by Epaminondas to take up an anti-Athenian stance as early as 364/3 (Diod. 15.79.1; cf. Isocrates 5.53 and [Demosthenes] 50.6). Cos too may have been a member of the Athenian alliance: though absent from what remains of the Decree of Aristoteles, the name is usually restored among the names lost at lines 85-90 (Cargill, p. 37). Nothing came of Epaminondas' approach at the time, though some scholars (e.g. S. Ruzicka, *Politics of a Persian Dynasty*, Norman and London, 1992, p. 91 with note 6) believe that it led to their secession from the Confederacy, and that Athens started the Social War seven years later by attempting to coerce them into rejoining. Byzantium's links with Boeotia became even closer when she entered some sort of confederacy based on Thebes and even sent contributions to help the Boeotians defray the expenses of the Sacred War (Tod 160, Harding 74).

Three years: most modern scholars reject Diodorus' date of 358/7- 356/5 in favour of 357/6-356/5, that given by Dionysius of Halicarnassus (*Lysias* 12. So R.Sealey, *Athens after the Social War*, JHS 75, 1955, pp. 74-81), while yet others (e.g. N.G.L. Hammond, *Diodorus' Narrative of the Sacred War*, JHS 57, 1937, pp. 44-78 and G.L.Cawkwell, *Notes on the Social War*, Classica et Mediaevalia 23, 1962, pp. 34-49) opt for Diodorus' three year war, but date it to 357/6-355/4. The scholiast on Demosthenes 21.17 states that it broke out in the same year as the Euboean expedition, but its date is no less controversial (see note on section 3 above). For sound arguments in support of Diodorus' dating of the Social War, see D.M.Lewis, *Notes on Attic Inscriptions: XIII. Androtion and the Temple Treasures*, ABSA 49, 1954, pp. 39-49. At ch. 22.2 below Diodorus wrongly states that the Social War lasted four years.

Chares: See J.K.Davies, *Athenian Propertied Families 600-300 BC*, Oxford, 1971, no. 15292; W.K.Pritchett, *The Greek State at War*, II, Berkeley and Los Angeles, 1974, pp. 77-85. He is first mentioned as general in 366, when he assisted Phlius against Argos (Xen. *Hell.* 7.2.18ff, Diod. 15.75.3). In 361/0 he was sent to Peparethus and from there to Corcyra (Diod. 15.95.3), and served subsequently in Euboea and the Chersonese (Dem. 23.173) before his despatch to Chios. Diodorus comments unfavourably on his generalship at 85.7 below.

Chabrias: See Davies, no.15086; Pritchett pp.72-7. First mentioned in 393 at Corinth (Diod. 14.92.2), he had a long and varied career as general, serving at different times in Aegina (388, Xen. *Hell.* 5.1.10-12), Euboea (377/6, Diod. 15.30.5), Abdera (372, Diod. 15 36.4, where he erroneously has him killed off), Corcyra (372, Xen. *Hell.* 6.2.39), Epidaurus (369, Xen. *Hell.* 7.11.5) and Egypt (Diod. 15.29.2, date uncertain). His most celebrated exploit was his victory over the Spartans at Naxos in 376 (Xen. *Hell.* 5.4.61, Diod. 15.34.3), though the degree of success achieved under his generalship fluctuated widely. While Demosthenes stresses his reputation for caution (20.82), he nevertheless accords him a place among the most famous men of the day (20.76-8). For a more detailed account of Chabrias' death, see Nepos, *Chabrias* 4, according to whom he was not general at the time but a private citizen (trierarch?), 'whose influence was greater than that of all who held command, and the soldiers looked to him rather than to their own leaders'. Some support for his fall from grace (perhaps for his failure at the Hellespont?) may be found in Demosthenes (20.81-2), who refers to the Athenians' robbing him of part of his reward for former services, and in the erasure of his name from the list of generals who took the oath appended to the treaty made with the Euboeans (see note on section 2 above).

Mausolus, son of Hecatomnus, the Carian dynast appointed satrap of Caria by Artaxerxes II in 392/1. On his father's death in 377/6 (see ch. 36.2, below), Mausolus inherited what became a hereditary position. He moved his capital from Mylasa to Halicarnassus and was ambitious to expand his rule. Since this could best be achieved by weakening Athenian influence in the eastern Aegean, he supported the rebels in the Social War. Demosthenes indeed (15.3) blames him for instigating the war, but though he undoubtedly had influence in Rhodes and perhaps even designs on the island, he had no known links at the time with Cos or with Chios, to say nothing of Byzantium. He did profit from Athens' defeat, as subsequent events were to show, but the most that can safely be said of his part in provoking the war is that its outbreak was not unwelcome to him.

8.1 In a great battle: see ch. 4.5-7, above.

8.2 Amphipolis: garrisoned by the Macedonians under Perdiccas but freed in 359, when Philip was seeking to conciliate Athens (3.3, above). Her preoccupation with Euboea and the Social War afforded him the opportunity to regain the city without Athenian interference.

Afforded him many opportunities for war: fearing attack from Philip, the Amphipolitans sent an embassy to Athens earlier in the year led by Stratocles and Hierax, offering to hand the city over (Theopompus, Frag. 42J, Dem. 1.8), but the Athenians were too distracted by events elsewhere to take any action. They did however send Antiphon and Charidemus on a diplomatic mission to Philip, but the envoys seem to have been deceived or to have deluded themselves as to his intentions. According to Theopompus (Frag. 30), they concluded a secret deal with Philip by which he was to hand over Amphipolis in return for Pydna, but Ste. Croix (see note on 4.1 above) has shown that there could be no place for secret diplomacy in a democracy, and that envoys who concluded unauthorised pacts on their own initiative would be disowned and prosecuted. Theopompus' view finds some support from Demosthenes, who refers at 2.6, in the context of negotiations about Amphipolis, to 'the secret that was on everyone's lips', but the real nature of this secret, if there ever was one and if it really was connected with

Amphipolis, cannot now be determined. Philip was undoubtedly master of the diplomatic promise and ambiguous utterance, and whether or not he pledged in in the presence of the ambassadors to hand Amphipolis over, the Athenians subsequently believed that he did (see Dem. 7.27 and 23.116). Philip's deception, real or imagined, was to poison relations between the two powers for many years, if not permanently.

He exiled those ill-disposed towards him, including Stratocles the leader of the embassy to Athens. An Amphipolitan inscription (Tod 150, Harding 63) records a decree of the people ordering the the exile of Stratocles and Philon.

Treated the remainder with lenience: the democracy was left intact, but it is likely that the property and estates of the anti-Macedonian exiles were assigned to Macedonians either now or at a later date. Demosthenes (1.8, delivered in 349) implies that Philip treated the pro-Macedonians badly, and in 346 Isocrates (5.5) mentions that Philip derived some sort of revenue from the city (some kind of tax or tribute?). At some time Philip established a mint there, and by Alexander's reign at latest no fewer than three naturalised Macedonians (Nearchus, Laomedon and Androsthenes) owned estates situated in Amphipolitan territory (Arrian, *Indica*, 18.4).

8.3 Well situated in regard to Thrace and the adjacent regions: Amphipolis was situated in a horseshoe bend of the river Strymon and was thus easily defended, while its position on the main land route from Epidamnus and Apollonia on the Adriatic to Byzantium at the point where the route crossed the Strymon made it an important strategic centre. It had a good port in Eion at the Strymon mouth, and was well located for trade with the Thracian interior by way of the Strymon valley. In addition the proximity of silver and gold producing areas made it a significant mining centre, while control of vast wooded areas enabled the city to export a fair amount of the timber and pitch which were badly needed by the shipyards of Greece.

Pydna: a Greek city on the Thermaic Gulf, five miles south of Methone, and an Athenian possession since its acquisition by Timotheus in 364. Besieged by Philip (Dem. 1.9), it fell by treachery (Dem. 20.63), but details are lacking. Demosthenes implies that, as with Amphipolis, the inhabitants were treated harshly, and in 326, two of Alexander's trierarchs at the Indus had estates there (Arrian, *Indica*, 18.5). It was the fall of Pydna, if not already that of Amphipolis, which induced Athens to declare war.

He concluded an alliance with the Olynthians: the Chalcidians had for some time been hostile to Athens, which was suspected of having designs on their territory, and were consequently on good terms with Philip. However his capture of Amphipolis, a former ally of theirs, must have set the alarm bells ringing, and Philip was anxious to forestall a possible Atheno-Chalcidian alliance. A badly mutilated inscription (Tod 158, Harding 67) records what was the last part of the treaty of alliance, the oaths sworn by the contracting parties, though the terms of the alliance itself are missing. In addition to the clause concerning Potidaea mentioned here, we know from other sources that Philip ceded the city of Anthemus to the Chalcidians (Dem. 6.20) and that both parties bound themselves not to make a separate peace with a third party (in effect Athens) without the consent of the other (Libanius, Hypothesis to the First Olynthiac 2).

Potidaea, a Corinthian colony on Pallene, situated at the narrowest part of the isthmus, formerly a member of the Chalcidian League, but won for Athens by Timotheus in 364 (Isocr. 15.113; Deinarchus 1.14 and 3.17; Diod. 15.81.6). The city requested the despatch of Athenian cleruchs to its territory in 361 (Tod 146, Harding 58), presumably in an attempt to strengthen it from possible Chalcidian retaliation, and the cleruchs were reinforced by the installation of an Athenian garrison (see section 5, below).

8.4 A significant city: Olynthus was relatively unimportant before the formation of the Chalcidian Confederacy in 432, but in the synoecism which created the federal state Olynthus was designated as the headquarters of the League, and the population of some of the smaller coastal cities which were too exposed to Athenian attack was transferred to Olynthus (Thucydides 1.58.2). Though retaining their existing lands, they were now citizens of the enlarged and well fortified capital.

In competition for the Olynthian alliance: an indication that diplomatic negotiations had been taking place between Athens and the Chalcidians.

8.5 When Philip reduced Potidaea: in 356, in order to implement his promise to deliver it to the Chalcidians. Neither Diodorus nor any other source preserves details of the siege, which the Athenians, despite their involvement in the Social War, resolved to break, only to abandon the attempt when news arrived of the city's fall (Dem. 4.35).

Treated them humanely: Philip is known to have released Athenian prisoners without ransom on two other occasions: the defeat of Argaeus in 359 (Dem. 23.121), and after Chaeronea in 338 (ch. 87.3 below; Plut. *Moralia* 177e, Polyaenus 5.10.4). One suspects that his generosity was motivated less by his respect for the Athenian people or by the importance of the city than in the hope of being able to influence public opinion there in his favour: since Athens was a democracy and less inclined to heed the advice of the prominent men whose services Philip utilised in influencing oligarchic regimes, he may have hoped that the collective gratitude of many ordinary families might succeed in swinging public opinion his way.

Sold the citizens as slaves: Philip's unusually harsh treatment should in this instance be explained by the need to recover the cost of the siege, for, as the city and its territory had been promised to the Chalcidians, he would otherwise have been operating at a loss.

8.6 Crenides: see note on 3.7. Philip intervened ostensibly in response to an appeal for aid from the inhabitants, who were being attacked by Thracians (Stephanus of Byzantium s.v. Philippoi). These Thracians may possibly have been subjects of Cetriporis, who had succeeded Berisades as king of the most westerly of the three Odrysian kingdoms, but were more probably acting under orders from Cersobleptes of eastern Thrace, in an effort to secure funds for his bid to secure control of a united kingdom (Dem. 23.9-10). Hammond and Griffith (p. 246) make out a case for believing that Diodorus is wrong in dating the capture of Potidaea before the occupation of Crenides: it is clear from Tod 157 line 46 (Harding 70) that Philip had possessed himself of Crenides by the first prytany of 356/5 (i.e. July 356), whereas Potidaea fell shortly before he received news of his Olympic victory about the end of August (Plutarch, *Alexander* 3.4-5, with Hamilton's note on the passage in his *Plutarch, Alexander:a Commentary*, Oxford, 1969). If the siege of Potidaea was brief, Philip could have taken the city before he went to Crenides, but if it lasted some time (as is likely if the Athenians were able to learn of it and make preparations for an expedition to recover it) Philip is more likely to have embarked upon the siege of Potidaea and diverted to Crenides while it was still in progress, leaving the prosecution of the siege to deputies.

Paltry and unimportant: this refers only to the gold production: silver had been obtained from the area in considerable amounts for over a century.

8.7 Abundance of money: in addition to the Crenides and Pangaeus mines, Philip obtained precious metals from the mines of Damastion, to the north of Lake Prespa, an area taken from the Illyrians in 358.

Gold currency: such a currency was highly unusual in the Greek world, and unprecedented for a Macedonian king. Though he had coined in silver since the beginning of his reign, the numismatic evidence indicates that Philip's gold coinage dates only from the late 340s (G.Le Rider, *The Coinage of Philip and the Pangaion Mines*, in Hatzopoulos and Laikopoulos pp. 48-57), presumably to defray the huge expenditure of his later years (e.g. Theopompus, Frag. 224). If he is correct in linking the gold coins with the acquisition of Crenides, Diodorus may be confusing Philip's gold coinage with that of the new city of Philippi, which minted gold coins in limited quantities inscribed with the city's own name.

Named Philippeioi after himself: these were staters issued mostly from the mint at Pella. On the obverse was a laureate head of Apollo, on the reverse a two horsed chariot and driver with Philip's name at the base, perhaps in commemoration of one of his Olympic victories. The naming of a coin from a king is unusual, but there is a precedent in the gold coins of Darius I of Persia, which were known to the Greeks as *Darics* and believed to be named after the king (Pollux 3.87), though in fact the name is derived from *daranya*, the Persian word for gold.

Traitors: see note on 3.3 above.

9.1 M.Fabius and C.Poplius: M.Fabius Ambustus and C.Poetelius Libo Balbus (or Visolus according to the *Fasti Capitolini*) were consuls for the year 360. The name of the latter has been corrupted in Diodorus' text.

14.1 Alexander of Pherae: Pherae was a city in the south east of Thessaly, whose port Pagasae possessed the only good harbour in the country. Unlike the other Thessalian cities, it was not dominated by one or another of the aristocratic families who monopolised the office of *tagos* or head of state. About 405 a wealthy citizen Lycophron seized power as tyrant with some popular support. His son Jason, who subsequently came to power, extended his rule beyond Pherae and secured election as *tagos* in 374 (Xen. *Hell.* 6.1.18), thus bringing about for the first time in two centuries a virtually unified Thessaly. After his murder in 370, opposition to the rule of the tyrant family of Pherae gathered strength, and the leaders of the traditional aristocratic families from the other cities formed a rival Federal League with a head of state called the *archon*. Thessaly was now divided into two camps, the adherents of the new federation and the supporters of the *tagos*, each claiming to represent the legitimate government. Alexander, grandson of Lycophron and nephew of Jason, was *tagos* from 369 till his death, which should perhaps be placed in 358/7 rather than 357/6: his successor Tisiphonus was already in charge when the Athenians and Boeotians were involved in Euboea in 357 (Scholiast on Aristeides' *Panathenaic Oration* 179.6), and Diodorus himself elsewhere (15. 61.2) places his accession in 369/8 and gives him a reign of eleven years. His wife Thebe was his cousin, daughter of Jason and had personal grievances which she incited her brothers to avenge. More details of the assassination are preserved in the accounts of Xenophon (*Hell.* 6.4.35-7, Cicero (*De Officiis* 2.17.25) and Plutarch (*Pelopidas* 35), who implicates a third brother, Peitholaus. The eldest brother, Tisiphonus, succeeded to the tyranny.

Won much approbation: Isocrates (Epistle 6.11), in a letter addressed to the children of Jason, advises them to maintain a constitutional regime rather than the autocracy advocated by some members of their intimate circle.

The mercenaries: the standing army of mercenaries formerly employed by Alexander to keep him in power.

Those opposed to them, including both Pheraeans opposed to the tyrannical regime in that city and federalists who supported the rival Thessalian League.

14.2 Aleuadae, a long established aristocratic family from Larissa which, along with the Echecratidae and Daochidae of Pharsalus and the Scopadae of Crannon, had supplied the *tagos* from within their own ranks, and consequently despised the Pheraean tyrants as upstarts. The eponymous ancestor, Aleuas the Red (7th century B.C.?), according to the scholiast on Demosthenes 1.22 a descendant of Heracles, was regarded as the traditional unifier of the country and creator of the system of land ownership that formed the basis of the national army (Aristotle, Frag. 497).

They acquired as an ally Philip: this was nothing new, for Macedonian kings had been summoned in the past, including Archelaus, invited in 401 by Aristippus of Larissa in his struggle with Lycophron ([Herodes] *Peri Politeias* 16ff., cf. Aristotle, *Politics* 1311b), and Alexander II, called in by the Aleuadae in 369 against the Pheraean tyrants (Diod. 15.61.3-5).

He entered Thessaly: since the death of Alexander may belong to 358 (see note on 14.1 above), Philip's intervention which followed it should also be placed in that year. According to Justin 7.6.8, the Thessalian campaign occurred after the Illyrian victory of 358 and before Philip's marriage to Olympias, which should be dated at least nine months before the birth of Alexander the Great in either July (Plutarch, *Alexander* 3.3) or October (Aristobulus in Arrian, *Anabasis* 7.28.1) of 356. Thus both 358 and 357 are possible dates for Philip's intervention in Thessaly, with slight odds in favour of the former if Plutarch's date for Alexander's birth is correct. The initiative in extending the invitation to Philip was taken by Cineas of Larissa (Theopompus, Frag. 35).

Overcoming the tyrants and regaining freedom for the cities: since Jason's sons were still ruling Pherae in 353 (ch. 35.1), Diodorus cannot mean that Philip expelled them or regained freedom for Thessaly at this time. He seems to be anticipating his successes of 353/2, described in more detail at 37.3 below. The silence of our sources on further incidents in Thessaly till 354/3 ought to mean that Philip was able to effect a temporary reconciliation between the warring factions.

Showed much goodwill to the Thessalians: if not another anticipation of Philip's settlement of 353/2, Diodorus may be thinking of such things as the parties he threw for his Thessalian friends (Theopompus, Frag. 162) and of the friends he acquired from such widely different social backgrounds as the aristocratic Cineas of Larissa and Daochus of Pharsalus (Dem. 18.295, Theopompus Frag. 35) and Agathocles from the *penestai* or serf class whom he appointed governor of Perrhaebia (Theopompus Frag. 81). Diodorus may also have in mind Philip's marriage to Philinna of Larissa, mother of the Arrhidaeus who was of marriageable age in 337 (Plutarch, *Alexander* 10.1). Since Satyrus (Frag. 5) states that she was married in order to conciliate the Thessalians, she is likely to have been of a higher social standing than the smears of Justin ('prostitute', 9.8.2; 'dancing girl', 13.12.2, cf. Athenaeus 578a) would appear to indicate.

Philip acquired them as confederates: as the phrase 'in subsequent events' proves, Diodorus is once again anticipating his later narrative. He may be thinking of the role of the Thessalian League as his ally in the Third (ch. 35.2, 59.2) and Fourth (Demosthenes 18.151) Sacred Wars, or of Philip's election as Archon of the Thessalian League in 353/2 (see note on 1.4 above).

Alexander: at 17.4 Diodorus states that he persuaded the Thessalians to acknowledge him as *hegemon* of Greece in succession to his father, and may also be referring to the very important role of the Thessalian cavalry , greater than that of any other Greek state, in the conquest of the Persian Empire.

14.3 Demophilus son of Ephorus: the universal historian Ephorus, utilised by Diodorus as his principal source, died leaving his work unfinished. Because of the thematic treatment of his subject matter, he left unrecorded the narrative of events in mainland Greece during the reign of Philip while at the same time relating the contemporaneous happenings in Asia. The glaring gap which resulted was partially filled by his son Demophilus who himself wrote an account of the Sacred War and appended it to his father's History as Book Thirty.

Seized the Delphic temple: see chapter 23 below.

Eleven years: Diodorus is hopelessly muddled in his chronology of the Sacred War. Aeschines (2.31 and 3.48), Duris (Frag. 2), Pausanias (9.6.4, 10.2.4) and Diodorus himself at ch. 59.1 below all give the correct figure of 10 years, while at ch. 23.1 below Diodorus manages to produce yet another estimate, this time of 9 years.

Destruction of those who shared in the spoils: see chapters 61 and 64 below.

14.4 Callisthenes, of Olynthus, the son of Aristotle's niece (Plutarch, *Alexander* 54.4), best known as the historian of Alexander's campaigns, whose career was cut short in 327 by his execution for alleged conspiracy at Bactra (Arrian, *Anabasis* 4. 22.2, Curtius 8.6.24ff.). He also wrote a Hellenica or History of Greece beginning with the Peace of Antalcidas of 387/6 and ending with the outbreak of the Sacred War in 357/6 (see also Diod.14. 117.8).

14.5 Diyllus, son of the Atthidographer, religious expert and politician Phanodemus, who wrote a historical work used by Diodorus in both Book 16 (Hammond, CQ 31 and 32, 1937 and 1938) and Book 17 (Hammond, *Three Historians of Alexander the Great,* Cambridge, 1983, pp. 322-5). He published his work in 26 books and in at least two *syntaxeis. Syntaxis I* covered events in Greece and Sicily from 357/6 till 340/39, and was apparently a continuation of Ephorus, while *Syntaxis II* included the deeds of both Greeks and barbarians (i.e. presumably events in Asia) from 341/0 to the death of Philip (cf. ch. 76.6, below). Because his work contained a reference to the burial of Philip III and Eurydice in 316 (Athenaeus 4.41.155a) and was mentioned by Diodorus again in the remains of Book 21 which began with the events of the year 301/0, the Philip with whose death *Syntaxis II* terminated is usually thought to be Philip IV, who died in 297/6. Hammond however (*Three Historians of Alexander the Great,* p. 174, note 20) believing the reference to be to Philip II, is of the opinion that Athenaeus and Diodorus in Book 21 were referring to a hypothetical *Syntaxis III.*

15.1 M.Poplius Laenates and Cn. Mamilius Imperiosus: there is some corruption in Diodorus' text in the transmission of these names. The consuls for 359 were M. Popillius Laenas and Cn. Manlius Capitolinus Imperiosus.
The 106th. Olympiad: 356/5-353/2.

21.1 The Social War: continued from 7.2-4.
Chares: see note on 7.3 above.
Iphicrates: see Davies 7737, Pritchett pp. 62-72. One of the most enterprising and innovative generals of the period, he was of humble origin (according to Plutarch *Moralia* 186f the son of a shoemaker) and had a distinguished career in the Corinthian War, when he was put in command first of a troop of mercenaries at Lechaeum (Xen. *Hell.* 4.4.9; Diod. 14.86.3), and then of peltasts at Phlius and Sicyon (Xen. *Hell.* 4.4.15; Diod. 14.91.2). His most celebrated exploit was the annihilation of a whole *mora* of the Spartan army in 390 (Xen. *Hell.* 4.5.13; Diod. 14.91.3). Thereafter he operated in the Hellespont in 389 (Xen. *Hell.* 4.8.34), at Abydos in 388 and 387 (Xen. *Hell.* 5.1.7), in Thrace in the 380s in the service of Cotys (Dem. 23.130-2), in Persian service in the mid 370s (Diod. 15.29.4 and 41-2; Nepos, *Iph.* 2.12; Plutarch, *Artaxerxes* 24.1), in Corcyra in 373-2 (Xen. *Hell.* 6.2.14 and 27, 6.4.1), in the Peloponnese in 369 (Xen. *Hell.* 6.5.49) and in Macedonia in 368, when he received the appeal from Eurydice (see note on 2.2

above). In the course of his career he married into the Odrysian royal family (Dem. 23.129) and secured adoption by Philip's father Amyntas III (Aeschines 2.28). A strict disciplinarian (Nepos, *Iph*. 2.1, 2.4; Frontinus *Strat*. 3.12.21), he also introduced new equipment for the peltasts with whom he came to be closely associated, a smaller shield, a longer spear and sword, and light boots named after him (Diod.15.44).

Timotheus (Davies 13700), son of the celebrated general Conon who had been active in the last decade of the Peloponnesian War and in the 390s. Timotheus studied rhetoric under Isocrates, whose favourite pupil he became and who included a eulogistic summary of his career at 15.107-113. He was active in the Peloponnese in 377 (Xen. *Hell*. 5.4.63; Diod.15.29.7; Nepos, *Tim*. 2.1, in Corcyra and north west Greece in 376 (Xen. *Hell*. 5.4.64; Isocr. 15.109; Diod. 15.36.5), in Egypt in 372 (Dem. 49.25), in Asia in support of the rebel satrap Ariobarzanes in 367-6 (Dem. 15.9), at Samos on 366 and in the Hellespont in 365-4 (Isocr. 15.108, 111; Nepos *Tim*. 1.3), and in Thrace in 364-3 (Isocr. 15.111; Diod. 15. 81.6). According to Nepos *Tim*. 3.2, Timotheus and Iphicrates were not generals in this Social War campaign but present merely as advisors to Iphicrates' son Menestheus, who was married to Timotheus' daughter (cf. Dem. 49.66). Menestheus' generalship that year is confirmed by Isocrates 15.129, but there is no reason to doubt that Iphicrates and Timotheus were, as Diodorus says, generals who were in addition given a mandate to supervise the former's inexperienced son.

21.2 Together with their allies: the identity of these allies can only be a matter for conjecture, but they certainly included the Perinthians (Plutarch, Demosthenes 17.2; cf. Demosthenes 15.26).

Imbros and Lemnos, two islands in the north Aegean which had been Athenian possessions since their acquisition by Miltiades in the 490s (Herodotus 6.40, 140), apart from a brief period after the end of the Peloponnesian War, and which were currently administered as outlying districts of Attica (cf. Aristotle, *Ath. Pol.* 61.6, 62.2). The allies will have sought to occupy these islands in an attempt to deny them to Athens as bases for a possible counter attack.

Samos, acquired by Timotheus in 366 (see note on Timotheus above), the island became an Athenian cleruchy (Aristotle, *Rhetoric* 2.1384b; Diod. 18.18), soon to be reinforced by additional groups of settlers in 361/0 (scholiast on Aeschines 1. 53) and in 352/1 (Philochorus Frag. 154; Strabo 14.1.18). The choice of Samos as an allied objective will have been dictated by its wealth, its importance to Athens as a naval base and pressure from the large number of dispossessed Samian exiles.

Many other islands: there is no doubt some exaggeration here. Evidence does however exist for an attack on Amorgos: an inscripton of 366 of the city of Arcesine on this island honours the Athenian Atthidographer Androtion, who was governor of the city at the time, for ransoming citizens who had been captured by the enemy (Tod 152 lines 15-16, Harding 68). The allied coalition is the only plausible candidate for the enemy in question, and the geographical location of the island almost due west of Cos would have rendered it particularly vulnerable to attack. The installation of Athenian garrisons in both Amorgos and Andros (Tod 156, Harding 69) in 357/6, contrary to the charter of the Athenian Confederacy, may have been justified by the possibility of such an attack.

21.3 Lay siege to the city of the Byzantines: the need to secure the corn route through the Bosporus will have been seen as the top priority in the circumstances.

In the area of the Hellespont: according to Polyaenus (3.9.29), this battle was fought off the coast of Asia Minor at a place in the territory of Erythrae called Embata, mentioned by Thucydides (3.29.2) and Theopompus (Frag.14). Since there is no reason why such an obscure place should be chosen as the fictitious scene of this battle, Diodorus' statement should be rejected and ascribed to his faulty geographical knowledge: if he can locate near the Hellespont such a well known city as Olynthus (ch.53.2 below), he is just as capable of making the same mistake in the case of the unfamiliar Embata.

21.4 Chares wanted to engage: Diodorus' statement ought to mean that no battle took place, but Nepos (*Tim.* 3.4) informs us that Chares did actually engage with his sixty ships and was defeated.

Brought Iphicrates and Timotheus to trial: since Chares' rashness could be considered culpable, it was essential for him to accuse his colleagues of lack of cooperation before they could act against him. There are two distinct versions of the prosecutions of Iphicrates and Timotheus (and Menestheus). According to Diodorus and Nepos (*Tim.* 3.5), Chares merely wrote an accusing letter and was not personally involved in the prosecution, but remained in the eastern Aegean (so ch. 22.1 below and Dem. 4.24) while the other generals were recalled to stand trial immediately; the alternative account of Polyaenus (3.9.29) has the trial deferred till 354/3 (so Dionysius of Halicarnassus, *Deinarchus* 667), when he returned to Athens and himself served as one of the accusers. Support for Diodorus' version is to be found in a fragment of Iphicrates' speech for the defence (Lysias, Frag. 131) which refers to the war as still going on. There is also a conflict of evidence in our sources concerning the type of procedure used to bring the generals to trial: see M.H.Hansen, *Eisangelia: the Sovereignty of the People's Court in Athens in the Fourth Century B.C.*, Odense, 1975, pp. 100-102), who argues for *eisangelia*, and J.T. Roberts, *Accountability in Athenian Government*, Madison, 1982, pp. 45-9, who maintains that the trial arose out of the *euthyne* they underwent after deposition. The charges were *prodosia* or treason (Lysias, Frag. 128; Isocr. 15.129; Nepos, *Tim.* 3.5) and accepting bribes from the allied coalition Deinarchus 1.14 and 3.17), while the prosecutor was Aristophon (Lysias, Frag.131; scholiast on Aeschines 1.64; Aelian *Var. Hist.* 14.3).

Fined them a large sum: Diodorus is here in error. According to Isocrates (15.129) and Nepos (*Iph*.1.3), Iphicrates and Menestheus were acquitted and only Timotheus was condemned (because of the odium he incurred through his haughty manner, if Isocrates is to be believed). The fine imposed on him was 100 talents (Deinarchus, locc. citt.). Unable to pay the fine, he went into exile at Chalcis (Nepos, *Tim.* 3.5), where he died before the publication of Isocrates' *Antidosis* (5.101) in 353.

22.1 Eager to free the Athenians of the costs: Athenian finances were in an unsound condition for much of the fourth century, and the inability to pay the troops was an important factor in explaining their indifferent military record. Generals were forced to rely on their own ingenuity in providing the wages that held their armies and navies together, and all too often resorted to what was little better than piracy or extortion (see e.g. Dem. 2.28, 4.24, 8.25, 51.13; Aeschines 2.71). Chares in particular had a bad reputation in this respect (Diod. 15.95.3; Plutarch, *Phocion* 14.2; Aeneas Tacticus 11.13-15), but on this occasion found a more satisfactory way of dealing with the problem.

Fraught with risk, of involving Athens in a war with Persia.

Artabazus, satrap of Hellespontine Phrygia. The new king, Artaxerxes III Ochus, who had just come to the throne (358), was determined to stamp out the satrapal revolts that had so weakened his predecessor, and ordered his satraps to disband their private mercenary troops. Since Artabazus felt it unsafe to do so, he defied the order and rose in revolt (scholiast on Dem. 4.19, for which see Harding 72).

The satraps who had more than seventy thousand: the identity of the satraps who led the King's army is nowhere stated, but it is likely that they were those with satrapies in western Asia Minor, such as Autophradates of Lydia or Mausolus of Caria. According to the scholiast cited in the previous note, a certain Tithraustes, who commanded 20,000 men, was defeated by Chares at this time, while a fragment of the unknown historian preserved in Papyrus Rainer (Jacoby *FGrH*. 105 Frag.4) states that this same Tithraustes, whose land in Phrygia was ravaged by Chares, thereupon made peace with Artabazus. He may have been one of the loyal satraps, but this is far from certain: he could just as well have been merely a local fief holder.

Chares came to his aid: according to the scholiast previously cited, some of the mercenaries previously employed by satraps entered Chares' service, and, when Artabazus approached him for help, pressurised Chares into joining him in order to provide them with their wages.

Defeated the King's army: according to Plutarch (*Aratus* 16.2), Chares wrote a letter to the Athenians in which he described this victory as a sister to that of Marathon.

22.2 At first the Athenians approved: so too the scholiast on Demosthenes loc.cit., who states that they even encouraged Chares to raise more mercenaries. The vast amount of booty he sent to Athens from the capture of Lampsacus and Sigeum (scholiast on Dem. 3.31, for which see Harding 72; cf. Isocrates 7.29) doubtless helped to influence public opinion, as did belief that the King may have been behind Mausolus' reputed role in fomenting the Social War.

A story had been spread: rumours of possible Persian intervention in Greece are also mentioned by Libanius, Hypothesis to Dem.14.

A settlement: Diodorus gives no details of the terms of the peace treaty, but the effective loss of the rebels to the Confederacy must have been recognised. In the aftermath of the settlement Mausolus took advantage of the vacuum previously filled by Athens to enforce his own supremacy over Rhodes, Cos and Chios. By 351, the date of Demosthenes' speech *On the Liberty of the Rhodians*, the Rhodian democracy had been replaced by an oligarchy, and Mausolus' garrisons had been installed in all three islands (Dem. 15.3,15,19; Theopompus, Frag. 121; Libanius' Hypothesis to Dem.15; Athenaeus 10.445e).

Four years: on the length of the war, see note on 7.3, above.

22.3 Three kings: Cetriporis the Thracian, Lyppeius the Paeonian and Grabus the Illyrian, whose names are given in the text of the the treaty of alliance which they made with the Athenaians (Tod 157, Harding 70). Cetriporis was the successor of Berisades in western Thrace, Lyppeius the presumed successor of Agis (see 4.2 above). Grabus was probably not the son of the Illyrian king Bardylis defeated in 358, for a son of Bardylis named Cleitus is attested as an opponent of Alexander in 335 (Arrian, *Anabasis* 1.5.1) and it is unlikely that his tribe would have recovered from such a comprehensive defeat within a mere two years. Grabus was probably king of some other Illyrian tribe (perhaps the Taulantii who lived on the Adriatic coast inland from Epidamnus and were later to cooperate with Cleitus against Alexander, or the Grabaei who lived further north, to the east of Lake Labeatis (the modern Shkodër). It is clear from the treaty of alliance that the coalition enjoyed the blessing of Athens, which joined it but purely as a passive partner. The treaty was concluded in the first prytany of 356/5 (i.e.

July 356) and postdates Philip's capture of Crenides which the coalition promises to recover (line 45).

As they were still assembling their armies: this should mean that the kings were attacked separately before they could join forces, but only a battle with the Illyrians is otherwise attested.

He appeared on the scene: Philip's involvement in the simultaneous siege of Potidaea and the seizure of Crenides makes it impossible for him to have been a participant in this campaign. We know from Plutarch (*Alexander* 3.5) that a victory over the Illyrians was won in this year by Parmenio, presumably in his capacity as Philip's deputy. Whether a second battle against the Paeonians followed, as Diodorus' account would have us believe, or whether the Illyrian defeat forced them to sue for terms is unknown.

Compelled them to submit: for the subsequent status of the Illyrians and Paeonians, see Demosthenes 1.23. As we hear of no further hostilities against Cetriporis at this time, he too may have come to terms, as Diodorus says.

23.1 M.Fabius and C.Plotius: C.Fabius Ambustus and C.Plautius Proculus were consuls for 358.

Nine years: actually ten. See note on 14.3, above.

The war that culminated at Leuctra: the war of 379/8-371, which began with the liberation of Thebes from Spartan control and ended with the Common Peace of 371 (Xen. *Hell.* 6.5.1) or rather with that of 362 (Diod. 15.89.1, Plutarch, *Agesilaus* 35.3, Polybius 4.33.9).

23.2 The Thebans brought an accusation: at the autumn meeting of 357, some fourteen years after the date implied by Diodorus, though he may merely be anticipating later events. The date is based on epigraphical evidence (see J.Buckler, *Thebes, Delphoi and the Outbreak of the Third Sacred War*, in P.Roesch and G.Argoud (edd.), La Béotie Antique, Paris, 1985, pp. 237-46.

Before the Amphictyons: on this body, see note on 1.4 above. The present charge arose out of their supervisory role over the conventions of Greek warfare which Sparta violated by seizing the Cadmea in time of peace.

Seizing the Cadmea: Phoebidas seized the Cadmea, the Theban citadel, in 382 (Xen. *Hell.* 5.2.27-31; Diod. 15.20.2; Nepos, *Pelopidas* 1.2; Plutarch *Pelopidas* 5.2-3, *Agesilaus* 23.3). Why the Thebans waited 25 years before bringing the charge is unclear: since Sparta was no longer a threat, the motive can have been little more than a desire to embarrass an enemy now experiencing hard times.

A large sum of money: 500 talents, according to chapter 29.2 below, where the imposition of a deadline for paying the fine is implied.

23.3 The Phocians were prosecuted: Diodorus is silent on the identity of the prosecutors. Justin (8.1.4) claims that the Thebans charged the Phocians as well as the Spartans, but Buckler (*Philip II and the Sacred War* Mnemosyne, Supplement 109, Leiden, 1989, pp. 16-18), argues convincingly for the Delphians. Though geographically part of Phocis, Delphi was an independent community outside the Phocian Confederacy, enjoying a special status in the eyes of the Greeks because of its guardianship of Apollo's temple situated on its territory. Forever anxious to forestall a Phocian takeover, it would have been in Delphi's interest to divert Phocian attention to other matters.

Cirrhaean: Cirrha was a Phocian city in the rich plain to the south of the shrine, between Delphi and the sea, where the valleys of the Pleistus and the Hyaethus merge. The inhabitants originally exercised the guardianship of the Delphic sanctuary, but were, according to fourth century belief, found guilty of sacrilege and destroyed with their city in 596 in the First Sacred War (Aeschines 2.107). The plain was subsequently consecrated to Apollo and entrusted to the care of the Delphians, who would have been very much an interested party in the event of Phocian encroachment upon the plain.

23.4 Philomelus: according to Pausanias (10.2.2), whose account seems to be drawn from the same source as that of Diodorus, he was a citizen of the Phocian city of Ladon.

23.5 In ancient times: Philomelus could have pointed out that the Phocians had control of Delphi prior to the First Sacred War, and temporarily recovered it in the mid 5th century at the time of the Second Sacred War (Philochorus, Frag. 34; Plutarch, *Pericles* 21.1-2), perhaps as the result of her alliance with Athens (Thucydides 1.111.1) after the battle of Oenophyta in 457 (Thucydides 1.108.3). The Spartans then returned control of Delphi to the Delphians, only for the Athenians to return it to the Phocians (Thuc. 1.112). How long they retained control is uncertain, but it is unlikely to have outlasted the Athenian defeat at Coroneia in 447 (Thuc. 1.113.2).

Homer: the quotation is from *Iliad* 2. 517 and 519, two lines from the Catalogue of Ships describing the Phocian contingent that went to Troy. This document was believed in antiquity to preserve an accurate record of the political geography of Greece at the time of the Trojan War.

23.6 General with full powers: details of the Phocian federal constitution are obscure. Among the organs of government were a primary popular assembly and a chief executive, elected by the assembly, comprising three generals (chapter 56.3 below; Plutarch, *Moralia* 244c), though in times of crisis the assembly would elect a general with full powers, who held office for the duration of the emergency. He possessed at least one colleague (see 31.5 and 38.6 below), but outranked him, though he was still subject to some measure of control by the federal assembly, which retained the right to depose him (see 56.3 below). For more information on the Phocian constitution, see J.A.O. Larsen, *Greek Federal States: their Institutions and History*, Oxford, 1967, pp. 40-48.

24.1 Archidamus, Eurypontid king from 360 till 338, the son of Agesilaus and third king of this name.

24.2 Cooperate in secret: to avoid appearing to condone sacrilege. According to Theopompus, Frag. 312, Archidamus and his wife Deiniche were won over by Philomelus' bribes, but these were unnecessary since, from Archidamus' point of view, an alliance with Phocis would keep the Boeotians in northern Greece and avert a repetition of the series of invasions of Laconia which had plagued Sparta in the 360s. As a result of this understanding, she even secured 3000 troops from the Phocians for use in the war with Megalopolis in 352 (chapter 39.3 below). The secrecy with which Archidamus operated probably prevented him from going through the gerousia and assembly, but his subsequent immunity from prosecution should mean that he acted in consultation with the board of ephors, who controlled foreign policy.

Fifteen talents: given the manpower shortage which afflicted Sparta in this period, Archidamus' failure to provide troops is understandable, but it is surprising that in a financial crisis no less acute, he could afford such a large sum. Part may have come from his private resources, but the bulk is likely to have been drawn from what was left of the payment of 230 talents made to his father Agesilaus in return for services rendered to the Egyptian pharaoh Nectanebo II in 360 (Plutarch, *Agesilaus* 40; cf. Xenophon, *Agesilaus* 2.31).

Peltasts: peltasts would be particularly useful in any engagement in the immediate environment of Delphi, where the nature of the terrain did not favour the use of hoplites.

24.3 He seized the oracle: some time in the summer of 356, after the spring and before the autumn meeting of the Amphictyonic synod. See Buckler, Appendix 1, pp. 152-4.

Thracidae: a Delphic aristocratic family, who wanted to keep Delphi independent of the Phocian Confederacy, and whose confiscated wealth would help defray the wages of his mercenaries. Diodorus neglects to state specifically that Delphi was now forcibly incorporated into the Phocian Confederacy.

24.4 Locrians: presumably those living closest to Delphi, the western or Ozolian Locrians of Amphissa.

In the vicinity of Delphi: on the assumption that sections 4-5 are a doublet of 28.3 (see note on 28.1), the battle in question will have been that fought near the cliffs called the Phaedriades, which overhang the Delphic sanctuary to the north.

24.5 His intention was not to loot the sanctuary: since he had other sources of funding initially, this proclamation may even have been sincerely meant, but his need for an ever increasing number of mercenaries and the high wage rate he was obliged to pay (see 25.1 and 30.1) soon made a mockery of his claim. Diodorus is inconsistent in his treatment of the issue, perhaps because of his use of two contradictory sources (Demophilus and Diyllus?) that he fails to assimilate: at 28.2 and 56.5, he has Philomelus abstain from the treasures, but at 30.1, supported by Theopompus Frag. 248 and Plutarch, *Timoleon* 30.4, he states the opposite.

Ch. 25 This is one of the most unsatisfactory chapters in the book, being full of obscurities, confusions and statements that are contradicted elsewhere. Certainly the reader will have a clearer understanding of the course of events if this chapter is ignored. It is best understood as a doublet of chapter 30, where what appear to be the same events are narrated more competently from a different source. For a good discussion, see Buckler, p. 148; for arguments to the contrary, see N.G.L.Hammond, *Diodorus' Account of the Sacred War*, JHS 57, 1937, pp. 44-77.

25.1 The Boeotians: Diodorus' account of the chronology and sequence of events is muddled. There is no reference at this point to the condemnation of the Phocians at the autumn synod of the Amphictyons (described at 28.4). Prior to this, the Boeotians, contenting themselves with a diplomatic offensive, took no military action. If the view that this chapter is simply a doublet of chapter 28 is rejected, we would have to assume that he is merely anticipating the events of the next campaigning season.

Surrounded the shrine with a wall: Philomelus' wall was constructed from large blocks of limestone, some of which are still *in situ*, and as part of the same scheme a square tower and quarters for a permanent garrison were added.

By half as much again: to encourage the enlistment of better quality mercenaries, who might otherwise be deterred by religious scruples. His ability to meet these additional costs would have been much impaired had he found no extra sources of revenue, a fact which lends some support to the charge that he appropriated some of the sacred monies by the end of his generalship (see note on 24.5, above).

25.2 Marched into Locrian territory: this took place *after* the vote of the Amphictyons and is a doublet of the events described at 30.3 (see Buckler, p. 173). The Locrians in question were the eastern or Epicnemidian Locrians, and Philomelus' move will have been designed both to knock them out of the imminent war in a surprise attack and to deny the Thessalians an easy passage south.

Requested permission through a herald: the usual Greek practice for the vanquished side in a battle was to ask the victors, who retained control of the battlefield, for permission to recover the dead under truce.

Cast out temple robbers unburied: so Xenophon (*Hell.* 1.7.22, speech of Euryptolemus), 'Try them under the law applying to temple robbers and traitors which provides that those who are traitors to the state and who have stolen property sacred to the gods should be tried before the courts and, if found guilty, shall not be buried in Attica, and shall have their property confiscated.' Cf. the initial Boeotian refusal to hand back the Athenians killed at Delium in 424 on the grounds that they had committed sacrilege in seizing and fortifying Apollo's temple and in using the holy water belonging to the god (Thucydides 4.97. 2-3). This episode too suggests that Philomelus did appropriate some of the sacred treasures, or at least that the Locrians believed him guilty of this offence.

25.3 Engaged the Locrians in battle: if this is the same battle as that described at 30.3-4 below, it was fought at a place called Argolas, identified by Buckler (p. 41 with note 16) with the modern village of Mendenitsa.

Ch. 26 Diodorus' account of the origin of the Delphic oracle appears nowhere else, apart from brief mentions by Plutarch (*Moralia* 433c and 435d) and Pausanias (10.4.7). It is totally at variance with the archaeological evidence and amounts to little more than a rationalistic invention by his source.

26.1 Make consultations with a goat, a reference to the practice employed by the priests to ensure that the occasion was auspicious for the delivery of an oracle. A goat was fetched and sprinkled all over with cold water in order to induce in it a violent trembling; should the shudder fail to materialise, the occasion was deemed unfavourable and no oracle was pronounced.

26.2 Chasm: a chasm at the oracular site is mentioned by Apollodorus (1.4.1), [Longinus] *On the Sublime* 13.2, and by the scholiast on Lycophron 1419, but is conspicuously absent from Plutarch's abbreviated version of this incident at *Moralia* 435d. Excavations conducted at the site have failed to reveal any sign of a deep chasm in the ground, and references in ancient writers to the Pythia (Plut. *Mor.* 397a, 405c, 438d) or to the enquirer (Pindar, *Pyth.* 4.58; Plut. *Mor.* 407d, *Timoleon* 8.2) 'descending' seem to mean only that the tripod and its immediate surroundings were situated at a lower level than the rest of the temple.

Delphi was as yet uninhabited: archaeology has revealed that Delphi was inhabited long before the institution of the oracle. A village existed on the site from the second half of the second millenium B.C., and a Mycenaean cult centre (of Earth?) was established on what became in the classical period the site of the shrine of Athena Pronoia. The village was destroyed at the end of the Mycenaean period, and there was no further habitation till the revival of the village and the establishment of Apollo's cult centre in the early eighth century B.C.

26.3 The goatherd: according to Plutarch (*Moralia* 433d and 435d), his name was Coretas.

Seat of the Earth goddess: Greek tradition regularly, but not invariably (e.g. the Homeric Hymn to Pythian Apollo), speaks of the owners of the sanctuary in the sequence Earth – Themis – Apollo (e.g. Aeschylus, *Eumenides* 1-8, where the Titaness Phoebe is added as a fourth, between Themis and Apollo; Euripides, *Iphigenia in Tauris* 1235-83; Pausanias 10.5.5-6). The basis of this belief may have been a dim recollection of the Mycenaean cult centre at Delphi, albeit at a different location.

26.5 Fashioned in imitation of this mechanism: tripods existed long before the arrival of Apollo's cult at Delphi. The Delphic tripod, which had a bowl in the centre and served as the seat of the Pythia when giving oracles, was probably installed originally as a container for the offerings made to Apollo which were burned over a central fire. H.W.Parke and D.E.W. Wormall (*The Delphic Oracle*, Oxford, 1956, p. 25) also suggest that the lot oracles attested in later sources may have been stored in the bowl and shaken up by the Pythia before drawing one out.

26.6 Echecrates the Thessalian, presumably a member, perhaps even the eponymous ancestor, of the aristocratic family of Pharsalus known as the Echecratidae. Since Diodorus dates the alleged incident 'in more modern times', this Echecrates may even have been a historical person, though the story itself can be little more than an aetiology invented to explain why the Pythia was dressed in the classical period in the robes of a virgin.

An older woman of fifty, a statement supported by passages like Aeschylus, *Eumenides* 38 and Euripides, *Ion* 1324 which imply a woman of mature years. The Pythia's 'uniform' is likely to have been intended as symbolic of her ritual purity.

27.1 In the traditional manner: exactly why Philomelus' consultation was not in the traditional manner is not explained. Since it is unlikely that he was stupid enough to alienate the Pythia or the Delphic authorities by demanding a consultation on an inauspicious day or by neglecting the proper preparatory rituals, it may be that those guilty of serious offences like sacrilege or bloodguilt were denied the right to put questions (cf. the Pythia's refusal to give a response to Calondas the killer of the poet Archilochus (Plut. *Moralia* 560d). Philomelus' seizure of a chance remark as an auspicious prophetic utterance has a parallel in the story of Alexander the Great who supposedly demanded a response on a day of ill omen and, denied a response by the Pythia, proceeded to drag her forcibly to the tripod and accepted as prophetic her remonstrative utterance, 'You are invincible, my son' (Diod. 17. 93.4; Plut. *Alexander* 14.4). The story seems to have been invented by someone who wished to portray Alexander as no less violent and impious than Philomelus.

27.2 Summoning an assembly: meetings of the Phocian Confederacy were normally held at the Phokikon, on the road from Delphi to Daulis, but this meeting seems to have been held at Delphi, which is the scene both of what precedes and what follows. The choice of venue was a propaganda exercise serving to emphasise the finality of Delphi's incorporation into the Confederacy.

Omen in Apollo's temple: because of the gravity of the step which Philomelus was taking, it was important for him to convince the more superstitious of his compatriots that his action was acceptable to the gods. An oracle, especially one irregularly obtained, would be inadequate for this purpose, but could be strengthened by some additional divine sign. The appearance of an eagle was traditionally seen as auspicious (e.g. Xenophon, *Anabasis* 6.5.2, *Cyropaedia* 2.4.19; Plut. *Dion* 24.4, *Timoleon* 26.3, *Alexander* 33.2).

Doves reared in the sanctuary: Cf. Euripides, *Ion* 1197-8, where doves are said to live tame about the temple.

27.3 Sent on embassies, a diplomatic offensive intended to put the best possible interpretation on his actions; by emphasising the reasonableness of his behaviour, he hoped to reassure as many states as possible, though he can hardly have expected much from the embassy sent to Thebes.

27.5 Athenians: as old friends of the Phocians (Thucydides 3.95.1) and bitterly hostile to Phocis' enemy Thebes, they were seen by Philomelus as natural allies. Moreover, Athens had harboured Astycrates, the leader of a dissident Delphian faction who had been exiled in 363 and awarded him citizenship (IG II² 109, M.J. Osborne, *Naturalization in Athens*, Brussels, 1981-2, Decree 11), at the same time denouncing Astycrates' banishment as illegal (line 17). In the circumstances, Philomelus rightly calculated that the Athenians would back any steps he took against Delphi and the Amphictyony. The decree proposing alliance between the Athenians and Phocians was moved at Athens by Hegesippus (Aeschines 3.118).

Spartans: see 24.1-2 and note. This alliance with Phocis was an official act of the Spartan state, unlike the earlier negotiations conducted by Archidamus.

Some others, including the Achaeans (see 30.4 and 37.3 below), the Corinthians (see 60.2 below) and, at least in 353/2, the tyrant family of Pherae (35.1-3, below).

Some other states: for a more detailed list, see 29.1, where the names given include the Thessalians and the minor members of the Amphictyony which were Thessalian subjects. In addition some states aligned with the Boeotians made financial contributions, including Alyzea and Anactorium on the Acarnanian coast as well as Byzantium (Tod 160, Harding 74).

Went to war with the Phocians: the declaration of war by the Amphictyons was made at the synod held in the autumn of 356 (see Buckler, pp. 146-57).

28.1 C. Marcius and Cn. Mallius: C.Marcius Rutilus and Cn. Manlius Capitolinus Imperiosus were consuls for the year 357.

Collected large numbers of mercenaries: cf. 24.2-3, of which this passage is a doublet.

28.2 Abstain from the sacred dedications: see note on 24.5, above.

Levied from the Phocians: probably the Thracidae, the confiscation of whose property Diodorus has already recorded at 24.4.

28.3 The Locrians marched against him: this Locrian attack seems to be a doublet of that described at 24.4 above.

The Phaedriades: see 24.4 note.

28.4 The Boeotians: cf. 25.1, above.

The Amphictyons voted for war: cf. 27.5 above. The date of the declaration of war was the autumn of 356, not 354/3.

29.1 The Boeotians, Locrians, Thessalians, a fuller list of belligerents than that given at 27.5.

Perrhaebians, Dorians... : apart from the Boeotians, Locrians and Thessalians, the peoples listed were perioecic communities subject to Thessaly. The Perrhaebians lived in the area to the north of Thessaly proper, on the border with Macedonia; the Dorians were a small nation living on the north-western border of Phocis; the Dolopians and their northern neighbours the Athamanians lived to the west of Thessaly by the Pindus range which separated Thessaly from Epirus and Amphilochia; the Achaeans of Phthia lived to the south of Thessaly along the west coast of the Gulf of Pagasae; the Magnesians occupied the entire western seaboard of Thessaly from Macedonia to the Gulf of Pagasae; the Aenianians inhabited the Spercheius valley, having as neighbours the Dolopians and Phthiotic Achaeans to the north, the Aetolians to the west, and the Oetaeans to the south.

And some others: Diodorus presumably has in mind the Malians, the only perioecic people absent from the list who were members of the Amphictyony, and perhaps the Oetaeans, who, though at this time lacking representation on the Council, were closely linked with their perioecic neighbours under Philip's later Corinthian League, in which they were grouped with, among others, the Aenianians, Malians and Dolopians (Tod 177/Harding 99, Frag. B, lines 8-9). For the complete list of Amphictyonic members prior to the reform of 346, see Aeschines 2.116 and Pausanias 10.8.2.

The Athenians, Spartans and some others: see note on 27.5, above.

29.2 The Spartans: the events mentioned in this and the two following sections have already been narrated at 23.2.

30.1 One and a half times: this appears to be a doublet of the similar statement at 25.1.

30.3 Advanced into Locrian territory: this, the first event in the campaigning season of 355, goes over the same ground as the briefer account at 25.2. The attack on the Epicnemidian Locrians was designed to remove them from the contest before they could join forces with either the Thessalians or the Boeotians, and to impede the passage of the Thessalians into

Phocian territory.

The Boeotians came to help: there is no hint of Boeotian involvement in the corresponding passage at 25.2, or, in this passage, of their fate. They disappear from the scene as mysteriously as they make their appearance, and, when Diodorus narrates the arrival of the Boeotians in the next section, they are to all intents and purposes making their first entry into the war. Their role in the present passage is thus best disregarded.

30.4 Argolas, presumably in the vicinity of the modern village of Mendenitsa (see note on 25.2, above).

Thirteen thousand troops, an unprecedented number for the Boeotian levy, which normally amounted to around 7000. There were 7000 at Delium in 424 (Thuc. 4.93.3), 6000 with Epaminondas at Leuctra (Diod. 15.52.2) plus those with Bacchyllidas sent to guard the Cithaeron passes (Paus. 9.13.7), 7000 in 369/8 (Diod. 15.68.1), 8000 in 368/7 (Diod. 15.71.3) and 7000 again in 364/3 (Plut. *Pelop.* 35.2). If Diodorus' figure of 13000 is to have any credibility, it should indicate the entire strength of the Amphictyonic army, not just the Boeotian contingent. The Boeotians may have been commanded by Pammenes, if Polyaenus 5.16.4 is to be assigned to this campaign.

The Achaeans, hostile to Thebes ever since the overthrow of the Theban imposed democracies in the individual cities in 366 (Xen. *Hell.* 7.1.43) and now firmly in the Spartan camp.

31.1 Campaigned with temple robbers: this appears to be an alternative version of the incident described at 25.2, with Boeotians substituted for Locrians. The allegation makes more sense here than it does at 25.2, since in that passage the Phocians had not yet looted the sanctuary.

31.2 Captured the enemy who were roaming over the countryside: cf. 25.3, where this fate is meted out to the Locrians after a battle. Clearly if the two passages refer to the same incident, the 'battle' was no more than a series of skirmishes.

31.3 Another area: the topography is curiously vague. It seems that both armies withdrew from Locris into Phocis, Philomelus by way of a route over Mount Kallidromon to Tithronium and from there to Tithorea on the Cephisus, and the Amphictyons by way of the Fontana Pass (see Buckler, pp. 40-1).

A severe battle: it is apparent from this account that the two armies met where they did purely by chance. The battle, left unnamed by Diodorus, is called the Battle of Neon by Pausanias (10.2.4). Neon was the older name of the city of Tithorea (Herodotus 8.32; Paus. 10.32. 8-9), but was retained as the name of the citadel (cf. Dem.19.148).

31.4 Threw himself down from a rock: so too Pausanias 10.2.4.

31.5 His fellow general: the Phocians had a board of three generals, but in emergencies granted one of them supreme power (see note on 23.6). This sentence anticipates the reference to Onomarchus' election at 32.3 and 33.2.

31.6 Methone, a Greek city on the Macedonian seaboard a few miles north of Pydna, situated on the western coast of the Thermaic Gulf and an Athenian possession since its acquisition by Timotheus in 364 (Dem. 4.4). By now it was the sole Athenian possession on the coast of Macedonia, and its capture was essential to Philip to deny Athens a base in the area. See 34.5 below, where Diodorus repeats his note on the city's capture. The double entry may indicate that Philip's siege went on into a second archon year (355/4- 354/3), but, since the present entry is the less detailed of the two and occurs in a section which incorporates brief notes on events that took place in four geographical areas, it is more likely to derive from his chronological handbook, while the longer account at 35.4-5 will be based on his historical source. The protracted nature of the siege is clear from Demosthenes' statement that the Athenians had time to prepare a relief expedition, even though it arrived too late. An Athenian decree (IG2 130) dated to the fifth prytany of 355/4 (i.e. December 355) honours one Lachares of Apollonia for – inter alia – sending his son into Methone, thus proving that the city was by that date either threatened with or already under siege. The loss of Methone should therefore be placed some time in 354, but, though Diodorus' date for its capture is correct, he is certainly wrong in his belief that the entire siege belongs to this archon year. For further details of the siege, see the notes on 35.4-5 below.

Pagasae, the port of the city of Pherae and the only good harbour in Thessaly, previously under the control of Lycophron and Peitholaus, the two surviving sons of Jason. Thessaly had been relatively quiet internally since Philip's earlier intervention (see 14.2 and note), but the details of his current involvement are not given till 35.1, a passage based on Diodorus' principal narrative source. If 'Pagasae' is the correct reading (the manuscripts have the unknown name 'Pagae'), the chronological muddle will be due to the imperfect assimilation of material pertaining to Thessaly drawn from his chronological and historical sources. The context in which the present passage occurs suggests that the Thessalian appeal may have reached Philip while he was engaged in the siege of Methone, but the circumstances leading up to the capture of Pagasae are left undetermined. Its capture is also mentioned by Demosthenes at 1.9 and 4.35, but without any reference to the context in which it occurred. The note is best understood as an anticipation of the Thessalian narrative of chapter 35, and the capture of the place should be dated to 353, the year of Philip's second, and highly successful, Thessalian campaign (see note on 35.3, below).

Leucon king of the Bosporus: the kingdom of the Cimmerian Bosporus comprised parts of the Crimea and the adjacent areas of the mainland to the east, with its capital at Panticapaeum (the modern Kerch). It had a mixed population that included both native Scythians and Greeks from the city foundations within its borders. It had been ruled since 438/7 by the Spartocids, a hellenised native dynasty, who were careful to claim the royal title only in the non-Greek areas of their realm: Leucon's official title is given in a contemporary inscription (Tod 115, Harding 27C) as '*archon* of the Bosporus and Theodosia, king of the Sindoi, Toretai, Dardanioi and Psessoi'. Because of the region's importance as a centre of wheat production and distribution on a large scale, the Bosporus kings were assiduously cultivated by Athens and other cities dependent on imported grain.

Our main source for this dynasty is Diodorus, though his account is confused and incomplete. The information he provides may be tabulated as follows (facts to be inferred, but not specifically states are enclosed in square brackets):

KING	ACCESSION DATE	LENGTH OF REIGN	DATE OF DEATH
Spartocus I*	438/7 (12.31.1)	7** (12.31.1, 36.1)	433/2 (12.36.1)
Seleucus	433/2 (12.36.1)	40 (12.36.1)	[393/2]
Satyrus I	[437/6]	44 (14.93.1)	393/2 (14.93.1)
Leucon I	393/2 (14.93.1)	40 (14.93.1; 16.31.6)	353/2 (16.31.6)
Spartocus II*	353/2 (16.31.6)	5*** (16.31.6, 52.10)	349/8 (16.52.10)
Paerisades I	349/8 (16.52.10)	38 (16.52.10; 20.22.1)	311/0 (20.22.1)

* this name regularly appears in Diodorus' text as Spartacus, a name well

known to Diodorus (or his copyists) from knowledge of the gladiator who led the slave revolt against Rome in 73-1.

** an error for 5.

*** the dates given by Diodorus actually add up to 4.

This list is internally consistent apart from the problem raised by the overlapping reigns of Seleucus and Satyrus I: Diodorus' failure to record either the death of the former or the accession of the latter suggests that Seleucus and Satyrus refer to the same person, and, given the uniqueness of the name Seleucus as a Spartocid dynastic name, it is possible that Diodorus has carelessly substituted Seleucus for Satyrus at 12.36.1. Alternatively, Seleucus and Satyrus may have reigned jointly for the 40 years following Spartocus' death, with Satyrus ruling for a further four years alone. However this is not the only inaccuracy in Diodorus' list: it is clear that Spartocus II, who is given a reign from 353/2 till 349/8, was still alive in 346, when he, along with his brother Paerisades, was the recipient of an Athenian honorific decree proposed by the Atthidographer Androtion (Tod 167, Harding 82). Moreover the relief, which depicts both men enthroned by the side of a third brother Apollonius who is standing, should indicate that Spartocus and Paerisades were at that time ruling jointly. It is possible to reconcile Diodorus with the epigraphical evidence if it is assumed that what he had before him was a list of Spartocid kings and the lengths of their reigns: unaware that Spartocus and Paerisades ruled jointly, he gave as the date of the latter's accession as sole ruler what was really the date of the beginning of the brothers' joint reign, and thus antedated the accession of all kings up to and including Spartocus II by five years, the duration of the brothers' period of joint rule. We thus arrive at the following table for the reigns of the earlier Spartocids:

KING	LENGTH OF REIGN	DATE OF REIGN
Spartocus I	5	438/7-433/2
Satyrus I	44	433/2-389/8**
Leucon I	40	389/8-349/8
Spartocus I	5	349/8-344/3
Paerisades I	38	349/8-311/0

** with or without 'Seleucus' as joint ruler for part of the time.

For a good discussion of the chronology of the Spartocids, see R. Werner, *Die Dynastie der Spartokiden*, Historia 4, 1955, pp. 412-44.

32.1 The consulship: M. Popillius (not 'Poplius') Laenas and M. Fabius Ambustus, both for the second time, were consuls for the year 356.

Returned home: the failure of the Boeotians to follow up their victory is puzzling. Diodorus ascribes it to a belief that the badly mauled and demoralised Phocians would sue for peace, but if so, subsequent events demonstrate the grave effects of their miscalculation.

32.2 Went back to Delphi: the choice of venue demonstrated to the enemy the irrevocable nature of the integration of Delphi into the confederacy. See also note on 27.2.

Assembled the allies, including presumably the Athenians, Spartans and Achaeans, and perhaps also the sons of Jason, who certainly appear as allies in the following campaign (chapter 35.1, below).

Debated about the war: the first hint of serious opposition to current Phocian policy. Diodorus sees the dissension as a split on religious grounds between the devout and the impious, but political factors were also involved. Opposition to the policies formerly advocated by Philomelus were advanced by the moderates, who could cite the recent defeat at Neon as a good reason for changing them.

Onomarchus: as a colleague of Philomelus and one who shared his views, Onomarchus emerged as spokesman for the 'war' faction and employed the threat of possible Amphictyonic reprisals both to encourage his partisans and to intimidate the opposition. For many, resistance was the only sure means of survival.

33.1 He was elated by a dream: just as Philomelus relied on a dubiously obtained oracle and a portent to boost his credibility (see 27.1-2 above), Onomarchus too needed evidence of divine backing in order both to reassure his supporters and to convince the waverers.

The fines which had been paid by the Phocians: this statement is the only indication in Diodorus that the Phocians had paid any part of the fines which the Amphictyons had imposed on them: elsewhere (23.3-4 and 24.4) he states the exact opposite.

The fine would be increased: see 60.2 below.

33.2 Weapons of bronze and iron ... coins from the silver and gold: i.e. from the metals obtained by melting down the dedications. Among the weapons were machines for throwing stones (Polyaenus 2. 38.2), and among the coins a bronze issue bearing a bull's head on the obverse and on the reverse the name of Onomarchus himself, enclosed in a wreath (G.F.Hill, *Historical Greek Coins*, London, 1906, p. 59; B.V. Head, *Historia Nummorum*, ed. 2, Oxford, 1911, pp. 89-91). Plutarch (*Moralia* 401F informs us that the pious Opuntian Locrians collected as many of these coins as they could find and rededicated them to Apollo.

33.3 Induced the Thessalians to remain inactive: disheartened as they were by their defeat at Argolas (30.4), they will not have needed much inducement, and the imminent outbreak of hostilities with Pherae (35.1) were in any case to prove a sufficient distraction.

Thronium: a city of Epicnemidian Locris of strategic importance because of its command of the road from Thessaly through Thermopylae. In this campaign of 354, the Locrians will have been obliged to fight on their own, since the Thessalians were now preoccupied with the war against Pherae and a good part of the Boeotian levy was on its way to assist Artabazus in Asia (see 34.1 below). The occupation of Thronium will have split and weakened the eastern Locrians and rendered more difficult the entry into Phocis of troops from Thessaly.

The Amphissans, of western or Ozolian Locris. Since the city was not on Onomarchus' line of march from Thronium to Doris, his next objective, he can hardly have proceeded against the Amphissans militarily, and indeed Diodorus' language suggests a diplomatic rather than a military initiative (in the winter of 355/4 before the start of the campaigning season?). A threatened show of force may have been enough to bring the Amphissans to terms before they could recover from the disaster at the Phaedriadae (24.4 and 28.3 above). They now abandoned their alliance with the Amphictyons for one with Phocis (Plutarch, *Moralia* 241F).

33.4 The cities of the Dorians, the Tetrapolis of Cytinium, Erineus, Pindus and Boeum, erroneously believed by the Greeks to have been settled by those of the invasion force raised by the Heracleidae who remained behind when their army was passing through on its way to conquer the Peloponnese. Though on this occasion the Dorians did not submit, their powerlessness made it impossible for them to play any further role in the war and strengthened the security of the north western border of Phocis.

Orchomenus, a city in north western Boeotia near the border with Phocis and frequently at odds with the Thebans, who destroyed the city in 364 for allegedly attempting to overthrow the constitution of the Boeotian Confederacy (Diod. 15.79.3-6, Pausanias 9.15.3). The Phocians can have captured little more than a ruined city, which the Thebans had recovered by 353/2, the date of Demosthenes' speech *For the Megalopolitans* (Dem. 16.4 and 25), only to lose again to Phalaecus in 347/6 (chapters 56.2 and 58.1).

Chaeronea, a Boeotian city even closer than Orchomenus to the Phocian border. Despite the absence of much of the Boeotian army in Asia (chapter 34.1), they were able to mount enough resistance to deny Phocis either control of the entire Cephisus valley or the increased security for her eastern frontier which possession of the city would have afforded.

Returned to his own land: in order to meet Philip's troops in battle (see ch. 35.1).

34.1 Artabazus: the narrative is continued from 22.1-2 above.

Five thousand troops, some five sevenths of the total strength of the Boeotian levy (see note on 30.4), a clear indication that the Boeotians regarded the war as virtually over and that the Phocians would sue for peace.

34.2 Two major engagements: perhaps the episodes described by Polyaenus 5.16.2 and Frontinus *Strat.* 2.3.3 belong here. Diodorus is silent about Pammenes' subsequent activities and about the end of Artabazus' revolt. It appears that Artabazus came to suspect Pammenes of plotting to change sides and replaced him in the command with his own brothers Oxythras and Dibictus (Polyaenus 7.33.2). The Thebans in a complete reversal of policy not only made their peace with the King but in 351/0 even received a subsidy of 100 talents from him as a contribution to the costs of the Sacred War (chapter 40.1). Artabazus fought on alone for a time, but by 343, when he is next heard of, he had been compelled to seek refuge at Philip's court (see ch. 52.2).

Deserted by the Thessalians, who were currently preoccupied with a renewal of the war with Pherae (see ch. 35.1).

34.3 Orneae, a city situated to the north west of Argos and subject to that city. This incident is described again, and in greater detail, at 39.4, where it is dated to 352/1 and placed in its proper context as part of the more widespread disturbances in the Peloponnese in these two years.

Sestos, a city in the Thracian Chersonese, on the European shore of the Hellespont opposite Abydos on the Asian shore and situated where the strait is at its narrowest point. Prior to 364, it had belonged to Cotys of Thrace, but was captured by the Athenians under Timotheus in that year (Isocrates 15.108 and 112), but subsequently revolted (in the Social War?).

34.4 Cersobleptes, king of the most easterly of the three Thracian kingdoms.

Animosity towards Philip...friendship for the Athenians: though he had in the past been suspicious of Athenian activity in the Chersonese, Philip too had proved a troublesome neighbour, as in the Crenides incident (see 8.6 above, with note), and was becoming ever more powerful. Chares' occupation of Sestos may have reminded Cersobleptes, if he needed reminding, that Athenian interest in the area was not going to evaporate, and he may have convinced himself by now that Athens was a necessary counterweight to the ever increasing might of Macedon. His cession of the cities of the Chersonese was a gesture of goodwill to consolidate his rapprochement with the Athenians. For an attempt to date the cession to c.356, see G.L.Cawkwell, *Notes on the Social War,* Classica et Mediaevalia 23, 1962, pp. 34-49.

Apart from Cardia: situated as it was at the narrowest point of the isthmus, Cardia was of particular importance strategically. The city's close links with Cersobleptes are clear from Demosthenes 22. 183, yet it was at this time nominally a personal possession of Cersobleptes' brother-in-law Charidemus (Dem. 23.181), and as such, excluded from the gift. To safeguard itself from coming under Athenian control, it concluded an alliance with Philip (Dem. 8.58, 9.16, 12.11, 19.174), probably at this time, and its separate status is mentioned by Demosthenes at 5.25, 7.41-3 and 9.35.

Settlers, whose presence there is attested by an inscription (IG II^2 1613, line 297). The presence of the cleruchs served the double purpose of providing a livelihood for landless Athenians and to keep the Hellespont secure for the passage of corn ships from the Black Sea.

Methone: repeated, with additional details, from 31.6. On the date, see the note to that passage.

A base for his enemies: the pretext for Philip's attack. The identity of the enemies is left unstated, but they are clearly Athens and her Confederacy. Philip no doubt also remembered the use of Methone in 359 as a base for the attempt to instal the pretender Argaeus in his place (see 3.5-6 above).

34.5 On condition that they depart: more lenient terms than those obtained by the Potidaeans (ch. 8.5) and the Olynthians (ch. 53.3), but harsher than those offered to Amphipolis (ch. 8.2). The determined resistance of the inhabitants, combined perhaps with the receipt of intelligence of the Athenian relief effort and impatience to be rid of the siege in order to take up the invitation to intervene in Thessaly, may have induced him to offer terms.

Apportioned the territory among the Macedonians, including presumably small allotments for landless Macedonians as well as larger estates for newly appointed Companions.

Struck in the eye with an arrow: so too Theopompus Frag. 52 and Marsyas of Pella Frag. 16, who inform us that he was struck in the right eye as he was inspecting his siege engines. Strabo (book 7, Frag. 22) relates a more sensational story of a catapult bolt, while Duris (Frag. 36) has him hit by a javelin hurled by a man named Aster. Plutarch (*Moralia* 307D) repeats the story of Aster ('Star'), converting him back from Duris' javelin thrower into Theopompus' archer, and making him break into verse to utter the iambic trimeter:

> Aster to Philip launches forth a deadly shaft.

Plutarch (*Alex*. 3.2) even relates a story to the effect that Philip received an oracle informing him that he was destined to lose the eye which he had applied to a chink in the door of Olympias' bedroom through which he had looked to see her coupling with the god Ammon in the form of a snake.

Philip's wound was treated by the physician Critobulus of Cos, who made his reputation by successfully extracting the arrow head (Pliny, *Nat. Hist.* 7.124) and was subsequently elevated to the status of a Companion (Arrian, *Indica* 18.7).

35.1 Invited by the Thessalians: i.e. those of the Thessalian Confederacy, which had prompted the previous intervention of 358 (see 14.2, note). This second intervention, which is contemporary with the events described at 33.4, should be placed in 354, though scholars such as Ellis, Cawkwell and Hammond and Griffith, who date the beginning of the war to 355 rather than to 356, put it in 353.

Went to war with Lycophron: Philip's activities on entering Thessaly are obscure. Some scholars believe that he attacked Pherae, but as evidence for their belief can adduce only a dubious textual emendation in an undated and unlocated anecdote of Polyaenus (4.2.20), where the otherwise unknown and probably corrupt reading "Karae" has to be replaced by "Pherae". Others are of the opinion that this was the occasion on which Philip captured Pagasae (see 31.6 and note). The appeal of Lycophron to the Phocians certainly indicates some hostile action by Philip on Pheraean territory.

Called in his Phocian allies: Diodorus neglects to inform us about the conclusion of this alliance. Indeed the now deceased Tisiphonus, the eldest of Jason's sons, had contributed ships to the Theban war effort several years previously, when they were fighting the Athenians, now a Phocian ally, for control of Euboea (scholiast on Aristides, *Panathenaicus* 179.6). The new alliance with Phocis is likely to have been instigated by Onomarchus as part of his diplomatic initiative in the winter of 355/4 (chapter 32), in an attempt to distract the Thessalians from interfering in Phocis, and will also have brought about a rapprochement between Pherae and Athens. Given Philip's earlier intervention in Thessaly in 358, Onomarchus should have foreseen the likelihood of a second, but may have calculated that Philip was too preoccupied with the siege of Methone to consider involvement in Thessaly for the present.

Phayllus: presumably already one of Onomarchus' two colleagues in the generalship. The diversion of 7000 troops from the attack on Chaeronea reveals the seriousness with which Onomarchus took Philip's entry into Thessaly.

Defeated the Phocians: Diodorus' language suggests that Phayllus' defeat occurred before he could link up with the Pheraeans.

35.2 Onomarchus came with all speed: he had been besieging Chaeronea when the appeal reached him, and news of Phayllus' defeat will have made it all the more necessary for him to check Philip in Thessaly to forestall any possibility of a Macedonian invasion of Phocis. Unable to mount an effective campaign on two fronts simultaneously, Onomarchus had little choice but to abandon his Boeotian campaign for the present.

Taking his entire army: he must have left behind sufficient forces both to garrison the captured Boeotian cities and to protect Phocis from possible Boeotian retaliation in his absence.

Superior in numbers: this can be true only after he had joined up with his Pheraean allies, and even then his numerical superiority will hardly have been pronounced.

Two battles: since a second battle was necessary, the first can hardly have been decisive. Nothing is known of the location of either battlefield, but Diodorus' brief statement on the outcome can be supplemented from a passage of Polyaenus (4.2.20), which should refer to the second of the two battles. In this passage, Polyaenus describes how Onomarchus stationed his army in front of a ridge shaped like a crescent moon and concealed catapults on the high ground on the two flanks. By a simulated flight to the middle of the crescent, he lured the Macedonians into range of the artillery. They, caught between the Phocians in front and the missiles hurled from the engines stationed on the flanks, were forced to flee.

Philip was deserted by his despondent troops: this was one of the few defeats inflicted upon him in the course of his career, and the greatest military disaster of his reign. The despondency of his troops will have been aggravated by the reflection that their previously invincible king had been outgeneralled and outsmarted by a worthy adversary. Had a suitable pretender been waiting in the wings, even his throne would have been imperiled, but in the end he was able to rally them with the morale boosting statement reported by Polyaenus to the effect that he was not fleeing, but, like a ram, was retreating in order to butt harder the next time. He also sought to inspire his men with greater zeal for the campaign in the following year by distributing laurel wreaths for them to wear on their heads, thereby emphasising their personal involvement in the war as Apollo's champions (Justin 8.2.3).

35.3 Philip returned to Macedonia: scholars are unanimous in postulating the end of one and the beginning of a new campaigning season at this point. Since it is impossible for all the events narrated in chapters 32-6 to have happened within the space of a single archon year, Diodorus must have compressed the activities of two archon years into one. Given Philip's desperate situation after his two defeats in Thessaly, he needed an entire winter to recover and to restore the morale of his troops. As he was in no position to return to Thessaly till the next spring, the events of 35.3-36.1 should be dated to 353.

Marching into Boeotia: the first activity in the next campaigning season. With hindsight it can be seen that Onomarchus' decision to campaign in Boeotia rather than to deliver the coup de grace to the Thessalian Confederacy was an error of judgment, as was his underestimation of Philip's resilience. But a renewal of operations there may have been motivated by a desire to take advantage of Pammenes' absence in Asia and to achieve some measure of success before his return. For Onomarchus it was now or never to seize what he could in Boeotia, and Thessaly could wait.

Coronea, a city to the south of Orchomenus and to the south west of Chaeronea, of some strategic importance on the main route from Thebes into Phocis. Control of the city would allow Onomarchus to dominate western Boeotia and impede the despatch of Theban troops to the main theatre of war. Some details of its capture are provided by the scholiast on Aristotle's *Nicomachean Ethics* 1116b 6 in explanation of Aristotle's cryptic reference to a fight at the Hermaeum. We are told that when the Boeotarchs, the military leaders of the Boeotian League, came to the assistance of Coronea with a mercenary force, the acropolis and the rest of the city were delivered to Onomarchus by treachery, but that the loyal citizens, together with the Boeotarchs and the mercenaries, sought refuge in the temple of Hermes. However in the ensuing conflict, the mercenaries fled when the Boeotarch Charon was slain, but the rest of those inside fought on to the death. The presence of Charon and the mercenaries at Coronea would have been unthinkable had Pammenes already returned with his 5000 citizen troops.

Marched against Lycophron: it may have been on this occasion that Philip laid siege to Pagasae, the capture of which Diodorus has already mentioned at 31.6, a passage derived from his chronological handbook but dated wrongly to the year of the fall of Methone. The chronological order in which Philip's conquests are listed at Demosthenes 1.12 has been taken to mean that Pherae was captured before Pagasae, but the Thessalian part of this list (Pherae...Pagasae..Magnesia) is concerned with settlements, not with the sieges or with the capture of the cities. Moreover it was imperative for him to move against Pagasae quickly, to deny Athens use of the port to unload supplies or reinforcements, were he to launch an assault on Pherae.

35.4 Arrange things in Thessaly with them: a vague phrase which would surely give the Phocians some right in determining the shape of a future Pheraean dominated Thessaly.

To wage war in common: Diodorus' phraseology implies that some sort of joint consultation went on concerning questions of command structure and future policy making. Philip may have been created supreme commander of the Thessalian forces, and some discussion may even been held about the possibility of his appointment as Thessalian Head of State (see notes on 1.4 and 14.2 above and 38.1 below).

35.5 The Thessalian cavalry were superior: this superiority should indicate that the site was chosen by Philip rather than by Onomarchus, though the latter may have been quite happy to engage in a coastal battle in which the sea would protect one of his flanks and a possible Athenian presence off shore would help to negate Philip's superiority in cavalry.

A fierce battle, known in modern times (the ancient name is unknown) as the Battle of the Crocus Field (or Crocus Plain), from the only site in the area which meets the combined requirements of space for Philip's cavalry and proximity to the sea (Strabo 9.443c, Stephanus of Byzantium s. Demetrias).

Chares was by chance sailing past: few modern scholars believe that Chares' presence was fortuitous. It is more likely that he was in command of the relief force said by Demosthenes (4.35) to have arrived too late to save Pagasae, and that his arrival off shore was prearranged, in order to cooperate with Onomarchus in whatever way ships were likely to be most useful: as events proved, Chares' main function would be to rescue Phocian fugitives.

35.6 6000 Phocians were killed, including the general: Onomarchus' fate is unclear. According to Pausanias (10.2.5), he was run through by his own men in disgust at his inexperience and lacklustre leadership, surely an inappropriate description of the man who beat Philip so soundly the previous year, while Eusebius (*Praeparatio Evangelica* 8.14.33) has him drown in an attempt to escape by sea. Diodorus' language, both here and at 61.2, is somewhat ambiguous: in both places he is said to have been killed (and the contrast with those captured, alive should mean that Diodorus means by 'killed' – 'killed in battle'), and then hung up on display by Philip (in the present passage on the gallows, at 61.2 on the cross). This can only mean that he met his end in the battle, and that his corpse was subsequently hanged (or crucified) by Philip as an act of policy to publicise his current role of avenger of the god and punisher of sacrilege.

Drowned the remainder: Hammond and Griffith (pp. 276-7) discuss the identity of 'the remainder'. Were they the 3000 survivors, the 6000 corpses, or all 9000, both living and dead? Diodorus' language is once again ambiguous.

36.1 Phayllus, already a colleague of Onomarchus, who had sent him to assist Pherae the previous year (see 35.1 above).

Doubling the normal rate of pay: it is unclear whether Diodorus means that Phayllus provided twice, in place of Philomelus' wage of one and a half times the usual rate for mercenary pay in the Greek world (25.1 and 30.1) or whether he doubled Philomelus' rate to what was in effect three times the normal wage. If the latter, it was an indication of both Phocian desperation and the growing unattractiveness of mercenary service with criminals. In order to afford such a high wage, Phayllus must have resorted to ever increasing despoliation of the Delphic treasures.

36.2 Mausolus: see note on 7.3. His father Hecatomnus ruled Caria from 392/1 till 377/6, to be succeeded in turn by Mausolus (377/6-353/2) and by Mausolus' widow Artemisia (353/2-351/0). The date of 351/0 given for Mausolus' death by the Elder Pliny (*N.H.* 36.30.47) is clearly wrong, since he was dead by the time Demosthenes delivered his speech *On the Liberty of the Rhodians* (15.7) in 351; Pliny seems to have added Artemisia's two year sole reign to that of her husband. It was Artemisia who commissioned the building of the Mausoleum as his tomb, and who organised a competition for the best funeral eulogy. The latter attracted entries from the historian Theopompus of Chios and from Isocrates of Apollonia, both pupils of the Athenian Isocrates, as well as from Naucrates of Erythrae and Theodectes of Phaselis the tragic poet and Platonist, who delivered his panegyric in iambic verse: the prize was nevertheless awarded to Theopompus (Aulus Gellius 10.18; Suda s.vv. Theodectes, Isocrates of Apollonia).

36.3 Clearchus the tyrant of Heracleia: Heracleia Pontica was a Greek city founded in the 6th century on the southern shore of the Black Sea, on the coast of Bithynia. Clearchus in his younger days had spent four years in Athens as a pupil of both Plato's Academy and Isocrates' school of rhetoric (Memnon, *FGH* 434, Frag. 1.1.1). On his return to Heracleia, he was exiled by the democratic regime then in power, and entered Persian employment as a mercenary general. When approached by the oligarchically inclined Council of his native city to return and lead a coup against the democracy, he instead placed himself at the head of the democrats, expelled the oligarchs, freed the slaves and set himself up as tyrant (365/4). Once in power he is said to have called himself son of Zeus and demanded prostration from his subjects when they were in his presence (Memnon, loc.cit.; Justin 16.4).

Was assassinated on his way to a festival: according to Memnon 1.1.4, the assassins were a group of disaffected Heracleots led by Chion, Leon and Euxenon, who were all cut down by the tyrant's bodyguard.Timotheus ruled for 15 years, i.e. 353/2-338/7 (so too ch. 88.5 below). According to Justin (loc. cit.), Clearchus was succeeded by his brother Satyrus, while Memnon (1.2.1 and 1.2.5) states that Satyrus acted as regent for Clearchus' two sons Timotheus and Dionysius for seven years and handed over the tyranny to Timotheus in 346/5. In Memnon's opinion, Satyrus was the most bloodthirsty of tyrants, while Timotheus was beloved by his subjects. Timotheus maintained his father's friendship with Isocrates, who sent him a letter (Epistle 7) congratulating him on his enlightened rule and giving advice on its future development. The tyranny lasted till the city's absorption into Lysimachus' kingdom in the 280s. The remainder of the chapter consists of brief notices of events that took place in Italy and Sicily.

37.1 C.Sulpicius and M.Valerius: C.Sulpicius Peticus and M.Valerius Poplicola were the consuls of 355.

The 107th Olympiad: the 107th Olympiad ran from 352/1 till 349/8.

Phayllus restored the fortunes of the Phocians: in view of the decisive defeat and the loss of 9000 men on the Crocus Plain, the Phocians were in no state to renew the war till the next campaigning season (352), and the measures outlined in section 2 must have taken place in the winter of 353/2.

37.2 Collected many mercenaries: repeated from 36.1 above.

Spartans...Achaeans...Athenians: Phayllus' diplomatic offensive clearly produced results. However all these peoples had an interest in keeping the Boeotians (to say nothing of Philip) preoccupied and saw the necessity of stiffening the Phocian war effort. The Athenians may also have been encouraged by their success in holding Thermopylae the previous year (see 38.2 below).

Nausicles: Davies 10552. A friend of the orator Aeschines (Aesch. 2.184), his first known command was at Thermopylae in 353 (Justin 8.2.8). He was later an ambassador to Philip in 346 (2nd. Hypothesis to Demosthenes 19, section 4), and subsequently changed his political allegiance to the faction of Demosthenes (Aeschines 3.159; [Plut.] *Moralia* 844F).

Lycophron and Peitholaus, the two surviving sons of Jason, will have surrendered Pherae to Philip after his victory at the Crocus Field. The city was strongly fortified, but Philip, reluctant to embark on what might prove to be a protracted siege, offered terms which the tyrants found acceptable.

37.4 Minor cities: their identity is unknown, but among them should be numbered Ozolian Locris, a Phocian ally since the previous year (see Plut. Mor. 249F and note on 33.3 above).

37.5 Phayllus invaded Boeotia: in 352. Wisely abandoning Thessaly to Philip, he concentrated Phocian resources against the Boeotians, whom he saw as easier prey. Moreover if a showdown with Philip was to occur, it was essential for him to knock out the Boeotians first, to avoid the necessity of having to fight on two fronts simultaneously.

Beside the Cephisus, in the course of a withdrawal from Orchomenus on his way home to Phocis. The engagement will have been fought somewhere in the territory of Chaeronea.

37.6 A battle near Coronea: with his retreat along the Cephisus blocked by a hostile Chaeronea, Phayllus will have turned south, with the aim of withdrawing by way of Mount Helicon. None of the three battles can have been decisive, but the losses sustained on the campaign as a whole will have dented Phocian morale, especially since they enjoyed a numerical superiority. The ability of the Boeotians to face Phayllus on the field indicates that Pammenes and his troops must have returned from Asia Minor by the prevous winter at the latest.

38.1 A remarkable battle: Diodorus now reverts to the activities of Philip in Thessaly in the previous year (353), which are picked up by the reference to the Crocus Field.

Suppressed the tyranny at Pherae, by permitting Lycophron and Peitholaus to depart under truce with their mercenaries (ch. 37.3).

Restored freedom to the city: i.e. by the abolition of the tyranny. Diodorus omits the other arrangements Philip made with Pherae, which included the transfer of both the port of Pagasae and the subject territory of Magnesia from Pheraean to Macedonian control (Demosthenes 1.12, 1.22, 2.11; Isocrates 5.21). As the only port of any significance in Thessaly, Pagasae will have been of importance to Philip both for the revenue derived from its harbour duties and as a naval base: we have no evidence that he was planning to resuscitate Alexander of Pherae's fleet which had operated from there, but he may well have been concerned to deny its use to the Athenians as a possible base of operations against him. It was probably at this time that he sought to conciliate the Pheraeans by marrying Nicesipolis and to advertise his victory at the Crocus Field by naming his daughter by this marriage Thessalonice ('Victory in Thessaly') (Plut. *Mor.* 141B; Satyrus Frag. 5; Stephanus of Byzantium s.Thessalonice).

Arranging all the other affairs of Thessaly: these will have included procuring his appointment as *archon* of the Thessalian League, specifically attested only at Justin 11.3.2. This remarkable achievement is of interest in showing the close affinity between Thessalian aristocrats and the Macedonian king, as well as the despair of the former at their inability to suppress the Pheraean tyranny unaided. Philip was in their eyes no alien interloper but a kindred spirit and the only man capable of guaranteeing unity in the country. As archon, Philip seems to have been granted the right to certain revenues from market dues and harbour taxes to help defray the cost of running the Thessalian League (Dem. 1.22, 6.22). In addition he was able to exercise some measure of supervision over the Thessalian constitution, with which he interfered on more than one occasion (Dem. 6.22, 9.26), as well as over the *perioikesis*, which is best attested for Magnesia (see previous note) and for Perrhaebia (Isocrates 5.21; Strabo 9.5.19), where he appointed his drinking companion Agathocles as governor (Theopompus, Frag. 81). Philip also used the office to station garrisons in some Thessalian cities (Dem. 19.260) and to plant a settlement of Macedonians at Gomphoi, henceforth Philippopolis (Stephanus of Byzantium s. Philippi). Control of Thessaly made Philip much more formidable than he had been previously, in that it gave him – inter alia – lucrative sources of revenue, the use in war of the excellent Thessalian cavalry and control of decision making at meetings of the Delphic Amphictyony, where the archaic voting system guaranteed the ruler of Thessaly an inbuilt majority.

He advanced to Thermopylae, in the belief that, in their current state of demoralisation, the Phocians would be in no condition to block his advance: success would bring about the surrender of Phocis and the termination of the war.

38.2 The Athenians prevented him: cf. Dem. 19.84 and 319; Justin 8.2.8. The troops in question were the 5000 men under Nausicles sent north to aid the Phocians (chapter 37.3 above). Whether the Spartan and Achaean contingents arrived in time is unknown.

He returned to Macedonia: had he possessed the determination to end the Sacred War once and for all, he could have attempted to force his way through, or find some alternative route to bypass the defenders, as Xerxes had done in 480, but if the Peloponnesians had not yet arrived, he may not have been prepared to risk an engagement in which the enemy was likely to receive reinforcments. More probably he was reluctant to suffer the high casualty rate which a frontal attack on the Athenian position would entail, and defeat here would cause unrest in Thessaly. His advance to Thermopylae is best seen as a piece of opportunism: if the route lay open, he would take advantage of his good fortune, but if not, time was on his side, and he could try again at a later date. Had he really been determined to invade Phocis, he would surely have done so immediately after the Crocus Field, but at that time he preferred to give priority to the settlement of Thessaly.

38.3 Phayllus, taking the field: we are now at the beginning of the campaigning season of 351.

Locrians known as Epicnemidians, the more westerly of the two parts of Eastern Locris, a softer target than the Boeotians who had defeated his uncle so comprehensively the previous year. The Epicnemidians had already been overrun by Philomelus in 355 (ch. 30.3) and again by Onomarchus in 354 (ch. 33.3-4). The conquest of the area would also consolidate Phocian control of the Thermopylae corridor.

All their cities: i.e. Alponus, Nicaea and Scarpheia, the cities which the Phocians offered in 347/6 to hand over to Athens (Aeschines 2.132) along with Thronium, which had already fallen to Onomarchus in 354 (ch. 33.3). According to Memnon (Frag. 1.28.10), Nicaea was destroyed, probably in the course of this campaign. The three cities commanded the passes from the coast into the interior, and their capture will have made it possible for Phayllus to open up communications with the Athenians by sea.

Naryx, a Locrian city, reputedly the birthplace of the Lesser Ajax (Diod. 14.82.8), occupying an easily defensible site that offered access to the adjacent regions by way of four different routes.

38.4 Abae, a city in the north east of Phocis close to the Boeotian frontier, on the main route from Thermopylae to Orchomenus and Thebes, famous for its oracular shrine of Apollo (Pausanias 10.35.1). Alone of Phocian cities, its inhabitants were not implicated in the sacrilegious looting of Delphi, and the city was consequently spared at the end of the war. After his failure at Naryx, Phayllus left troops to prosecute the siege, while he retired to Abae with the presumed intention of invading Boeotia.

38.5 Phayllus routed them: the only success recorded for Phayllus' two year tenure of the generalship, and due more to Boeotian carelessness and overconfidence than to any great competence on his part. This victory at Naryx completed the conquest of Epicnemidian Locris and effectively ended Locrian participation in the war.

38.6 Wasting illness: according to Pausanias (10.2.7), Phayllus had a dream in which he saw among the Delphic offerings a bronze statue of a man in an emaciated condition, consisting of nothing but skin and bone, who bore a strong resemblance to himself: the dream image corresponded to a real statue reputedly dedicated by the celebrated physician Hippocrates. The dream was interpreted as a sign from the gods sent as a warning of his own imminent sickness, which was to prove fatal. Three Phocian generals in succession had now held brief tenures of office (Philomelus for one year, Onomarchus and Phayllus for two), and all three met particularly horrible deaths, which were seen by the devout as divine punishment for their sacrilegious crimes.

Phalaecus son of Onomarchus, or, according to Pausanias (10.2.7), son of Phayllus. He was to prove more machiavellian and more durable than any of his three immediate predecessors.

Mnaseas, father of Mnason, a friend of Aristotle the philosopher (Timaeus, FGH 566, Frag. 11), according to whom (*Politics* 1304b11) Mnaseas had been the leader of a faction hostile to Euthycrates the father of Onomarchus (and so also of Phayllus), with whom he quarrelled over possession of an heiress, a statement which indicates that the two men were blood relations. By 351 the feud must have been patched up.

Appointed as his guardian and as general: Diodorus is writing very loosely at this point: though Phayllus was indeed entitled by law to nominate his nephew's guardian, he cannot have appointed Mnaseas to the elective office of general. At best he can only have given Mnaseas his backing, and recommended both him and Phalaecus to the electorate.

38.7 The Boeotians attacked the Phocians: Diodorus has neglected to inform the reader that Mnaseas and Phalaecus invaded Boeotia. The Boeotian victory will have been due as much to the change in the Phocian leadership and the inexperience of the new board of generals as to the surprise attack by night.

39.1 At the same time: i.e. simultaneously with the events described in sections 37-8, and therefore covering the campaigning seasons of 352 and 351.

In the Peloponnese: the fighting developed out of a diplomatic initiative undertaken by the Spartans, who hoped to take advantage of Theban preoccupation with the Phocians to undo the arrangements made by Epaminondas for the Peloponnese in order to strengthen their own position. The Spartan aims can be recovered in good part from Demosthenes' speech *For the Megalopolitans*, delivered on behalf of a Megalopolitan embassy which arrived in Athens in the hope of winning her support against Sparta. According to the claims made in this speech, the Spartans wished to destroy Megalopolis (sections 4 and 30), and to recover Messenia (section 20). To aid their efforts, they suggested (section 16) the restoration of the ruined Boeotian cities of Orchomenus, Thespiae and Plataea in order to weaken Thebes, and, to attract allies, they proposed the return to Elis of Triphylia, seized by the Arcadians in 368 (Xen. *Hell.* 7.1.26; Diod. 15.77.1), and to Phlius of Tricaranum, a fortress the Argives had taken in 366 (Xen. *Hell.* 7.4.11); moreover, in the hope of winning the adherence of Athens, they proposed that the Athenians should recover Oropus, which the Thebans had occupied in 366 (Xen. *Hell.*7.4.1; Diod. 15.76.1)

Quarrel with the Megalopolitans: ostensibly perhaps over the disputed border territory of Belemina (cf. Pausanias 8.25.4; Livy 38.34.3), but in reality Sparta sought the destruction of the city which, ever since its foundation in 368, had blocked off their natural route to the north west.

Archidamus: see note on 24.1 above.

Called upon their allies: these are listed in section 2, but the Megalopolitans also cast their net more widely, and appealed unsuccessfully to Athens.

39.2 The Argives: the traditional enemies of Sparta could be guaranteed to join any anti-Spartan coalition, and they too had a boundary dispute with the Spartans over Cynuria (Paus. 7.11.1-2).

Sicyonians: they were too remote to be menaced by Sparta and were acting under the terms of their alliance with Thebes, which had been in force since 369 (Xen. *Hell.* 7.1.18; Diod. 15.69.1; Paus. 6.3.2-3).

Messenians: reduced to serfdom by the Spartans at the end of the 8th century, they recovered their independence in 370/69, but this independence had never been formally recognised by Sparta. They were under no misapprehension about their fate should the Spartans be victorious. Moreover, like their allies, they had a frontier dispute with the Spartans, in this instance, over the Denthaliatis (Strabo 8.4.6).

4000 infantry: more than half the normal strength of the Boeotian army (see 30.4, note). The remainder will have been needed to prosecute the war with Phocis.

39.3 With their allies, i.e. the Messenians (and perhaps the Sicyonians), since it is clear from what follows that neither the Argives nor the Boeotians had yet arrived.

Near the sources of the Alpheus: in the Maenalus range, not far from the city of Pallanteum on the road from Megalopolis to Tegea. They will have had no desire to tackle the Spartans without the support of their Argive and Boeotian allies, whom they expected to join them there.

3000 foot from the Phocians, in return for the 1000 men lent to Phayllus earlier in the year (ch. 37.3 above).

Cavalry from Lycophron and Peitholaus: having been expelled from Pherae, they retired to Phocis with their mercenaries (ch. 37.3). This token gesture was little more than a sign of their goodwill to the Spartans.

Mantinea, the capital of the dissident half of the former Arcadian Confederacy, hostile to Megalopolis and allied to Sparta since 362. The Spartan presence there will have been designed to cut off the Megalopolitans from their Argive and Boeotian allies.

39.4 Orneae: see 34.3, where the capture of the city is mentioned briefly in an extract from Diodorus' chronological handbook. Archidamus must have become tired of waiting at Mantinea and aimed at hitting the Argives before they could be reinforced by the Boeotians.

39.5 The Thebans...put in an appearance: their arrival in Argive territory emboldened the latter to renew the struggle for control of Orneae.

The Argives and their allies returned to their own cities: since the Megalopolitans and Messenians were not involved in the struggle for Orneae, the allies in question must be the Thebans, whose performance in the campaign had been unimpressive and unproductive, other than as propaganda designed to recall the great days of Theban intervention in the Peloponnese in the time of Epaminondas. Neither side had much to show for its efforts: the Spartans had failed to make any move against Megalopolis, while the numerically superior allies had failed to link up to exploit their advantage.

The Spartans invaded Arcadia, perhaps in a vain attempt to bring the Megalopolitans to battle.

Helissus, a city in Megalopolitan territory near the source of the river of the same name, a tributary of the Alpheus. Helissus was an insignificant place which had little to attract the Spartans other than the prospect of easily won booty which might defray the cost of the campaign. Lacking the strength or the confidence to assault Megalopolis, Archidamus had to his credit the capture of two minor cities, a victory over the traditional enemy and a draw against a more recent one, all in all something of a wasted effort.

39.6 Some time later: since Diodorus has just informed us that the Argives, Thebans and Spartans all went home, and it is difficult to believe either that the Thebans sent out a second army this season or that the Spartans replaced Archidamus with an otherwise unknown commander, the events of this section are best dated to the following year (351).

Telphousa, usually spelt Thelpousa or Thelphousa, a city on the river Ladon in the most westerly region of Arcadia, close to the Elean border. The Spartans will have been seeking to weaken Megalopolis by detaching some of her smaller Arcadian allies.

Two other engagements: their location is unspecified, and neither is mentioned elsewhere.

39.7 A battle of some significance: again Diodorus fails provide information on the site, the name of the commanders or the number of casualties. Clearly losing interest in these minor engagements, he is abridging his source more drastically than usual, indeed too drastically to be of much use to the student of this war.

Concluded a truce, which marked the end of this unsatisfactory episode which brought little in the way of glory for either the Spartans or the Thebans.

39.8 While occupying himself in Boeotia: resumed from 38.7 above.

The date is still 351.

Phalaecus captured Chaeronea: we last heard of him losing a cavalry engagement in the neighbourhood, but he remained in the area, to enjoy this ephemeral success.

Taking the field against Phocis: probably after the return of the troops who had won the battle at Telphousa, and with an army large enough for the Phocians to offer no resistance worthy of mention.

Seized some of the small townships, perhaps including Tithorea, in whose citadel of Neon Theban troops were lated stationed (Dem. 19. 149).

40.1 M. Fabius and T. Quintius: M. Fabius Ambustus and T. Quinctius Poenus Capitolinus Crispinus were consuls for 354.

Weary of the war with the Phocians: for other references to Theban discomfiture at the hands of the Phocians, see Isocrates 5.54-5 and Demosthenes 19.148.

40.2 Artaxerxes willingly heeded them: Artaxerxes III was not the most forgiving of rulers, and, in view of recent Theban support for the rebel Artabazus (see 34.1), the extent of his generosity is remarkable. Since he was currently planning an expedition to recover Egypt, which had maintained a precarious independence since the beginning of the century, it is likely that his subsidy was provided only in return for the despatch of Boeotian troops to take part in the Egyptian campaign.

No activity worth mention took place in this year: another indication of the boredom felt by Diodorus in recording the events of 351 and 350, at least those that took place on the Greek mainland. Compare 7.2 for an equally unilluminating sentence on the fighting in Euboea in 358/7. The rest of this chapter, and practically the whole of chapters 41-51, in which he purports to narrate the events of the years 351/0 and 350/49, are in fact devoted to a lengthy account of the Persian reconquest of Phoenicia and Egypt, which actually took place in the years 344 and 343. The chronological error is caused by Diodorus' inability to understand Ephorus' thematic combination, within the confines of one book, of two attempts to recover Egypt, the first (and unsuccessful) one taking place in 351/0, the second in 344/3. I have included in my translation only the very few passages from these chapters that are of relevance to the mainland and Asiatic Greeks.

44.1 The King sent ambassadors: this diplomatic mission to Greece took place in 344, not 351/0.

The Athenians: according to Philochorus (FGH 328 Frag. 157), they gave a reply more arrogant than was fitting, to the effect that they declined the King's request, while promising to remain at peace with him as long as he did not attack the Greek cities. This reply brought to the surface the latent feelings of hostility to Persia, thus making it impossible for them to win support when they in turn sought his support for the war with Philip. If Jacoby's doubtful restoration of a lacunose text is accepted, the Atthidographer Androtion was one of the politicians who advocated a reply along these lines.

44.2 The Thebans sent 1000 troops, partly out of gratitude for the subsidy of 351/0 (ch. 40.2, above), and indicative of continued pro-Persian sympathies even at a time when they were allied to Philip, though they cannot then have been aware of his long term plans.

The Argives sent 3000: like Thebes, Argos had a long tradition of medism.

44.3 Nicostratus, a larger than life, even eccentric individual, nick-named the second Heracles, who carried his obsession with this hero to absurd lengths. Plutarch has a story (*Moralia* 192A, 535D) according to which Archidamus offered him any Spartan non-royal woman of his choice as an inducement to commit a treasonable act, whereupon Nicostratus denied Archidamus' Heraclid descent on the grounds that while Heracles went around chastising the bad, Archidamus was bent on making good men bad. In a typical piece of abusive characterisation, Theopompus (Frag. 124) denounced him for avarice and gross flattery of the King by invoking the King's *daimon* as a preliminary to eating his meals.

The Greeks who lived in the coastal areas of Asia Minor: as subjects of the King since the Peace of Antalcidas, they had no choice in the matter, and were scarcely in the same position as the Thebans and Argives.

45.1 Artemisia: see 36.2, where her accession is noted.

Idrieus: he was officially co-ruler with his sister-wife Ada, who continued the dynastic tradition of brother and sister marriages initiated by their siblings and predecessors Mausolus and Artemisia.

Ruled for seven years: so chapter 69.2 below. On his death in 344/3, Ada continued to function alone.

46.1 M. Valerius and C. Sulpicius: C.Sulpicius Peticus and M.Valerius Poplicola were consuls for 353. Diodorus is so absorbed in his account of Artaxerxes' Egyptian campaign that he neglects to mention any of the events of this archon year that took place in Greece or Macedonia. Compare his account of the archon year 339/8, where he lets himself be carried away by his narrative of Timoleon's exploits in Sicily to the extent of omitting the simultaneous happenings on the Greek mainland. Some of the events recorded at 56.1 may perhaps belong to 349 (see notes on this section below).

52.1 C. Marcius and P. Valerius: P.Valerius Poplicola and C.Marcius Rutilus were the consuls of 352.

Mentor, a mercenary commander from Rhodes, who had previously been employed by the Egyptian pharaoh Nakhtharehbe (in Greek Nectanebo), who had lent his services to Tabnit (Tennes in Greek), the king of Sidon who was in revolt from the King. Tennes and Mentor together plotted to betray the city to the King (chapter 45), whereupon Artaxerxes employed him to lead, in cooperation with the Persian Bagoas, one part of the army he was assembling to reconquer Egypt (ch. 47.4, 7-8). The two men were subsequently rewarded for their services, and Bagoas was raised to the rank of *hazarapatish* or vizier, the second man in the kingdom and commander of the elite corps of the royal bodyguards, the Immortals.

In his war with the Egyptians: Diodorus erroneously dates the war to 349/8 (see 40.2 above), when it really belongs to 344-3. The three main reasons for belief in the latter date are as follows:

(a) The revolt of Phoenicia, which was recovered before Egypt (ch. 43-4), ended in 344. This is established from the fragmentary Babylonian Chronicle, which dates to the seventh month of the fourteenth year of the reign of Artaxerxes III (i.e. the second half of the year 345/4) the entry into Babylon of booty and captives won from Sidon. Numismatic evidence also testifies to the recovery of Phoenicia by 343,when Phoenician coins were again minted in the name of Mazaeus, the satrap of Syria.

(b) The last pharaoh before the Persian reconquest, Nectanebo II, who was installed by Agesilaus in 361/0 (Plut. *Ages.* 38.1, 40.1) is given by Manetho a reign of 18 years, a statement confirmed by the evidence of papyri, which continue to date events to the reign of Nectanebo till a day that corresponds to 5/6th July 343.

(c) The letter written to Philip by Speusippus, the current head of the Academy, in recommendation of his pupil Antipater of Magnesia the historian, dated on internal evidence to the winter of 343/2, ends with the excuse that Speusippus cannot write at greater length because of the papyrus shortage caused by the King's reconquest of Egypt.

52.2 The choicest of estates: perhaps including the territories of Scepsis, Cebren and Ilium given to him by Artabazus by 362 (Dem. 23. 155) and still in the possession of his brother Memnon in 334 (Arrian, *Anabasis* 1.16.8).

Satrap of the coastal areas of Asia Minor : whatever Mentor's title may have been, it was not satrap, an office to which no King ever appointed a Greek. At 50.7, he is more accurately termed *hegemon* 'leader' or 'commander' (cf. the use of this title for his brother Memnon at Arrian, *Anab.* 1.16.8). Artaxerxes did not remove any existing satrap from office to make way for him, but gave him something like the Roman concept of a *maius imperium*, which conferred on him a supervisory role over the coastal satraps Arsites of Hellespontine Phrygia, Rhosaces of Lydia and Ada of Caria, a role that has precedent of a kind in the appointments given to the Younger Cyrus in 407 (Xen. *Hell.* 1.4.3, *Anab.* 1.1.1), and perhaps to Orontes in 362 (Diod. 15.90.3).

Those in revolt: since Artabazus' revolt was now over, (see section 3 below), this must be an allusion to Hermias of Atarneus (see section 5 below) and his allies (including perhaps Erythrae, cf.Tod 165, Harding 79).

52.3 Mentor was related to Artabazus and Memnon: Memnon was Mentor's brother, and their sister (name unknown) was married to Artabazus by 362, when he was still satrap of Hellespontine Phrygia (Dem. 23.154). The two families were linked still more closely when Memnon married Artabazus' daughter (Plut. *Alex.* 21.4).

Who had fought against Persia in the past, following the accession of Artaxerxes III in 358 (see chapters 22.1 and 34.1 with notes).

Were living at Philip's court, where Artabazus was made a *xenos* of Philip (Curtius 6.5.2).

52.4 Eleven sons and ten daughters: it is difficult to credit Diodorus' assertion that one wife could have given birth to all twenty one children: the report may be an exaggeration of the tradition that when Artabazus surrendered to Alexander in Hyrcania in 330, he was accompanied by nine sons, all born of the same mother (Curtius 6.5.4). The names of several of Artabazus' offspring are known: among the sons were Pharnabazus who succeeded Memnon as commander of the Persian fleet in the Aegean in 333 (Arrian, *Anab.* 2.1.3), Ariobarzanes, Cophen and Arsames who surrendered along with their father in 330 (Arrian, *Anab.* 3.23.7) and Ilioneus, captured by Parmenio at Damascus in 333 (Curtius 3.13.3), while the daughters included Memnon's wife (named Barsine by Plutarch at *Alex.* 21.4, but see W.W.Tarn, *Alexander the Great* II, Cambridge, 1948, Appendix 20, pp. 330-7), and Artacama and Artonis who were married at Susa in 324 to Ptolemy and Eumenes respectively (Arrian, *Anab.* 7.4.5).

52.5 Hermias, formerly slave of the banker Eubulus who obtained possession of Assos, a city in the Troad, as security for an unpaid loan made to the satrap of Hellespontine Phrygia. Impressed by Hermias' talents,

Eubulus had him freed and given a philosophical education, then appointed him his business partner. On Eubulus' death, Hermias became owner of the banking house and ruler of the district. His philosophical interests were further developed through his friendship with Erastus and Coriscus, pupils of Plato who were natives of the area and who, like all true Platonists, sought to deepen their ruler's interest in the philosophical life. Their efforts proved so successful that he gave them the city of Assos, where they set up a branch of the Academy on Plato's death in 347. They were joined there by other Platonists, including Aristotle, Callisthenes and Xenocrates. Aristotle became a close friend of Hermias, who even gave him his niece and adoptive daughter Pythias in marriage. Contemporary opinion on Hermias was divided, as we are told by Didymus in a surviving fragment of his Commentary on Demosthenes (columns 4.59-5.21 and 5.66-6.18): whereas Aristotle saw him as an outstanding example of virtue and patriotism, he is depicted characteristically by Theopompus (Fragments 250 and 291) as a crook, a barbarian, a eunuch and a tyrant of the most savage and oppressive kind. (See also Tod 165 = Harding 79; Strabo 13.1.57 and 67; Athenaeus 696A-697B; Diogenes Laertius 5.1.3 ff.)

Who was in revolt from the king: his immunity up till now suggests that he had not actively taken up arms, though he may well have been in sympathy with the Phoenicians and Egyptians. More seriously from the King's point of view, he may have been intriguing with Philip, as Demosthenes (10.22) believed: certainly Philip, who was already casting his thoughts towards a future war in Asia, was actively searching for possible allies (cf. his later negotiations with Pixodarus of Caria in 337, described by Plutarch at *Alex.* 10). Hermias' principality, though not on Philip's direct line of march, would be of value if he could effect a rising in the Persian rear, and thus severely embarrass the King's troops should they seek to contest a Macedonian crossing of the Hellespont or Bosporus. Modern scholarship (e.g. W. Jaeger, *Aristotle: Fundamentals of the History of his Development*, ed. 2, Oxford, 1948, pp. 105-23; A.H. Chroust, *Aristotle Leaves the Academy*, Greece & Rome 14, 1967, pp. 39-44 and *Aristotle's Sojourn at Assos*, Historia 21, 1972, pp. 170-6) has even seen Aristotle's presence at Hermias' court as a front for negotiations between Hermias and Philip. It is also possible that Artabazus, who had recently spent some time at the Macedonian court, was able to communicate to Mentor information on Philip's intrigues with Hermias: certainly it is difficult otherwise to explain the magnanimity of Artaxerxes, who was not the sort of ruler to forget or to forgive disloyalty, towards a former rebel.

A large number of strongholds: the identity of these can only be a matter of guesswork, but Atarneus, Hermias' capital, was itself particularly well fortified (Xen. *Hell.* 3.2.1; Diod. 13.65.4).

52.6 A parley at which he had him arrested: cf. the epigram written by Aristotle for Hermias' cenotaph at Delphi (D.L. Page, *Epigrammata Graeca* lines 623-6),

> This man was slain by the bow-bearing Persians who impiously transgressed the sacred ordinances of the blessed gods, not by openly mastering him with the spear in the murderous contests of war, but by making use of the pledged word of a treacherous man.

Diodorus characteristically neglects to inform the reader of Hermias' fate. Didymus' commentary (cf. Theopompus Frag. 291) informs us that he was delivered to the King, who at the instigation of Mentor and Bagoas had him tortured to death with the famous last words "I have done nothing unseemly or unworthy of philosophy" on his lips. Hermias' death greatly affected Aristotle who, in addition to erecting the aforementioned cenotaph at Delphi, commemorated him in his Ode to Virtue (Page, *Lyrica Selecta Graeca* 432), in which Hermias is compared to Heracles, the Dioscouroi, Achilles and Ajax and depicted as the latest in the long line of panhellenic heroes who toiled for Greece against the barbarian. Whatever the King may or may not have learned from his interrogation, he undoubtedly began to take Philip more seriously. To deny him control of the entire European shore of the Bosporus and Hellespont, he sent troops across to Thrace (Arrian, *Anab.* 2.14.5) and despatched aid to Perinthus and Byzantium in 340 when Philip put them under siege (see ch. 75.1).

52.7 Mentor was held in high favour: despite this, we hear no more of him, and by 334, when Alexander crossed into Asia, he was dead and his command entrusted to his brother Memnon (17.7.2; Arrian, *Anab.* 1.12.9; Plut. *Alex.* 18.3). Diodorus narrates the entire Hermias affair as part of the events of 349/8, presumably because it was described by his source as a tailpiece to the recovery of Egypt. As the true date of the latter is 343, the Hermias affair should be placed in 342: at Athens, Demosthenes, addressing the assembly in 341 (10.22), knows of Hermias' arrest, but not yet of his death.

52.9 In Europe Philip: the narrative of Philip's activities, broken off at 38.2, where he is said to have returned to Macedonia after being frustrated in his attempt to penetrate Thermopylae in 353, is here resumed. There is however a gap of three years (352-0) for which Diodorus supplies no information whatsoever. In 352 Philip campaigned in Thrace (Dem. 1.13), where he came to the assistance of Amadocus II, the new king of central

Thrace, and the Greek cities of Perinthus and Byzantium (scholiast on Aeschines 2.81), all of whom were being threatened by Cersobleptes, now an Athenian ally. In the course of this campaign Philip laid siege to the fortress of Heraion Teichos to the west of Perinthus, which Cersobleptes had recently seized, only to abandon the enterprise because of illness (Dem. 3.4-5). Despite this, he forced Cersobleptes to come to terms, took his son hostage to Macedonia (Aeschines 2.81) and, according to Demosthenes, expelled some Thracian chieftains and replaced them with others more to his liking. The years 351 and 350 Philip seems to have spent in the west against the Illyrians, Paeonians and Epirots (Dem. 1.13, cf. Isocr. 5.21), if indeed Demosthenes is listing his campaigns in chronological order. The Illyrians and Paeonians had been quiet since the crushing defeats inflicted on them earlier in Philip's reign (see 4.2-7 and 22.3 above), but may have grown restive following Onomarchus' victories of 354. Epirus had been ruled since c.360 by Arybbas, the uncle of Philip's Molossian wife Olympias, but Philip now removed from his court and brought to Macedonia Olympias' young brother Alexander, the son of Arybbas' elder brother and predecessor Neoptolemus (Justin 8.6.5), to be groomed as a possible replacement for Arybbas should the latter's policies give Philip any cause for concern.

Marched against the Chalcidians: unlike the earlier sections of this chapter, Philip's Chalcidian campaign, derived from his chronographic source, really does belong to the year 349 (Philochorus Frag. 49), though Diodorus supplies no motivation for the attack. The *casus belli* was the harbouring by the Chalcidians of Philip's two surviving half-brothers Arrhidaeus and Menelaus, sons of Amyntas III by Gygaea (Justin 8.3.10), a third brother having already been eliminated. However relations between Philip and the Chalcidians had been deteriorating for several years: the alliance concluded in 357 (ch. 8.4 above), though successful as long as Athens was the common enemy of both parties, broke down when the Chalcidians, fearing the great increase in Philip' power, made peace with Athens contrary to the terms of their treaty with Philip (Dem. 23.109, delivered in 352; cf. 3.7 and Libanius' Hypothesis to *Olynthiac* 1, section 2). In the first of these three passages Demosthenes even claims that the Chalcidians were aiming at an alliance with Athens: Philip too seems to have believed this, and retaliated with a sudden attack on Chalcidian territory (Dem. 4.17, spoken in 351), wherupon they in alarm sought to appease him by exiling the pro-Athenian leader Apollonides and electing to the office of hipparch Philip's guest-friend Lasthenes (Dem. 9.56, 66). Having averted a Chalcidian rapprochement with Athens, Philip withdrew for the moment, hoping that the Chalcidians were sufficiently chastened. The welcome they now gave to his half-brothers convinced him otherwise and exhausted his patience.

Zereia, a small Chalcidian township of uncertain location, if indeed this is the correct emendation for the corrupt manuscript reading *Zeira* or *Geira*. The alternative of *[Sta]geira*, the birthplace of Aristotle which Philip also destroyed (Plut. *Alex*. 7.2, *Mor*. 1126F) is excluded by the description of the place as a stronghold rather than a city.

Forced them to submit: Philip's stratagem was to attack the smaller Chalcidian towns one by one and so weaken the capital, in the hope that it too might submit without putting him to the trouble and expense of a siege. Most of the Chalcidian towns did in fact surrender, according to Demosthenes (19.266) through treachery. Diodorus omits the visit in this year of a Chalcidian embassy to Athens, which led to the conclusion of an alliance between the two states thanks in part to the advocacy of Demosthenes, and to the despatch to Olynthus of Chares with 2000 peltasts and 30 ships (Philochorus Frag. 49). A second embassy followed in the winter, which obtained further reinforcements in the shape of eighteen ships and 4000 peltasts under Charidemus. With these added to their own troops, the Olynthians undertook an expedition in the spring of 348 to the isthmus of Pallene and the territory of Bottiaea occupied by Philip the previous season (Philochorus, Frag. 50).

He drove out Peitholaus: Peitholaus and his brother Lycophron had been expelled from Pherae after the battle of the Crocus Field in 353 and sought refuge in Phocis (see 37.3), from where they sent troops to aid Sparta in the Peloponnesian campaign of 352 (ch. 39.3). They subsequently turned up in Athens, where they received a grant of citizenship which was later withdrawn because of their earlier anti-Athenian record ([Dem.] 59.91; Aristotle, *Rhetoric* 1410a 17). There was indeed unrest in Thessaly in 349 caused by Philip's continued occupation of Magnesia (Dem. 1.22, 2.11), and, since Magnesia had formerly been subject to Pherae, it would have been among the Pheraeans that the ill-feeling was strongest. Whether Peitholaus was able to take advantage of the situation to effect his return is uncertain. Though Philip i likely to have visited Thessaly each year in the capacity as *archon*, it i doubtful if, with a major Chalcidian war on his hands, he would have ha the leisure to undertake the full scale siege operations necessary for him t recover Pherae, and Demosthenes is suspiciously silent about the return of Peitholaus, if indeed he did return at this time. Westlake, who accepts that I did, dates it to 350 (p. 183) on the grounds that Demosthenes had it in min when he delivered the Second Olynthiac in 349, where in section 14 mentions as 'recent' an intervention by Philip against the Thessalian tyran However the earlier expulsion of 353 was surely recent enough to qualify the incident referred to by Demosthenes in this passage. The allusion to expulsion of Peitholaus is seen by most scholars as a misdated doublet either Philip's earlier settlement of 353 (ch. 37.3) or of a later expulsior Pheraean tyrants (in which Peitholus is not named), dated by Diodoru 344/3 (ch. 69.8 below).

52.10 Spartacus...Paerisades: see note on 31.6. The dates of the reign of Spartocus (the correct form of the name) are 349/8-344/3 and of Paerisades 349/8-311/0.

The king of Pontus: a glaring anachronism. These kings were rulers of the Cimmerian Bosporus: in Spartocus' day the district of Pontus, which embraced the central part of the southern coast of the Black Sea between Bithynia and Paphlagonia to the west and Colchis and Lesser Armenia to the east, was included in the Achaemenid Empire and divided for administrative purposes between the satrapies of Paphlagonia and Cappadocia. The kingdom of Pontus was founded by Mithridates I only in the first half of the 3rd century B.C. Diodorus is thinking of the situation in his own day, when the kings of Pontus also ruled over the Cimmerian Bosporus, situated due north across the Black Sea. Unable to withstand the constant pressure of the adjacent Scythian tribes led by Scilurus, Paerisades V, the last ruler of the Spartocid dynasty, voluntarily ceded his kingdom to Mithridates VI Eupator (also known as the Great) of Pontus c.114 B.C. (Strabo 7.4.3ff). The murder of Paerisades by Saumacus, who was opposed to his agreement with Mithridates, led to a full scale invasion by Mithridates' general Diophantus, who merged Paerisades' kingdom with Pontus c. 109 (Strabo loc. cit.; Justin 38.7.4-5). Mithridates governed the Bosporus through the agency of his son Machares from 81-66, and after Mithridates' death, the Romans allowed his son Pharnaces to rule the Bosporus (63-47). The Pontic connection was continued by the next ruler Asander (47-27), who married Pharnaces' daughter Dynamis.

53.1 C. Sulpicius and C. Quintius: C. Sulpicius Penticus and T. (not C.) Quintius Poenus Capitolinus Crispinus were the consuls of 351 BC.
The 108th Olympiad: 348/7-345/4.

53.2 To subdue the cities on the Hellespont: since the Hellespont (the modern Dardanelles) is the strait separating the Chersonese from the Troad in Asia Minor, Philip's attack on Chalcidice, some 150 miles to the west, can hardly have been motivated by the reason given by Diodorus, whose geographical knowledge is here extremely shaky. Cf. 21.3, note.

Mecyberna, a Chalcidian city on the Gulf of Torone some 2 miles to the south east of Olynthus, to which it served as the port.

Torone, a Chalcidian city on the west coast of the peninsula of Sithonia, not far from its southern tip. Philip's capture of these cities was part of his strategy of isolating Olynthus from its hinterland. The loss of Mecyberna in particular was a severe blow which made it difficult for the Olynthians to bring in provisions or reinforcements by sea. However they had already sent

off a third embassy to Athens, begging for citizen troops rather than mercenaries. Despite the outbreak of fighting in Euboea (Aeschines 3.85-8; [Dem.]
59.4; Plut. *Phocion* 12-4), the Athenians, urged on by Demosthenes, responded with 17 triremes, 2000 citizen hoplites and 300 cavalry (Philochorus, Frag. 51), but by the time of their arrival, Olynthus had already fallen.

Instituted a siege: excavations at Olynthus have unearthed a large
number of arrow heads and sling shots of which some are inscribed with the
name of Philip. It was probably at this point that 500 Olynthian horse fell
into Philip's hands through the treachery of their officers (Dem. 9.56 and
19.266). The Olynthians in despair at last consented to negotiate with Philip,
only to receive the ominous reply that either they must cease to live in
Olynthus or he in Macedonia (Dem. 9.11): his failure to procure their
submission earlier and the necessity of conducting a costly and time-con-
suming siege will have exhausted his patience.

Euthycrates and Lasthenes, two of the Chalcidian hipparchs (Dem.
9.60; Hyperides Frag. B 19).The two men were prominent members of the
pro-Macedonian faction opposed to the policy of confrontation with Philip.
In addition they were both guest-friends of his (Dem. 8.40, 18.48), and were
allegedly bribed to betray their city (Hyp. loc.cit.). According to Demosthenes
(19.205), Euthycrates received from Philip a gift of cattle and Lasthenes
timber for roofing his house. They subsequently became infamous for their
treachery, and their names came to bear much the same notoriety as the
modern word Quisling (Dem. 19.342, Plut. *Mor.* 178A, 510B). As time went
on, the stories of their villainy improved in the telling: according to Hyperides (loc. cit.), Euthycrates even advised Philip on the amount of money
each of his enslaved fellow citizens would fetch on the open market.

53.3 Plundered the city: the destruction of Olynthus is also mentioned
by Demosthenes (9.26) and Justin (8.3.11).

Enslaved the inhabitants: cf. Dem. 19.194-8 and 305-10, where Philip
is said to have distributed Olynthian women as gifts to his guest friends and
other supporters in the Greek states. See also note on 55.4 below. Among
those enslaved were members of the two Athenian relief expeditions caught
up in Philip's siege (Dem. 19.230; Aeschines 2.15). Diodorus tells us nothing
about the fate of the other Chalcidian cities. It would be reasonable to
conclude that he dissolved the Chalcidian League, since it is not heard of
subsequently, but many, if not most of the cities survived, some to be
incorporated by Cassander in 316 into Cassandreia and Thessalonica. The
territory of Olynthus was probably assigned, like that of Amphipolis and
Methone in the past, to Macedonian settlers: an inscription (Syll.[3] 1.332)
attests the award by Philip of an estate at Spartolus to the north west of
Olynthus to a Macedonian named Ptolemaeus, and if the Apollonia which
later gave its name to a squadron of Companion Cavalry (Arrian, *Anabasis*

1.12.7) is the Apollonia in northern Chalcidice, we have further evidence for the grant of land in Chalcidian territory to Macedonians.

The other cities which were at war with him, including presumably the Phocians and their allies, as well as the Athenians and the members of her Confederacy.

He honoured...the soldiers who had distinguished themselves: cf. note on 3.1 above.

Distributed...money among influential friends: among these were his guest-friends and prospective guest-friends. See 54.4 and note. Diodorus is here referring to the charge made by Demosthenes and his partisans that Philip made use of hirelings to promote his interests in the Greek states. See also chapters 3.3, 8.7, 54.2-4.

Increased his kingdom more by gold: for a similar story, see Plut. *Aemilius* 12.6.

54.1 The Athenians would come to the aid: the despatch of three expeditionary forces to the relief of Olynthus probably afforded Diodorus' source the opportunity to indulge in praise of Athens' anti-Macedonian stance, but it is ironic that the Athenian aid to Olynthus is ignored by Diodorus himself.

They sent to the cities ambassadors: this is palpably false in the case of Olynthus, which initiated all three appeals, and up till this time and beyond, the Athenians were content to respond to the initiatives of others rather than to take them themselves. However Diodorus' source may have been thinking of later actions which the Athenians did initiate, such as the diplomatic missions to the Peloponnese in 344 (Dem. 6.19ff. with Hypothesis 2-3) and in 342 (Dem. 9.72, 18.79; [Plut.] *Mor.* 841E), to Ambracia in 342 (Dem. 18.244), a mission or missions to Euboea (Dem. 9.65, 18.79, Aeschines 3.100), the diplomatic initiative which created the Hellenic League of 340 (Dem. 18.237; Aeschines 3.95-8; Plut. *Dem.* 17.3-4, *Mor.* 845A), the mission to Byzantium in 340 (Dem. 18.80 and 88; Plut. *Phocion* 14.2) and the embassy to Thebes in 339 which concluded the alliance with Boeotia (Dem. 18.211-4; Aeschines 3.141-2; Diod. 16.84.5-85.1; Plut. *Dem.* 18.2-4).

They undertook to fight alongside them: Diodorus (and his source?) conveniently forgets that the relief expeditions sent out up till this time had arrived too late, though he may also have in mind those sent subsequently, and with greater success, to Megara in 343 (Plut. *Phocion* 15), to Euboea in 341 and to Byzantium in 340.

54.2 Demosthenes the orator: born in 384, he began to make a name for himself in the 350s as a professional speech writer who composed the speeches for the prosecution in the trials of Androtion (355), Timocrates (353) and Aristocrates (352). He embarked on a political career by delivering his first speech before the assembly (*On the Symmories*) in 354, followed by the speeches *For the Megalopolitans* (352), *On the Liberty of the Rhodians* and the *First Philippic* (both 351). Diodorus' source seems to have dated his emergence as an orator of the first rank to the year of the delivery of the three *Olynthiacs* in 349, if, as is probable, it was in this context that Diodorus found the eulogistic remarks which he is here summarising. Most of the diplomatic initiatives undertaken by the Athenians in the period 344-39 which are listed in the last note but one were indeed proposed by Demosthenes, who also participated personally in many of the missions.

Crop of traitors: Diodorus (or his source) is here echoing the actual words of Demosthenes as spoken in the oration On the Crown (18.61), where he claims that

> in every single state there sprang up the most prolific crop of traitors, recipients of bribes and abominations to the gods within the memory of mankind.

The impulse of its citizens to treachery: from the viewpoint of Demosthenes, pro-Macedonian politicians were regarded as traitors, and in the case of Athens, he had in mind men such as Aeschines (Dem. 18.21, 41, 51, 282ff.; 19.145, 167, 253, 314), Philocrates (Dem. 18.21; 19.189, 229), Phrynon (Dem. 19.189, 230) and Pythocles (Dem. 19.225), all of whom are denounced for selling their country to Philip.

54.3 When Philip wanted to capture some city: a similar anecdote is recounted by Plutarch (*Moralia* 178B).

54.4 Guests and friends: the reference here is to the institution of guest-friendship (*xenia, xenia kai philia*), the subject of an illuminating study by G.Herman (*Ritualised Friendship and the Greek City*, Cambridge, 1988). Originating in a tie of shared hospitality between two individuals, the institution developed into a sort of fictitious kinship which was hereditary and was cemented by gift exchange and mutual assistance when needed. Like most Greek aristocrats, Philip had his guest-friends, but few possessed resources sufficient to maintain the vast network of *xeniai* which he was able to construct. Some of his *xeniai* were inherited, like that made with the family of Eumenes of Cardia (Plut. *Eumenes* 1.2), but the great majority he established in person. Among influential Greeks said by our sources to be linked to him by ties of *xenia* were Aeschines (Dem. 18.51, 284; 19.248, 314) and

Pythocles (Dem. 19.225) of Athens, Python of Thebes (Dem. 19.140; Plut. *Mor.* 178C), Perillus and Ptoeodorus of Megara (Dem. 19.295) and Demaratus of Corinth (Plut. *Alex.* 9.6). To these may be added those described as 'friend', such as Lasthenes and Euthycrates of Olynthus, Eudicus and Simus of Thessaly and Aristratus of Sicyon (Dem. 18.48), Thrasydaeus of Thessaly (Theopompus, Frag. 115), Hipparchus of Eretria (Plut. *Mor.* 178F) and (at one time) Callias of Chalcis (Aeschines 3.89). A fair number of the rogues gallery of traitors listed by Demosthenes at 18.295 may also have been guest-friends of Philip. In the hands of a shrewd individual like Philip the institution was open to abuse, and, given the vast resources which he had at his disposal, an exchange of gifts was very much a one way transaction. Money (Dem. 19.137, 167), timber (Dem. 19.145, 265), grain (Dem. 19.145), cattle and other livestock (Dem. 19.265), estates (Dem. 18.41, 19.145), objects wrought in precious metals (Dem. 19.137) and slaves (Dem. 19.306) all had a part to play in Demosthenes' sorry tale of Philip's handouts. In return, he had no need for any gifts of a tangible nature, but instead used the institution to extend his influence and patronage abroad: in such a situation the distinction between the gifts of a *xenos* and the bribes of a paymaster became distinctly blurred. What Philip badly needed, and what his *xenoi* could provide without difficulty, was information, and when the time came to call in his favours, he would expect his *xenoi* to provide him with intelligence on matters like the relative strengths of the various factions in the Greek cities, the degree of internal stability afforded by their constitutions, the conclusions to be drawn from the outcome of important political trials, or the existence of any inter-state tension which Philip might be able to exploit. In such circumstances, the obligations of *xenia* and the national interest could conceivably clash, and *xenoi* who gave priority to the former could be denounced as traitors by their anti-Macedonian rivals.

By the wickedness of his company he corrupted men's characters: the sentiment is similar to the famous line of Menander (*Thais*, Frag. 216) "bad company ruins a good character".

55.1 The Olympia, the principal festival of Macedonia, held at Dium. Among the events were a sacrifice to Zeus, who gave his name to the festival, and dramatic and musical competitions in honour of the Muses (Dem. 19.192 with scholiast; Dio Chrysostom 2.2). Arrian (*Anabasis* 1.11.1) mistakenly gives the venue as Aegae.

Many non-Macedonians who had come to visit: doubtless Philip took advantage of the conviviality to cultivate men of influence who might be useful to him in the future.

55.2 The gifts he distributed: apart from illustrating Philip's generosity, the gifts would in some cases mark the first stage in the establishment of a link of *xenia*.

55.3 On one occasion: the story is based ultimately on a passage of Demosthenes (19.192-5), where a much more detailed account is given.

Satyrus the actor, an Athenian who was presumably one of the participants in the dramatic contest. Quite apart from being fond of the theatre, Philip found actors extremely useful in gathering information, since their contracts required them to visit many cities and, as Aeschines says (2.15), "the profession naturally wins friends". Two other actor friends of Philip, also Athenians, are known, Neoptolemus, described by Demosthenes (5.6) as "Philip's agent and spokesman at Athens" and Aristodemus. Both men first made an impression on Philip when sent to Macedonia to negotiate for the release of the Athenians captured at Olynthus (Dem. 19.12, 18, 315; Aeschines 2.16-7) and Aristodemus again as a member of the embassy which concluded the Peace of 347/6 (Dem. 19.97; Aeschines 2.19). Neoptolemus subsequently went off to live in Macedonia on a permanent basis (Dem. 5.8), and was one of the star performers at the wedding of Philip's daughter Cleopatra to Alexander of Epirus (see ch. 91.3-4 below).

Daughters of a friend of his: the friend in question was Apollophanes of Pydna, one of the assassins of Philip's eldest brother, Alexander II, who was himself subsequently murdered (Dem. 19.195).

55.4 Philip granted the request: another example of Philip's generosity to a friend. In this instance the story had a happy ending, but not all captive Olynthian women were so fortunate. Tales were told of plight of those given by Philip to Atrestidas of Mantinea (Dem.19.305-6) and of one owned by the Athenian exile Xenophron (Dem. 19.196-8): such stories could be, and were used by anti-Macedonians in the Greek cities to blacken the reputation of both Philip and the recipients of his bounties.

56.1 C.Cornelius and M.Popilius: M. Popillius Laenas and L. Cornelius Scipio were the consuls of 350.

Plundering a large part of Phocis: the narrative of the Sacred War continues from 40.2 (i.e. from the events of 350). Diodorus records nothing of the war under the archon years 350/49, 349/8 and 348/7, and the natural assumption would be that he has omitted the events of the war that took place in 349 and 348. However it is by no means certain that all the events recorded in this chapter belong to 347. The reference to the destruction of grain by the Phocians at the beginning of the invasion described in section 2 ought to indicate the start of a new campaign in the spring, and it is possible that Diodorus, rather than omitting the events of two campaigning seasons, has compressed three such seasons (349, 348 and 347) into one. The ability of the Boeotians to overrun a large part of Phocis (section 1) should be compared to the statement of Demosthenes in the *First Olynthiac* 26 that at the time of the speech (349), the Phocians were unable to protect their own territory and to the remark in the *Third Olynthiac* 8 that financial exhaustion rendered the Phocians incapable of preventing any possible encroachment by Philip. If there is some connection between the situation described by Demosthenes in the Olynthiacs and that presented by Diodorus in the present passage, the events of this section should belong to 349 rather than to 347.

Hya, also called Hyampolis, a Phocian city in the north east of the country, situated not far from the Boeotian border. It was of strategic importance for its command of the pass connecting Thermopylae and Eastern Locris with the Cephisus valley and the Phocian heartland.

56.2 Near Coronea: see note to 35.3 and 37.6.

Seized several sizeable cities: these were Orchomenus, Coronea and Corsiae (or Chorsiae) (chapter 58.1), together with the fortress of Tilphossaeum (Dem. 19.141, 148). The first two had been captured by Onomarchus in 354 and 353 respectively (33.4 and 35.3, above), but were in Boeotian hands again by the time Demosthenes delivered his speech *For the Megalopolitans* in 352 (scholiast on Dem. 16.4). Chorsiae was a city in south west Boeotia to the south of Mt. Helicon, overlooking the Corinthian Gulf. The site of Tilphossaeum is unknown, and it is variously identified with the modern Palaeotheva, a peak on the range of Mt. Libethrion or with the rock of Petra to the south of Lake Copais. As a result of these successes, the Phocians now held much of south western Boeotia, and the campaign marked a high point in the Phocian war effort.

Destroyed the grain: since the grain ripens in Greece in the spring, this invasion should mark the beginning of the next campaigning season (348?). Instead of attempting to recover the cities lost the previous year, the Boeotian invasion of Phocis was aimed at diverting the Phocians from further inroads into Boeotia by compelling them to defend their home territory.

On the way home suffered a defeat: this was near the mountain range of Hedylium that separates Orchomenus from Abae and Hyampolis: in this engagement the Phocians were superior in cavalry, and the Boeotians lost some 270 men (Dem. 19.148 with scholia).

56.3 Phalaecus...was...relieved of his post: given the remarkable run of Phocian successes in the years 349 and 348, the removal of Phalaecus from office in the winter of 348/7 is inexplicable, but is much more comprehensible if it took place in the following winter. With the Boeotian victory at Abae in 347 and the loss of 500 Phocian troops (chapter 58.4), morale had been undermined, and the imminent entry of Philip into the war in response to a Boeotian appeal (59.2) will have weakened Phalaecus' position even more. Up till now such opposition as had existed was muted and ineffectual, but the threat for the first time of a combined simultaneous invasion of Macedonians and Thessalians from the north west and Boeotians from the south east will have made it imperative to reach a settlement, and the sacrilege of Phalaecus will have cast him in the role of an obstacle to that settlement.

Philon, otherwise unknown, but clearly the holder of an important financial post, and so, like Phalaecus, a suitable scapegoat.

56.5 Philomelus abstained from the dedications: see 28.2 with note and 30.1.

A brother of Philomelus named Onomarchus: since Philomelus was the son of Theotimus (Pausanias 10.2.2) and Onomarchus' father was Euthycrates (Aristotle *Politics* 1304a 12), Diodorus' statement can be correct only if they were half-brothers by the same mother. However there is no reference to this alleged relationship in any other source, and even Diodorus is unaware of it when he records the transfer of power from one to the other at 31.5. His error is caused by confusing Philomelus with Phayllus, Onomarchus' successor who really was his brother (see 36.1, 37.1 and Pausanias 10.2.6).

Spent a large part of the god's funds: see 33.2.

Converted a good part of the dedications: see 36.1.

56.6 120 gold bricks: according to Herodotus (1.50), these bricks or ingots were 117 in number, of which only four were of pure gold, the remainder being of 'white gold', i.e. electrum or a gold/silver alloy of which some 70-80% consisted of gold: these bricks were used as a base for the lion, the bottom layer comprising 63, the second 35, the third 15, with the four bricks of refined gold positioned directly under the lion.

Weighing two talents each: if the measurements were in Euboean talents, each would have weighed around 115 lb. or 52 kg., if in Aeginetan talents, 167 lb. or 76 kg.

Dedicated by Croesus: Croesus, who ruled Lydia from 560 till 546, was as celebrated for his generosity to Greek shrines as for his vast wealth.

360 gold drinking bowls: there is no mention of these in Herodotus, who refers instead to a pair of huge mixing bowls and another pair of vast sprinkling bowls, in each case one of the pair being of silver and the other of gold (1.51.1-3). However Herodotus does state that Croesus sent to Delphi many more gifts than those he describes (1.51.5).

Weighing two minae each: since a mina was one sixtieth of a talent, two minae on the Euboean standard would be equivalent to approximately 870 grams or just under 2 lbs., while the corresponding value on the Aeginetan standard would be $1^1/4$kg. or $2^3/4$lbs.

A lion: see Herodotus 1.50.3. The lion was the symbol of the Lydian monarchy, and as such appeared on the Lydian coinage: the word *walwet*, which also occurs on some Lydian coins, is believed to mean 'lion'. According to Herodotus, the lion was of refined gold and originally weighed 10 talents, but $3^1/2$ talents were melted off in in the heat of the fire of 548.

A woman of gold: see Herodotus 1.51.5, where it is stated that the statue was 3 cubits (roughly $1^1/3$ metres or 53 inches) in length, and believed by the Greeks to be a representation of Croesus' baker, who saved his life when his half-brother Pantaleon attempted to have him poisoned (Plut. *Mor.* 401E).

Weighed 30 talents: i.e. 1123 kg. (2476 lb.) on the Aeginetan standard or 785 kg. (1730 lb.) on the Euboic.

When converted into its equivalent in silver: the ratio of silver to gold fluctuated in antiquity. In Herodotus' day (3.95.1) it was 13:1, as it was in the third century, though it sank as low as 10:1 for a time in the fourth (see H. Michell, *The Economoics of Ancient Greece*, ed. 2, Cambridge, 1957, pp. 323-6).

4000 talents: this figure appears to be based on the 13:1 ratio. The total weight in talents of the gold objects melted down by Phalaecus, if we accept Diodorus' claim that the bricks were of refined rather than white gold and also Herodotus' figure for the weight of the lion which Diodorus omits, the following total is obtained:

ITEM	WEIGHT (IN TALENTS)
120 bricks @ 2 tal. each	240
360 bowls @ 2 minae each	12
1 lion (after heat damage)	$6^1/2$
1 woman	30
TOTAL	$288^1/2$

Multiplication by 13, to convert the gold into its equivalent value in silver, produces a figure of 3750, or 4000, when rounded upwards. If Diodorus and his source were unaware of the damage to the lion and took its weight to be 10 talents, the total amounts to 4088 talents of silver. In actual fact, since the bricks were only of white gold, usually reckoned to be ten rather than thirteen times as valuable as silver, the total would have been closer to 3000 than to 4000 talents.

56.7 The sums acquired by Alexander in the treasuries of the Persians: Alexander acquired huge sums of gold and silver in the course of his Asian conquests (334-23), but, even allowing for some exaggeration on the part of the Alexander-historians, Diodorus is guilty of gross hyperbole in suggesting comparability between the two treasures. Alexander came across large quantities of gold and silver in various places in Asia, but it will suffice to restrict the evidence to the two biggest treasuries of the empire. At Susa in 331, he came into possession of 50,000 talents of silver (Arrian, *Anabasis* 3.16.7; Curtius 5.2.11), and at Persepolis no less than the equivalent of 120,000 (Diod. 17.71.1; Curtius 5.6.10). Of this immense sum, 180,000 talents were subsequently sent to his treasury at Ecbatana (Diod. 17.80.3). Compared to this vast fortune, whatever Phalaecus may have appropriated from Delphi was chickenfeed. The comparision with Alexander will have been invented by Diodorus' source in order to increase the enormity of Phalaecus' sacrilege.

Phalaecus' supporters on the board of generals: since the current board was hostile to Phalaecus, Diodorus must be referring to an incident that took place prior to his deposition (i.e. at some time between 352 and 347).

Homer: the citation is from *Iliad* 9, lines 404-5, where Achilles, in reply to the embassy of mollification sent by Agamemnon, spurns all his gifts with the declaration that no wealth, however great, will be enough to compensate for his shameful treatment. Pytho is a poetic name for Delphi derived by the Greeks variously from the verb *pythomai* ('I rot'), with reference to the rotting corpse of snake slain by Apollo at the site, or from *pynthanomai* ('I enquire'), with reference to the questions put to the oracle.

56.8 The gods were...indicating the punishment: Diodorus regularly explains the events of the Sacred War from a theological viewpoint. Thus Philip is depicted as the pious and devout instrument of the god who punishes the impious and sacrilegious Phocians (1.4, 38.3, 58.5-6); at the same time the gods are no less capable of acting on their own to achieve the same results (31.4, 38.6, 60.4, 61, 64).

57.1 The Athenians and the Spartans: for their alliance with Phocis and participation in the Sacred War, see 24.1-2, 27.5 and 29.1. Both states sent contingents to assist Phayllus after the Phocian defeat at the Crocus Field (37.3), and the Athenians also blocked the pass of Thermopylae at this time (38.2), but there are no other references to the receipt of Phocian subsidies in exchange for troops, apart from suggestions that Delphic monies may have lined the pockets of some individuals (33.2, 37.2), including Archidamus of Sparta and his wife (Pausanias 3.10.3).

57.2 A little before the Delphic crisis: in 373 (Xen. *Hell*. 6.2.33-7; Diod. 15.47.7).

Iphicrates: see note on 21.1.

Dionysius the ruler of Syracuse: Dionysius the Elder, tyrant from 405 till 367.

Sending to Olympia and Delphi: probably as thank offerings from the booty acquired in the Third Carthaginian War of 383-375.

Having secured possession of them: since Dionysius was an ally of Sparta, with whom Athens was then at war, the statues could be legitimately regarded as the spoils of war, though if they had already been consecrated to the gods, the Athenian action could equally be construed as sacrilege.

57.4 Their patron deity and forefather: strictly speaking, the patron deity of Athens was Athene, but no fewer than five of the Attic months were named after festivals of Apollo. In describing Apollo as their forefather, Diodorus has in mind the cult title Patroos ('Ancestor God') enjoyed by Apollo as father of Ion, the ancestor of all the Ionian peoples and the progenitor of the four sons who gave their names to the four pre-Cleisthenic Athenian tribes.

Though they consulted the oracle...and acquired...their constitution: the Spartans believed that their constitution had been prescribed for them by the Delphic oracle given to their legendary lawgiver Lycurgus (Tyrtaeus, Frag. 4; Herodotus 1.65.2-4; Diod. 7.12.6; Plut. Lycurgus 6.1; Pausanias 3.2.4).

58.1 Three strongly defended cities: a recapitulation of 56.2, with the addition of the names of the cities.

58.2 Lack of financial resources: the subsidies they had previously received from Persia (see note on 40.2) were presumably exhausted. Cf. Dem. 18.19, who confirms that the Thebans had fallen from arrogance to humiliation and were distressed by the prolongation of the war.

Sent envoys to Philip with a request for aid: Pausanias (10.2.4) claims that Philip concluded an alliance with Thebes after the death of Philomelus (i.e. in late 355 or early 354), and, if this is correct, the Theban request will have been made in accordance with the terms of that alliance. However Diodorus (ch. 59.2) dates the alliance to 346, and there is no positive evidence in favour of an earlier date. Philip and Thebes are not known to have cooperated prior to 347, and all that can be said of their previous relationship is that they had common allies in the Thessalians and common enemies in the Phocians. The Boeotians will have hoped that

Philip might intervene now that his success in Chalcidice had left him at leisure.

58.3 Deflate their Leuctric arrogance: Demosthenes (18.18) also refers to abuse by the Thebans of the position they had gained after their victory at Leuctra over Sparta in 371. The Theban request put Philip in a quandary: if he ignored it, especially after his earlier claim to be the god's champion (see note on 35.2), he would alienate public opinion in the Greek world, but if he acceded to it, he was merely buoying up Theban prestige. His real interests required him to wear out both sides and win for himself the credit for ending the war.

58.4 Abae: see note on 38.3. The object of the fortification was to block the only route from Boeotia to Phocis which they did not already control, as well as to facilitate communication with their garrison at Orchomenus which they had captured the previous year (see 56.2 and 58.1, above).

58.5 Divine manifestations to fall upon Phocis: see note on 56.8.

58.6 The straw caught fire: perhaps an attempt by Diodorus or his source to exculpate the Boeotians from sacrilegiously seeking to burn out the fugitives.

59.1 M.Aemilius and T.Quintius: these names should correspond to the consuls of 349, but the Roman tradition (e.g. Livy 7.24.11) offers L.Furius Camillus and Ap.Claudius Crassus Inregillensis.
   The Phocians had been humbled: it was probably now (winter 347/6) that Phalaecus was replaced by a new triumvirate (see ch. 56.3), which appealed for assistance to Athens and Sparta. Diodorus is silent on the appeal to Athens, which is attested by Aeschines (2.132), who informs us that the Phocians offered to place in their hands Thronium, Alponus and Nicaea, the first of which had been captured by Onomarchus in 354 (see ch. 33.3), and the two latter by Phayllus in 351 (see note on 38.3). Since the three Locrian cities controlled the route to and from Thermopylae, the Phocians were in effect relying on Athens and Sparta to keep Philip out of central Greece. The Athenians responded in the spring of 346 by sending a force under Proxenus, who met up with Archidamus and his Spartans at Nicaea, only to be rebuffed by Phalaecus.

59.2 Concerning an alliance: see note on 58.3. The initiative came from the Boeotians, who hoped that the conclusion of a formal alliance would oblige Philip to involve himself more enthusiastically in the war. The visit of the Thebans coincided with the arrival in Macedonia of an Athenian embassy including Demosthenes, who graphically describes (19.139-42) what he construed as a shameless attempt by Philip to bribe the Boeotian delegates.

Who had once again been deemed worthy of the generalship: Phalaecus had already occupied the three cites which his opponents were offering to the Athenians and Spartans, and declined to hand them over (Dem. 19.73, 77; Aeschines 2.133-5). This so exasperated the Athenians and Spartans that they withdrew in frustration and the Phocian government, thus deprived of allies, had no option other than to turn to Phalaecus and reinstate him in his command.

Entered into negotiations with the king: Phalaecus had no intention of playing the role of scapegoat for which his opponents had cast him, and aware that his control of the Thermopylae corridor was a useful bargaining counter in any deal he might make with Philip, preferred to negotiate with him rather than with the domestic enemies whom he mistrusted.

59.3 Permitted Phalaecus to depart: the concession he secured from Philip as the price of handing over Thermopylae. The self-styled champion of Apollo was cynically prepared to overlook Phalaecus' sacrilege in exchange for this major prize: after all, he could play Apollo's avenger again when the time came to settle with the Phocian government, which, unlike Phalaecus, had nothing to offer him that he wanted.

The Phocians...surrendered to Philip: for the first time in this war, the Phocians found themselves caught in a pincer operation: while the Boeotians were preparing an invasion from the south east, Philip and the Thessalians, now that they controlled Thermopylae, would attack from the north. Of their allies, Sparta had been alienated by the rebuff from Phalaecus, while Athens was concluding a treaty of peace and alliance with Philip. Diodorus is so preoccupied with the fate of the sacrilegious Phocians that he omits the signing of the Peace of Philocrates between Philip and the Athenian Confederacy in 346. Philip had made clear his desire for peace with Athens as early as 348 through the agency of both Euboean ambassadors and Phrynon of Rhamnous, an Athenian he had captured and subsequently released (Aeschines 2.12-3). At first, the Athenians were incredulous, and it was only after the failure of their mission to the Peloponnese in an attempt to build up an anti-Macedonian coalition that they began to take his proposal at all seriously (Dem. 19.10-2). They then sent Aristodemus the actor to sound out his intentions (Dem. 19.12; Aeschines 2.15-7), and, on receiving a favourable report, dispatched ten envoys to Pella (Dem. 19.12-3; Aeschines 2.18ff.) in the winter of 347/6 to conduct the negotiations. On returning to Athens, they reported that he insisted on alliance as well as peace, and on a treaty in the form of a bilateral agreement between Philip and the Athenian Confederacy, under which both sides should keep what belonged to them at the date of the conclusion of the peace. In other words, the Athenians had to recognise the loss of Amphipolis and their other former possessions now in Philip's hands, while Philip was given a free hand in Phocis (significantly not mentioned in the treaty). So great was the desire on the part of the Athenians to avoid a Macedonian invasion of Attica conducted by the divinely ordained avenger of sacrilege that even Demosthenes argued in favour of acceptance, however much he sought to deny it afterwards. The peace, named for Philocrates, the proposer of the decree recommending acceptance, was approved, and a second embassy, including Philocrates, Demosthenes and Aeschines, was sent to Macedonia to ratify the agreement and receive Philip's oath. The Phocians, now totally isolated, surrendered to Philip unconditionally.

59.4 Met in deliberation with the Boeotians and Thessalians: these were only informal deliberations between Philip and his chief allies concerning the Phocian settlement, which, it was decided, should be entrusted to the Council of the Amphictyons. Doubtless the line to be taken by the allies at that meeting was discussed and a common policy agreed upon.

60.1 Philip and his descendants should be members of the League: cf. Pausanias 10.3.3. The two votes were given to Philip personally, not to the Macedonians, and the two delegates appointed by him regularly appear in second place on Amphictyonic documents as 'those from Philip', the Thessalians retaining pride of place.

The two votes which had formerly belonged to the Phocians: Speusippus' Letter to Philip of 343/2 informs us that the historian Antipater of Magnesia 'discovered' precedents for depriving a league member of its votes, two from mythological times (the Phlegyans whose eponymous ruler Phlegyas impiously destroyed Apollo's temple in revenge for the rape of his daughter Coronis, cf. Pausanias 9.36.2, 10.7.1, 10.34.2, and the Dryopes, who attacked Delphi in the reign of king Phylas, cf. Diodorus Book 4.37), and one (the Crisaeans) allegedly at the end of the First Sacred War in 582 (cf. Aeschines 3.107-9, 114-7).

The walls of the three cities controlled by the Phocians: presumably the three Boeotian cities mentioned at 58.1 above, which had been refortified by the Phocians during their period of occupation. Also relevant is Demosthenes' reference at 19.325 to the enslavement of Orchomenus and Coronea at this time.

The Phocians should have no share in the Amphictyonic Council: Diodorus omits the exclusion of the Spartans (Pausanias 10.8.2). The Athenians, as Philip's new allies, were spared this ignominy.

Denied the use of horses and weapons, to ensure that they were incapable of resisting the conditions imposed on them by the Amphictyons.

Liable to seizure: i.e. to enslavement. The reference is to Phalaecus and his associates who had fled (see 61.3-62.2, 64.4), as well as to those who had sought refuge in Athens (Dem. 5.19).

60.2 Destroy...the Phocian cities and split them up into villages: i.e. they should suffer what the Greeks called dioecism. Cf. Dem. 19.325 and Paus. 10.3.1-2, who lists twenty by name, adding that Abae with its Apolline oracle was spared because of its previous opposition to the sacrilege. Many of the cities were rebuilt after the conclusion of the Atheno-Boeotian alliance of 339 (Paus.10.3.3).

Sixty talents: the epigraphic evidence from Delphi (Tod. 172, Harding 88) together with the fragmentary list of payments erected by the Phocians at Elatea, confirms the payment in semi-annual instalments of 30 talents, commencing in the archonship of Cleon (344/3 or 343/2). After Chaeronea, Philip softened this harsh line and secured a reduction in the payments from 60 to 10 talents per year, which the Phocians continued to pay till 322.

Philip was henceforth to celebrate the Pythian festival: i.e. to preside at the ceremonies. The Pythian festival, at which musical and athletic contests were held, took place at Delphi every four years.

Because of Corinthian involvement: Diodorus seems to imply, if the text is sound, that the presidency of the Pythian Games was transferred to Philip from the Corinthians, but they had no known connection with this festival except as members of the Amphictyony who played an active role in the affairs of the League. They did however preside at the Isthmian Games which were held on Corinthian territory, but if Philip ever presided at these, it can only have been at the meeting of 336, when as *hegemon* of the League of Corinth, he may have been present at the League synod timed to coincide with the festival (cf. Aeschines 3.254; Curtius 4.5.11; SEG I 75 = Harding 138 line 12). If so, he will have been given the presidency on this occasion out of a desire to honour the *hegemon* rather than to punish the Corinthians for an act of sacrilege perpetrated more than a decade previously.

60.3 Dashed the weapons...against the cliffs, because of the impious uses to which they had been put. Though inanimate objects, they were deemed to merit the traditional punishment for sacrilege (cf. the Oetaean proposal mentioned at Aeschines 2.142 to throw the adult Phocian males from a cliff and the self-inflicted fate ascribed to Philomelus at ch. 31. 4).

60.4 Made a name for himself for his piety: Diodorus is thinking specifically of his role as Apollo's champion, not in general terms.

60.5 He was eager to be nominated commander-in-chief of the Greeks: the date when Philip first seriously contemplated a pan-Hellenic crusade against Persia is uncertain. Though some modern scholars think that this wish did not evolve till after Chaeronea, in favour of Diodorus' date is the fact that in his second letter to Philip written after Chaeronea, Isocrates expresses the belief that he sent the *Philippus* in 346 to a man who had already made up his mind to attack Persia (*Epistle* 3.13). Moreover Philip's decision in the same year to conclude an alliance with Athens at a time when he had no obvious need of one, is more intelligible if he was already thinking of a war with Persia in which he would not only need the cooperation of the Athenian fleet but also the goodwill and diplomatic support of the state which enjoyed the longest and staunchest anti-Persian record of all Greek cities.

61.1 The punishment which the god inflicted: see note on 56.8. Most of the first and second sections of this chapter consists of a recapitulation of incidents which have been previously described.

61.2 Philomelus...threw himself from a rock: see 31.4.

His brother Onomarchus: the mistaken belief that Onomarchus was Philomelus' brother is repeated from 56.5, and the story of his death from 35.6.

61.3 Phayllus...fell victim to a lingering illness: see 38.6.

61.4 After the conclusion of the compact: i.e. with Philip. On this, see 59.3.

In the Peloponnese: perhaps on the peninsula of Taenarum in Laconia, the normal place of assembly for unemployed mercenaries, inaccessible and difficult to attack (see. e.g. Diod. 17.108.7, 17.111.1, 18.9.1, 18.21.1; Plut. *Moralia* 848E; Arrian, *Anabasis* 2.13.6). The desire to retain command of such a large force will have led Phalaecus to invent an unnamed paymaster in the west. The chronic instability in both Sicily and Magna Graecia, where the mixed population of the cities produced frequent stasis, and where the cities were frequently at war with either a rival city or a barbarian neighbour, in Sicily the Carthaginians, in Italy one or another of the Italic peoples, lent plausibility to the claim.

Lucanians, an Oscan speaking people who inhabited the south west of Italy, the modern region of Basilicata, stretching from the Tyrrhenian Sea in the west to the Gulf of Tarentum in the east. According to Plutarch (*Agis* 3.2), it was not the Lucanians who were involved in this war but the Messapians, an Illyrian speaking people who had migrated to Italy and settled in Calabria,

137

where they were Tarentum's eastern neighbours.

The Tarentines: the inhabitants of the Greek city of Taras (in Latin Tarentum), a Spartan colony on the north shore of the Gulf of the same name, due east of Lucanian territory. In the fourth century the Lucanians exercised constant pressure on the Tarentines, who became increasingly dependent on mercenary leaders summoned from Greece to maintain the city's autonomy.

62.3 They assembled at Cape Malea: the Malea peninsula in the extreme south east of Laconia is not mentioned elsewhere as a recruiting base for mercenaries, and it is possible that Phalaecus and his men were excluded from Taenarum either by the Spartan authorities or by the mercenaries already there who were anxious to avoid the taint of sacrilege. Not all of Phalaecus' mercenaries in fact remained with him: according to Plutarch (*Timoleon* 30.4), some entered the service of Timoleon when he was recruiting troops for his projected expedition to Sicily (see ch. 65).

Cnossos, a city in the north of Crete, the site of the former Minoan palace, at that time a shadow of its glorious past, but still a city of some significance in the island.

Lyctos, also known as Lyttos, another Cretan city and a neighbour of Cnossos, situated some 15 miles to the south east.

62.4 Since they were the founders of their race: Tarentum was a Spartan colony, founded in 706, allegedly to remove from Sparta subversive malcontents termed Partheniai, who had been excluded from the rights of citizenship because they were either bastards or the sons of Spartiate women by helots (Aristotle, *Politics* 1306b 31; Diod. 8.21; Pausanias 3.12.5; Justin 3.4.3ff.). The recent decision of Corinth to assist her colony of Syracuse (see ch. 65) may also have influenced the Spartans, as did hopes of rich Italian booty sufficient to replenish a virtually empty treasury.

The Spartans were persuaded: the similarity of Spartan and Cretan institutions was a reminder of their common Dorian origin (Strabo 10.4.17 ff.), and the Spartans had in the past found in Crete a useful recruiting ground for mercenaries. Both factors contributed to the forging of close links between Sparta and Crete (cf. the presence in Crete of Agesilaus the brother of Agis III in 333 (Arrian, *Anabasis* 2.3.16) and of Areus I in 272 (Plut. *Pyrrhus* 27.1).

63.1 After this: if the activities of Phalaecus and his mercenaries in the Peloponnese belong to the year 345, his arrival in Crete, and the departure of Archidamus from Sparta should belong to 344. The decision of the Argives in the winter of 344/3 to send 3000 men to assist the Persians in Egypt (see ch. 44.2) can only have been taken if Sparta was no longer seen as a threat, i.e. if Archidamus had already departed. Also relevant is the Spartan inability to undo the pro-Macedonian coup in Elis in 343 (see note on section 4 below). Archidamus will in this event have arrived in Italy in 343.

Meet an illustrious death in battle: Archidamus was slain in battle at a place called Mandurium (Plut. *Agis* 3.2), according to Diodorus (ch. 88.3) and Plutarch (*Camillus* 19.5) on the very same day as the battle of Chaeronea (338). Since the purpose of this and the following chapter is to illustrate the divine punishment of the sacrilegious, it is strange that Diodorus should omit to inform us that Archidamus' corpse missed burial owing to the anger of Apollo (Pausanias 3.10.5).

63.2 King of Sparta for 23 years: Archidamus succeeded to the throne upon the death of his father Agesilaus, which Diodorus records under the archon year 362/1 (15.93.6). However this represents the year of his arrival in Egypt, not of his entire campaign. Since he was involved in the deposition of the pharaoh Tachos (Plut. *Agesilaus* 37.6), which is dated by Egyptian sources to 361 or 360, he must have spent a year at least there. If the figure 23 is correct, and we also give credence to the story that Mandurium was fought in the same year (even if not on the same day) as Chaeronea, his reign should be dated to the years 361-38. If 360 is preferred for the death of Agesilaus (see G.L.Cawkwell, *Agesilaus and Sparta*, CQ 26, 1976, p. 63 note 8; P. Cartledge, *Agesilaus and the Crisis of Sparta*, London, 1987, pp. 20-1), Diodorus' figure of 23 will be an error for 22.

His son Agis ruled for 15 years: Agis III was killed at the battle of Megalopolis, which was fought in either 331 or 330 (Diod. 17. 63.4; Curtius 6.1.13-5; Plut. *Agis* 3.2; Pausanias 3.10.5). Reckoning back from this year would put his accession in either 346 or 345, but he only became king when Archidamus died, probably in 338. Diodorus contradicts himself by giving Agis a reign of 9 years in ch. 88.4 below and at 17.63.4. Clearly a reign of some 7 or 8 years is indicated, and it is possible that Diodorus arrived at the figure of 15, if indeed it is not a simple blunder, by adding to his reign the years he served as regent on behalf of his absent father: in effect Agis did rule Sparta for around 15 years, but for only the last 7 or 8 of these as king.

Attempted to besiege Cydonia: Cydonia, the modern Khania, was a city in the west of Crete, on the north coast. There is no hint in Diodorus that he was hired to attack the city, and it is more than likely that he was acting on his own initiative, with the aim of securing enough loot to enable him to keep his band of mercenaries together as an effective fighting force. Isocrates (4.168, 5.96 and 120; 8.24; *Epistle* 9.9) attests to the trouble bands of unemployed wandering mercenaries could cause to Greek cities; for a specific example, see Xenophon, *Anabasis* 7.1.15-21, where some of the Ten

Thousand force their way inside the walls of Byzantium and offer to instal him as tyrant. Phalaecus may even have been looking for a similar occurrence at Cydonia.

63.4 Exiles from Elis: the pro-Spartan government had been overthrown by a pro-Macedonian faction (Dem. 19.260 and 294; Pausanias 5.9.4) in receipt of Messenian support (Pausanias 4.28.5-6) and driven into exile. These exiles hired the former mercenaries of Phalaecus in order to stage a forcible return, but were thwarted, as Diodorus says, by the Arcadians. The Messenians and Arcadians, who shared a border with Laconia, were the natural allies of any anti-Spartan regime in the Peloponnese. The date of the revolution should be 343, since there is no mention of it in the *Second Philippic* of 344, and it is referred to in Demosthenes' speech *On the Embassy*, delivered in 343, as 'recent' (19.249). The abortive attempt of the pro-Spartans to return should therefore belong to late 343, or, more probably, to the following year.

64.1 The most famous cities were later vanquished by Antipater: Diodorus here refers to Antipater's victories over Sparta at Megalopolis in 331 or 330 (see note on ch. 63.2) and over Athens and her coalition in the Lamian War at Crannon in 322 (Diod. 18.17). Markle (*Diodorus' Sources for the Sacred War*, in I.Worthington, *Ventures into Greek History*, Oxford, 1994, p. 49) argues that this passage must derive from a source who wrote later than 322 (Duris?), but it could equally well be an addition of Diodorus himself from his own knowledge of later events.

64.2 The one which had belonged to Helen: many Greek temples preserved what passed for relics handed down from the Bronze Age as votive offerings. Compare the preservation in the temple of Ismenian Apollo at Thebes of tripods allegedly dedicated by Laodamas the grandson of Oedipus and by Amphitryon the step-father of Heracles (Herodotus 5.19-21) and of the lyre of Paris and armour dating from the Trojan War in the temple of Athena at Ilium (Arrian, *Anabasis*, 1.11.7; Diod. 17.18.1; Plut., *Alexander* 15.5). Helen's necklace was believed to have been dedicated by Menelaus in the temple of Athena Pronoia in response to an oracle (Ephorus, Frag. 96 = Athenaeus 6.232D). Ephorus/Demophilus goes on to describe how the wives of the Phocian leaders cast lots to determine who should receive which piece of jewellery: the winner of Helen's necklace was, like Helen herself, as notorious for her promiscuity as for her beauty. Whereas Ephorus/ Demophilus has her fall in love with an Epirot youth and accompany him back to his home, Diodorus goes one better and converts her into a whore. Since

Helen was the 'woman of many men/husbands' (Aeschylus, *Agamemnon* 62) (Theseus, Menelaus, Paris, Deiphobus, Menelaus again, and finally, on the White Island at the mouth of the Danube, Achilles), the promiscuous life of the woman who wore the necklace is a not inappropriate invention.

The wearer of Eriphyle's: she was the mistress of Phayllus and wife of Ariston, an Oetaean mercenary commander (Phylarchus, Frag. 70; Plut. *Moralia* 553E; Athenaeus 6.232D). Eriphyle's necklace was originally crafted by Hephaestus and given by the gods as a wedding present to Harmonia the daughter of Ares and Aphrodite when she married Cadmus the founder of Thebes. It remained as an heirloom in the possession of the Theban royal line till the time of the expedition of the Seven against Thebes, when it was offered by Polynices as a bribe to Eriphyle wife of the seer Amphiaraus who refused to participate in the war because he foresaw his own death. Yielding to Eriphyle's entreaties, he gave way, but not before ordering his son Alcmaeon to avenge him. The latter duly avenged his father's death by killing his mother, only to be driven mad by the Erinyes. On receiving absolution, he dedicated her necklace in the temple of Athena Pronaia. The fate of Phayllus' mistress has to some extent been assimilated by Diodorus' source to that of Eriphyle, though the parallel is only partly apposite. According to Ephorus (Frag. 96), she plotted her husband Ariston's death and was subsequently killed by her younger (eldest, according to Diodorus) son in a fit of madness: whereas Eriphyle was murdered by a son who later became insane, Phayllus' mistress was killed by one who was already mad. All in all we are treated to a cautionary moral tale which is historically worthless.

64.3 Piety towards the god: cf.1.4, 60.4 above.
Designated commander-in-chief of the whole of Greece: i.e. *hegemon* of the League of Corinth (338/7). See ch. 89 below.

65.1 Slaves to many diverse types of tyranny: in the fourth century, Syracuse had been ruled by the Elder Dionysius (405-367), then by his son Dionysius the Younger (367-57). There followed a period of faction fighting (Dion against Heracleides, Dion against Callippus) which was in turn succeeded by the tyrannies of Callippus (353-2), Hipparinus (352-0), Nysaeus (350-46) and Dionysius II restored (346-4).

Sent envoys to Corinth: the appeal, made in 345, was the work of Syracusan aristocrats hostile to the tyranny and was supported by Hicetas, a former adherent of Dionysius who was now living in exile at Leontini, where he had installed himself as tyrant (Plut. *Timoleon* 1.3, 2.1-2). Corinth was the metropolis of Syracuse with which she retained close ties. Though involvement in Sicily was for her virtually without precedent since the defeat of the Athenian Sicilian expedition of 415-3, the forces she sent initially (7 ships and 1000 men: see Plut. *Tim.* 8.3 and 11.3) hardly constituted a strong commitment, and it was only after Timoleon won some measure of success that the Corinthians began to show enthusiasm for the expedition (ch. 69.4 and Plut. *Tim.* 16.6).

65.2 Son of Timaenetus: according to Plutarch (*Tim.* 3.1), his father was Timodemus.

65.3 Timophanes...had...been aspiring to tyrannical rule: though Diodorus insists that Timophanes was never actually tyrant, he is specifically given this appellation by Aristotle (*Politics* 1306a 23): according to Nepos (*Tim.* 1.3) and Plut. (*Tim.* 4.2-3), he was a legally elected general who seized power with the aid of 400 mercenaries entrusted to his command.

64.4 Timoleon slew him as he was walking about: Nepos (*Tim.*1.4) and Plut. (*Tim.* 4.5) both deny that he took any active part in the assassination, and state that he merely stood to one side weeping while the killers (whom Plutarch names as Timophanes' brother-in- law Aeschylus and either Satyrus or Orthagoras) cut him down. Either Plutarch's source is attempting to free Timoleon from the odium of fratricide or Diodorus is embellishing the story for dramatic effect.

65.6 When the council of elders met: Diodorus seems to have in mind a trial before a political body sitting in a judicial capacity, which once more converts itself into a political gathering when the Syracusan envoys arrive. The story, though exciting dramatically, lacks internal plausibility.

65.7 While the issue was...undecided, envoys from Syracuse sailed in: Diodorus' chronology, which requires the murder of Timophanes to have taken place in 345 not long before the arrival of the envoys, is certainly erroneous. Plutarch, who dates Timoleon's mission some twenty years after Timophanes' death (*Tim.* 7.1) implies a date for the latter of around 365, a date that is fully consistent with the circumstances of Timophanes' coup. We know from Plut. *Tim.* 4.2 that the mercenaries with whom he staged his coup had been recruited by the Corinthians through fear of possible treachery on the part of their allies, and from Xenophon (*Hell.* 7.4.4-10) that the incident in question arose in 366 from Corinthian alarm that the Athenian garrisons stationed on her territory might be used to reduce her to an Athenian dependency. If Athenian behaviour in 366 necessitated the recruitment of mercenaries, the ambitious Timophanes will have sought to use them as soon as possible rather than wait the twenty years that Diodorus' narrative requires.

65.8 They laid before him alternatives...both novel and unbelievable:
this story seems to have originated in a private remark made by one Tele-
cleides after Timoleon's election (Plut. *Tim.* 7.2): as the actual verdict of a
court of law, it is indeed, as Diodorus says, unbelievable.

65.9 Timoleon directed the affairs of Sicily: here Diodorus gives a
brief, eulogistic summary of Timoleon's achievements in Sicily, which he
describes in more detail in chapters 66-68.2, 72-3 and 77.4-84. These
chapters have been omitted from this edition. For more details on Timoleon's
career and achievements, see Plutarch's *Life*. See also H.D.Westlake,
Timoleon and his Relations with Tyrants, Manchester, 1951 and
R.J.A.Talbert, *Timoleon and the Revival of Greek Sicily 344-337 B.C.*,
Cambridge, 1974.

66.1 M.Fabius and Ser.Sulpicius: M.Fabius Dorsuo and Ser.Sulpicius
Camerinus Rufus were the consuls of the year 345. The consular list used by
Diodorus gives for the first time in Book 16 names which cover at least part
of the correct archon year.

66.2 He had 700 mercenaries, presumably as much as Corinth's
limited financial resources would allow. Some of these were formerly in
the employment of Phalaecus (Plut. *Tim.* 30.4). Plutarch (*Tim.* 11.3) and
indeed Diodorus at 68.9 gives him 1000 on his arrival in Sicily, i.e. the
original 700 of Diodorus, together with 300 picked up at Leucas and Corcyra
en route. Plutarch (*Tim.* 12.3) assigns to him 1200, which must include the
Tauromenians, who joined him on his arrival in Sicily (see 68.8).
Four triremes and three fast sailing ships: Diodorus appears to be
making a distinction between two types of trireme. Fast triremes are occasionally (e.g. Thucydides 6.43; Xenophon, *Hell.* 1.1.36) contrasted with
stratiotides, literally 'ships for carrying troops', but the contrast is probably
more apparent than real, for the difference was not so much one of weight,
construction or workmanship as in the number of rowers. See H.T.Wallinga,
Ships and Sea-Power before the Great Persian War, Leiden, 1993, pp. 175-7,
where it is argued that the term *stratiotis* is used of a ship which lacks its full
complement of oarsmen (adequate for the transportation of troops), whereas
the same vessel becomes a 'fast sailer' whenever the oarsmen are brought up
to full strength. In Timoleon's case, it would have been fully in keeping with
the cheese-paring Corinthian war effort to provide him with inadequate
funding to provide a full complement of rowers for all seven of his ships.
Three ships from the Leucadians and Corcyreans: of these, two were
Corcyrean and one Leucadian (Plut. *Tim.* 8.3). Both Corcyra (the modern

Corfu) and Leucas were Corinthian colonies on the route from Greece to Sicily which might be expected to contribute to an expedition of the mother city, and it is possible that other colonies in the north west also contributed: fragments of a commemorative memorial to Timoleon's success have been found on the site of Corinth (SEG II 126A), which certainly named the people of Apollonia and may also have referred (in a restored passage) to the Ambraciots. However it is possible that their contribution was made not to the original expedition but to the reinforcements that were subsequently dispatched.

Ionian Gulf: othewise known as the Ionian Sea, the name given to the southern part of the Adriatic which separates Greece from Sicily and Magna Graecia. The rest of this chapter and the two that follow are devoted to Timoleon's arrival in Sicily and to his victory over Hicetas at Adranum.

69.1 M. Valerius and M. Poplius: M. Valerius Corvus and M. Popillius Laenas were consuls for the year 348.

The 109th Olympiad, which ran from 344/3 till 341/0.

The first treaty was made between the Romans and the Carthaginians: this treaty is also mentioned by Livy (7.27.2), who dates it to 348: clearly it came to be attached to the consulship of Valerius and Popillius. Full details of the content of the treaty (but not its date) are recorded by Polybius at 3.24. Neither Diodorus nor Livy is aware of an earlier treaty said by Polybius (3.22) to belong to the first year of the Roman republic (509/8), and Livy (9.43.26) mentions under the year 306 a third treaty which is unknown to Polybius and Diodorus. Yet another treaty was concluded in 279/8 (Polybius 3.25, cf. Diod. 22.7.5 and Livy, Epitome 13). For a discussion of the various treaties and their chronology, see F.W. Walbank, *A Historical Commentary on Polybius*, Vol. I, Oxford, 1957, pp. 336-56.

69.2 Idrieus the ruler of Caria: see 45.7, where his accession is recorded under the year 351/0.

Ada: like Mausolus, Artemisia and Idrieus, she was a child of Hecatomnus, and was officially joint ruler in the reign of her brother/husband. Her sole reign terminated in 341/0, when she was driven from power and replaced by her youngest brother Pixodarus (see ch. 74.2).

69.3-6: these sections, which describe the three way contest at Syracuse between Timoleon, Dionysius and the Carthaginians, have been omitted in my translation.

69.7 An ancestral enmity with the Illyrians: Diodorus has in mind the two Illyrian invasions during the reign of Philip's father Amyntas III in 393/2 and 383/2 (see Diod. 14.92.3 and 15.19.2), the war of 359 which led to the death in battle of Perdiccas III (see ch. 2 4-5), Philip's victory over Bardylis in 358 (see ch. 4.3-7) and the Illyro-Thraco-Paeonian coalition of 356 (see 22.3).The reference in the present passage to ancestral enmity should mean that the tribe now under attack was the Dardanians (currently ruled by Bardylis' son Cleitus - see note on 4.3), and indeed Justin (8.6.3) names them specifically as Philip's objective. However Didymus (*Commentary on Demosthenes* col. 12.64), citing the Macedonian historian Marsyas (Frag. 17), informs us that Philip campaigned against a king called Pleuratus, who was probably ruler of the Ardiaei (Hammond, *BSA* 61, p. 245), a tribe living on the Adriatic coast between the Naron (the modern Nereta) and Lake Labeatis (now the Lake of Shkodër). If Justin is correct in naming the Dardanians at this point, it is possible that Philip campaigned against both peoples. His initial objecive will have been the Dardanians, whom he reduced to dependent status, but the Ardiaei may have intervened and obliged him to attack them as well. Diodorus' date for this Illyrian war is 344, but there is no reference to it in the *Second Philippic* delivered in that year, and Philip was much preoccupied with Thessaly at the time. On the other hand 345 is for Philip a blank, and since it would be unusual for such a restless individual (Dem. 1.14) to spend a whole campaigning season in inactivity, the Illyrian war is best slotted in at this point to fill the vacuum.

69.8 He passed through Thessaly: the settlement made after the Crocus Field (ch. 38.1) was by now in need of a thorough overhaul. The end of the Sacred War will have made the Thessalians less dependent on Macedonian support, and led some to question Philip's behaviour as archon: he was suspected of diverting some of the archon's revenues to illegal uses (Dem. 6.22), while the transfer of Pagasae and Magnesia from Pherae to himself (Dem. 2.12; Isocrates 5.21) caused dissatisfaction in that city. He accordingly decided to intervene and make whatever changes were necessary to strengthen his control.

He expelled the tyrants from the cities: there is evidence for Macedonian intervention at Pherae (Dem. 8.59, an assault on its walls; [Dem.] 7.32, the installation of a garrison; Dem. 9.12, Philip's recent seizure and retention of the city) and at Larissa (Aristotle, *Politics* 1306a30, stasis within the ruling oligarchy headed by Simus; scholiast on Dem. 1.22, translated in Harding 62D, Philip's expulsion of Simus). In addition, Demosthenes (19.260) refers in 343 to the stationing of Macedonian garrisons in unspecified cities. Presumably the 'tyrants' Diodorus has in mind include Simus and whoever was currently ruling Pherae. For the possibility that it was Peitholaus, and that his return was misdated by Diodorus to 349/8, see note on 52.9 above. It was in the course of his intervention of 344 that Philip established a decadarchy or governing board of ten (Dem. 6.22). If the singular is to be taken literally, he will have instituted one such body for the whole of Thessaly, though the analogy of Lysander's decadarchies suggest that Demosthenes' singular is collective (i.e. a board of ten for each Thessalian city, presumably consisting of hand-picked pro-Macedonians). By 341, the date of the *Third Philippic*, Philip imposed yet another constitutional change on Thessaly, the tetrarchy of Group of Four (Dem. 9.26). These were old geographical units (Histiaeotis, Thessaliotis, Pelasgiotis and Phthiotis) which had been abolished or at least had their political significance reduced by Pelopidas: the office of tetrarch had been replaced by the polemarchy, attested in the treaty of alliance of 361/0 between Athens and Thessaly (Tod 147, Harding 59. Cf. Theopompus, Frag. 208, from Book XLIV, which covered the year 342). At 9.26 Demosthenes states that the Thessalians were now slaves not only city by city but also people by people. Since the peoples are the four tetrarchies, the reference to enslavement 'by city' must be an allusion to the decadarchies of 344, which were still in existence. The reintroduction of tetrarchies was probably an attempt to regain something of the earlier popularity which Philip had forfeited by the establishment of decadarchies, as well as provision for some of his Thessalian friends: of the tetrarchs he appointed, we know of Daochus (of the Daochidae of Pharsalus), described as 'tetrarch of the Thessalians' on an inscription, and Thrasydaeus (Theopompus Frag. 209), who appears on Demosthenes' list of traitors at 18.295.

The adjacent Greeks...concluded an alliance: Diodorus may be referring to the perioecic peoples removed from Thessalian control, perhaps at this time. By 339, the Aenianians, Dolopians and Phthiotic Achaeans were able to send embassies to Thebes in their own right (Philochorus, Frag. 56).

70.1 C.Plautius and T.Manlius: the consuls of 347 were C. Plautius Venno (or Venox) and T. Manlius Imperiosus Torquatus. The rest of chapter 70 describes the expulsion of Dionysius the Younger from Syracuse and Timoleon's introduction of a new constitution for the city.

71.1 An expedition against Thrace, which took up much of the campaigning seasons of 342 and 341. Philip's most recent Thracian campaign had been in 346, when he was involved in hostilities with the central and eastern kingdoms at the time he was negotiating the Peace of Philocrates with the Athenians. By the end of the campaign of 346, both Teres (the successor of Amadocus in central Thrace) and Cersobleptes had been reduced to vassal status.

To subdue the cities on the Hellespont: since the European shore of the Hellespont belonged to Athens and the Asian shore to Persia, it is difficult to see how and why any actions of Cersobleptes in the Chersonese can have been of any concern to Philip. Diodorus is probably using the term 'Hellespont' loosely to mean the Thracian coast: cf. his inaccurate uses of the term at 21.3 to refer to Embaton and at 53.2 to Chalcidice. Cersobleptes' attacks on some of the Thracian coastal cities captured by Philip in 346 will have been used by Philip as a *casus belli*.

71.2 Defeating the Thracians: Diodorus fails to explain which of the Thracian kingdoms was the objective of Philip's attack. Cetriporis of western Thrace is not heard of after 352, and his kingdom was probably incorporated into Macedonia either then or in 346. Central Thrace was currently ruled by Teres, the successor of Amadocus II, while Cersobleptes still ruled the eastern part. It is likely that both kings were attacked by Philip, who enjoyed the support of the Getae, a tribe living between the Odrysian kingdoms and the Danube, thanks to the marriage he contracted at this time with Meda, the daughter of Cothelas, the Getic king (Jordanes, *Getica* 10.65; Satyrus, Frag. 5; cf. Theopompus, Frag. 217).

He ordered the subjugated barbarians to pay tithes: Diodorus' account of the settlement is brief and vague. It is clear from [Dem.] 12.8 that both Teres and Cersobleptes were dethroned and the country turned into a dependent territory of tributary status. It was probably now that Philip appointed a military governor (*strategos*), though the office is first attested under Alexander (Arrian, *Anab.* 1.25.2; Diod. 17.62.5; Curtius 10.1.44).

Founding significant cities, with the aim of opening up the country, developing its resources, and contributing to its pacification by occupying areas of strategic importance and planting garrisons in those that gave trouble. Among the places occupied by Philip at this time were Drongelus, Mastira and Cabyle (Dem. 8.44, 10.15), of which the latter, situated on the river Tonsus near modern Yambol, became a foundation of some importance. Among the cities founded on a new site were Philippopolis (modern Plovdiv) and probably Beroe (the modern Stara Zagora). To inhabit the new cities Philip imported Macedonian and Greek settlers (cf. Theopompus, Frag. 110) to dwell alongside the native Thracians, thus creating a mixed population analogous to that which subsequently came to inhabit Alexander's foundations in Asia.

71.3 Among the historians, a bibliographical note which is inaccurate even by the Diodorus' usual standards.

He included a period of 50 years: since the Elder Dionysius became tyrant in 405/4 and the Younger was expelled in 344/3, the period covered was 61 years, not 50. Diodorus seems to have confused the second expulsion of the Younger Dionysius with the earlier one of 356/5. Reckoning back from this date to the beginning of the tyranny gives a period of 49 years (similarly rounded up to 50 at ch. 11.2).

The 3 books in question are the 41st to the 43rd: Theopompus devoted 5 books (39-43) to the history of the western Mediterranean, using as an excuse for the digression Philip's arrival on the Adriatic coast during his Epirote campaign of 343. Surviving fragments of these books indicate that Books 39 and 40 (no named fragments survive from Book 41) dealt with Sicily, while Books 42 and 43 were devoted to Italy, Liguria and Spain. If Diodorus is correct in stating that Sicily was covered in three books, they must have been 39-41, not 41-43. His carelessness about matters concerning his native Sicily is particularly surprising.

72.1 M.Valerius and M.Popilius: M. Valerius Corvus and C. Poetilius (not Popilius) Libo Visolus were the consuls for the year 346. Diodorus has confused the consuls of 346 with those of 348, who have similar names (see 69.1 above).

Arymbas the king of the Molossians: the correct spelling of the name is Arybbas (confirmed by epigraphical evidence, see below). He was the younger son of Alcetas I and grandson of the Athenian educated Tharyps. On Alcetas' death, he shared power with his elder brother Neoptolemus I (Pausanias 1.11.3), and became sole king when Neoptolemus died. The date of his accession must precede 357, since he was already on the throne when Philip married his niece Olympias (Plut. *Alex.* 2.2). Arybbas himself married Troas, another of Neoptolemus' daughters (Plut. loc. cit., *Pyrrhus* 1.3). In 351/0, Philip intervened in Epirus, reduced Arybbas to dependent status and transferred Neoptolemus' young son to Macedonia, where he was given an education worthy of a Macedonian prince (see note on 52.9 above).

Died after a reign of ten years: this statement is doubly erroneous. In the first place Arybbas did not die in 342/1, but was expelled by Philip and replaced by his nephew Alexander. Arybbas sought refuge in Athens, where he took up the grant of citizenship previously conferred on his father and grandfather (Tod 173; Wickersham and Verbrugghe 71; not in Harding). The Athenians gave him their protection and instructed their generals to effect his restoration to his native land. Since no opportunity for doing so presented itself, Arybbas remained in exile till his death (Justin 7.6.12). Diodorus' error is due to a hasty reading of his chronographic source and a mistaken assumption that a king's reign invariably terminates with his death. Secondly, Diodorus errs in giving Arybbas a ten year reign: since he was already on the throne in 357, a sole reign of at least 14 years is called for, and an even longer reign if the period of joint rule with Neoptolemus is taken into account.

Leaving a son Aeacides the father of Pyrrhus: so Diod. 19.11.1, 36.2, 88.1; Plut. Pyrrhus 1.3; Pausanias 1.11.1). Aeacides was in fact Arybbas' younger son, who ruled Epirus briefly in 317 and again from 313 till 312 (Diod. 19.11.1, 36.3, 74.3-5). Arybbas had an elder son Alcetas, whom he detested and banished from the kingdom. Alcetas ruled Epirus from 312 till 311, when he was murdered by disaffected subjects along with two of his sons (Diod. 19.89.3).

Thanks to the involvement of Philip: Philip's intervention in Epirus belongs to the year 343 or early 342, and (despite the order of events in Diodorus) before and not after his Thracian campaign. Philip installed as king Olympias' brother Alexander, whom he had been grooming for the succession since 351/0, in the expectation that he would prove a more accommodating ruler. At the same time he could plead by way of excuse that he was merely restoring the rightful king, for Alexander, as the son of Arybbas' elder brother, had a better claim to the throne. While in Epirus, Philip attacked Pandosia, Boucheta and Elatreia, three autonomous Greek cities and incorporated them into Alexander's kingdom ([Dem.] 7.32; Theopompus, Frag. 207). Because of the proximity of these cities to the territory of the Corinthian colony of Ambracia, the alarm bells began to ring in Corinth (Dem. 9.34), the Ambraciots went to war with Philip (Dem. 10.10) and were visited by Demosthenes in person (Dem. 18.244) with the offer of an alliance. The way was now open for the Atheno-Corinthian alliance of 340 (Dem. 18.237; Plut. *Dem.* 17.4). The remainder of this chapter and chapter 73, omitted in this edition, describe the warfare between Timoleon and Hicetas, the liberation of Engyum, Apollonia and Entella and Carthaginian preparations for prosecuting the war with Timoleon more vigorously.

74.1 C. Marcius and T. Manlius: C. Marcius Rutilus and T. Manlius Imperiosus Torquatus were consuls for the year 347.

Phocion...defeated Cleitarchus the tyrant of Eretria: Diodorus' account of the Euboean campaign of 341 is excessively brief. The situation in Euboea was complicated, arising from strife between the factions in the various cities, who sought to resolve things in their favour by calling in external aid. In Eretria, Cleitarchus (along with Hipparchus and Automedon) had seized power in 343 with the aid of a force of 2000 mercenaries under Hipponicus sent by Philip (Dem. 9.58, cf. 19.87, 204, 326, 334), and at Oreus, a similar coup was staged in 342 by Philistides, Menippus, Socrates, Thoas and Agapaeus, also with Macedonbian backing (Dem. 9.12 and 59, cf. 8.18). By 341, Callias of Chalcis, a former Companion of Philip (Aeschines 3.89), was so thoroughly alarmed that he sent an embassy to Athens to solicit Athenian aid in expelling the pro-Macedonian regimes (Aesch. 3.91ff.). Athens responded with the despatch of two successive forces, the first under Cephisophon which, in concert with the Chalcidians and Megarians, freed Oreus and put Philistides to death (Philochorus, Frag. 159; Charax of Pergamum, Frag. 19) and the second under Phocion, which liberated Eretria at the start of the new archon year (Philochorus, Frag. 160)

Raised to power by Philip: Cleitarchus is first heard of in 348 as a political enemy of the tyrant Plutarchus (Philochorus, Frag.160), but Diodorus is here more likely to be referring to the role of Hipponicus in Cleitarchus' coup of 343 (see previous note).

74.2 Ada: see note on 69.2. Following Pixodarus' coup, Ada was forced to withdraw from Halicarnassus, the seat of government. She retained control of the fortress of Alinda, where she resided till the arrival of Alexander in 334, whereupon she handed over Alinda and adopted Alexander as her son. He then reinstated her as satrap of Caria (Arrian, *Anab.* 1.23.8; Diod. 17.24.2). She must have died by 324 at latest, when Philoxenus held the office ([Aristotle], *Economica* 2.1351b).

Pizodarus, usually spelt Pixodarus. Since his title to the throne was at best tenuous, he sought to strengthen his position by suggesting to Philip a marriage between his daughter (Ada the Younger?) and Philip's son Arrhidaeus. This plan was however frustrated by Alexander (Plut. *Alex.* 10). According to Strabo (14.2.17), Pixodarus thereupon made his peace with the King and asked for a Persian nobleman to be his son-in-law and co-ruler. The King sent Orontobates, who subsequently succeeded him on his death and was satrap by the time Halicarnassus was put under siege by Alexander (Arrian, *Anab.* 1.23.1 and 7).

Ruled for five years till Alexander's crossing: both parts of this statement cannot be true. If the figure of five is correct, his rule will have lasted from 341/0 till 336/5, but must have been over by the time Alexander crossed to Asia in 334; alternatively if he lived to see Alexander's crossing, his reign must have lasted six years.

Perinthus, the modern Eregli (derived from its alternative name of Heracleia), was a city on the north shore of the Propontis about half way between the Chersonese and Byzantium, situated on a headland approachable only along a narrow isthmus. The city had been a member of the Second Athenian Confederacy (Tod 123, 1.84, Harding 35), but was occupied for a time in the 360s by the Persian satrap Ariobarzanes (Dem. 23.142), though she still remained on sufficiently friendly terms with Athens in 359 to allow her ships the use of her harbour (Dem. 23.165). However she defected in the Social War (Plut. *Dem.* 17.2), perhaps under pressure from Byzantium. When attacked in 352 by Cersobleptes, Perinthus was aided by Philip (scholiast on Aeschines 2.81), and it was probably at this time that the city became Philip's ally.

Which was opposed to him: we do not know the cause of the breach, but the Perinthians will have felt menaced by Philip's conquest of Thrace, and perhaps refused to contribute to his Thracian campaign. From Philip's point of view, it was unacceptable for him to subdue the interior while leaving independent the Greek cities on the coast, particularly if they were proving refractory. The attacks on Perinthus and Byzantium should be seen as consolidating the conquest of Thrace, and necessary both to deny Athens use of them as bases in the event of war (Didymus, Commentary on Demosthenes, col. 10.34) and to facilitate the crossing for his projected war with Persia, especially if Athens continued to hold the Chersonese and chose to deny him passage across the Hellespont.

74.3 Eighty cubits in height: if the measurement is in Attic cubits, their height would be some 35 metres or approximately 116¹/₂ feet.

74.4 Their allies the Byzantians: Byzantium, like Perinthus, had been a member of the Second Athenian Confederacy (Tod 123, line 83), but was showing a markedly pro-Theban stance as early as 364, when she gave Epaminondas a friendly welcome (Diod. 15.79.1), and in both 362 ([Dem.] 50.6) and 361 ([Dem.] 50.17) she interfered with Athenian grain ships. At the beginning of the Social War, if not before, the Byzantians formally seceded (see ch. 7.3), and henceforth the two cities tended to cooperate on issues of foreign policy. Like Perinthus, Byzantium became an ally of Philip in 352, but grew increasingly disenchanted with the expansion of Philip's power. She now realised that if Perinthus were to fall, her turn would come next.

74.5 A quantity of machines that...could not be bettered: Diodorus is here referring to the diversity and effectiveness of Philip's siege train, and in particular to the availability of battering rams, stone throwers, mobile wooden siege towers, mantelets, long scaling ladders, and, above all, to the newly invented torsion catapults operated by springs of sinew or horse hair, which were perhaps still at the experimental stage. These catapults were invented by Philip's chief engineer, Polyeidus of Thessaly, assisted by his pupils Diades and Charias (Vitruvius 10.13.3; Athenaeus Mechanicus, *On Siege Engines* 10.5). On Philip's siege train, see E.W. Marsden, *Greek and Roman Artillery*: I *Historical Development*; II *Technical Treatises*, Oxford, 1969, 1971, and I 56ff. in particular.

75.1 News...had reached Asia, partly through information elicited from the captured Hermias (ch. 52.5), and perhaps also from reports brought back from Macedonia by the pardoned Artabazus (ch. 52.3).

Wrote to the satraps on the coast: these were Arsites of Hellespontine Phrygia, the Lydian satrap (either Rhosaces, if still in office – he is last heard of in 343 during the Egyptian campaign, ch. 47.2 – or his successor Spithridates, first attested in 334, Arrian, *Anabasis* 1.1.28; Diod. 17.19.4), and Ada (or Pixodarus, if he had seized power by this time) of Caria. Persian intervention in Europe had been unprecedented since Xerxes' invasion, and the reversal of policy is an indication of the seriousness with which Philip's conquest of Thrace was viewed at Susa. The Persians will also have taken into account the impossibility of finding a Greek state both able and willing to curb him, since of the two major powers both Athens and Thebes were not only at peace but also in alliance with him.

75.2 The satraps sent...a force of mercenaries: Arsites, as the nearest to the theatre of war, assumed responsibility for carrying out the King's instructions, and gave command of the mercenaries to Apollodorus, an Athenian condottiere (Paus. 1.29.10, cf. [Dem.] 11.5). A second force was sent to Thrace (Arrian, *Anab.* 2.14.5), where Antipater and Parmenio were waging war against the Tetrachoritae (Theopompus, Frag. 217), and perhaps cooperated with the Athenian general Diopeithes, who was based in the Chersonese but was guilty of aggression in Thrace ([Dem.] 12.3). The Persian intervention in Thrace and at Perinthus, at a time when Persia and Macedonia were at peace, was later used by Alexander to justify his invasion of Asia (Arrian, *Anab.* 2 14.5).

76.1 The nature of the city...assisted the besieged: the description of the site of Perinthus, like the entire account of the siege, occurs only in Diodorus, who is here condensing his source much less drastically than is his wont.

A stade in breadth: the Attic stade was equivalent to 117.4 metres or 194 yards.

76.3 He divided his troops into two parts, perhaps rather into three, if he instituted a siege of Selymbria at the same time. Selymbria (the modern Silivri) was a city on the Propontis to the east of Perinthus which had been a member of the Second Athenian League (Tod 123, line 125) but had been detached by the Byzantines, probably during the Social War, and made an ally of the latter (Dem. 15.26). The evidence for a siege is poor (Hypothesis to [Dem.] 11; scholiast on Dem.18.76; the bogus letter of Philip at Dem. 18.77), but it is difficult to believe that it would have been invented, and, if Selymbria were still allied to Byzantium, Philip cannot possibly have tolerated the threat it would pose to his communications if he left it unsubdued in his rear.

76.5 Concluded his work with the siege of Perinthus: cf. note on 14.3, where we are told that he did not write about the Sacred War. The two passages are not mutually contradictory, for Ephorus wrote thematically or topic by topic, and though he reached 340 in his account of some topics (presumably including Macedonian and Persian affairs), his account of Greek history terminated with the events of 357.

Beginning with the return of the descendants of Heracles: the 'return of the Heracleidae' is the mythological equivalent of the Dorian invasion of the Peloponnese, interpreted as the recovery of Heracles' Peloponnesian heritage by his descendants in the third generation, Temenus, Aristodemus and Cresphontes (Isocrates 6.17; Apollodorus 2.8.2; Pausanias 2.18.7, 3.1.5, 3.3.3).

He covered a period of nearly 750 years: so Diod. 4.1.2. Ephorus (Frag. 223) dated the return of the Heracleidae 735 years before the crossing of Alexander to Asia in the archon year 335/4 and so to the year 1070/69. Diodorus' 750 is a round figure.

Wrote 30 Books: strictly speaking, only 29, since the thirtieth (on the Sacred War), though published along with his work, was written by his son Demophilus. See ch. 14.3, above, and Athenaeus 6.232D.

Introducing each with a preface: Diodorus clearly regards Ephorus' prefaces as significant, and it was under Ephorus' influence that he himself regularly began each book with a similar composition of his own. See Sacks, chapter 1, pp. 9-22.

Diyllus: see note on 14.5.

77.1 M.Valerius and A.Cornelius: M.Valerius Corvus and A.Cornelius Cossus Arvina were consuls for the year 343.

The 110th Olympiad: it ran from 340/39 till 337/6.

77.2 The Athenians resolved that he had broken the peace, i.e. the Peace of Philocrates of 347/6, which Diodorus omits to mention in its proper context. On the outbreak of war between Philip and Athens, see Philochorus, Frag. 55 (translated by Harding, 55A). Diodorus and Philochorus are in agreement that it was the Athenians who declared war, though Diodorus gives only one explanation, namely Philip's siege of Byzantium. Since Byzantium was not at the time an Athenian ally, the siege in itself did not constitute an act of war by Philip, but the Athenians saw it as a hostile act designed to facilitate Philip's ability to interfere with the passage of corn ships through the Bosporus on the way to Athens. Philochorus (Frag. 53) indicates that each party had grievances against the other. Philip could complain of the ravaging of territory in Thrace by Diopeithes ([Dem.] 12.3), the kidnapping of Nicias, a Macedonian herald, also by Diopeithes ([Dem.] 12.2), and the beating up of Amphilochus, a Macedonian envoy sent by Philip to negotiate ([Dem.] 12.3). The Athenians too had their petty grievances, including the ravaging of Peparethos, an Athenian ally ([Dem.] 12.12; Dem. 18.70) and Philip's support for Cardia in its dispute with the Athenian settlers in the Chersonese ([Dem.] 7.41-44; Dem. 8.58, 9.35, [Dem.] 12.11). More seriously, Athens could complain of his seizure of some 180 Athenian and 50 allied grain ships (Theopompus, Frag. 192; Philochorus, Frag. 162), ostensibly because some of the grain on board was destined for the city of Selymbria, then under siege by Philip ([Dem.] 18.78). This act on Philip's part was probably due mainly to his need to recoup some of the expenses of the costly sieges currently in progress, but, as he must have known that nothing was more calculated to enrage the Athenians, he may also have been trying to goad Athens into a declaration of war which he was keen to avoid having to do himself lest he tarnish the image he enjoyed in the eyes of Greek public opinion.

Sent a naval force...to assist the Byzantians: this force was commanded by Chares, who was already operating in the neighbourhood (Hesychius of Miletus, Frag. 1). However, because Chares had been the most vigorous of the Athenian generals in the Social War (see ch. 7.3 and 21.1-4), and because he had a bad reputation for extorting money from allies and neutrals alike (Aesch. 2.71; Plut. *Phocion* 14.2), the Byzantines, despite their plight, refused him admission to their city. He remained in the vicinity, but the Athenians replaced him with Phocion (Plut. *Phoc.* 1.3, cf. *Mor.* 188B, 851A) and his political ally Cephisophon (IG 2^2 1628 lines 436-8 and 1629 lines 957-60).

The Chians, Coans, Rhodians and some others: the three states named had been allies of Byzantium in the Social War, and may have sent aid under the terms of that alliance, but Rhodes, and perhaps Cos, were now satellites of the Carian satrap (see note on ch. 22.2), and can hardly have acted without Pixodarus' approval. This seems to have been the limit of Persian assistance to Byzantium, and it may be that the King was content to leave the rescue of the city to Athens, now that she had entered the war. Among the other cities which sent help to Byzantium was the island of Tenedos, a loyal member of the Athenian Confederacy (Tod 175, line 10, Harding 97).

77.3 Philip abandoned the siege: not because of alarm at the size of the coalition as Diodorus would have us believe, but because he appreciated the difficulty, even the impossibility, of capturing a strongly fortified city without the sea power necessary to impose an effective blockade. Philip's fleet was defeated by that of the Byzantians alone (Hesychius of Miletus, Frag. 1), and certainly no match for the Athenian ships stationed in the harbour and off the Asian coast opposite.

Concluded peace with the Athenians and the...Greeks opposed to him: this statement, though consistent with 84.1, where we are told that Philip won over most of the Greeks to friendship, is manifestly untrue in the case of the Athenians, who remained at war with him till the conclusion of the Peace of Demades in 338 after Chaeronea. A passage in Frontinus (1.4.13A) supports the statement that peace negotiations of a sort were held, and if Philip did make peace with anyone at this time, it will have been with the Chians and Rhodians, who are not known to have opposed him subsequently, and perhaps also with the Byzantians and Perinthians, though [Plut.] *Mor.* 851B suggests that Byzantium at least was still allied to Athens down to Chaeronea. The remainder of this chapter and chapters 78-81 narrate the continued warfare between Timoleon and the Carthaginians, culminating in Timoleon's victory at the Crimisus.

82.1 Q.Servilius and M.Rutilius: Q.Servilius Ahala and C.Marcius Rutilus (not Rutilius) were consuls for the year 342. Diodorus devotes the entirety of this archon year to Timoleon's activities in Sicily (the death of Hicetas, peace with Carthage, the despatch of new settlers to Sicily from the Peloponnese, and the final settlement of Sicily. So absorbed is he in his native island that he has nothing whatever to narrate about events in Greece and Macedonia in this momentous year (cf. the similar omission of the events of the archon year 350/49, for which see the note on ch. 46.1). Omitted are the Athenian blockade of the Macedonian coastline (Dem. 18.145), Philip's campaign of 339 against his former ally Ataias, king of the Scythians (Justin 9.2.1, cf. Plut. Mor. 174F), and against the Triballians, who ambushed him on his return and stripped him of much of his Scythian booty (Justin 9.3.1-3) and the outbreak of the Fourth Sacred War, when the Locrians of Amphissa, at the instigation of Thebes, accused the Athenians before the Amphictyons of sacrilege, only to have the tabled turned on them by the Athenian delegate Aeschines. The Amphissans were in turn accused and found guilty of sacrilege by the Amphictyons, who organised a feeble and incompetent attack on them. To extricate themselves from an embarrassing situation, they invited Philip to conduct the war on their behalf on his return from Scythia (see Dem. 18.143-153; Aesch. 3. 113-29, which are necessary reading to plug the yawning gap in Diodorus' narrative). Whether Philip instigated the Sacred War from his Scythian headquarters or merely profited from the opportunity offered of legitimately passing through Thermopylae with all the moral authority of an Amphictyonic invitation is a matter of dispute, but once again he was able to don the mantle of Apollo's champion and seize the Phocian city of Elatea (see ch. 84.1) before the Greeks realised what had happened.

84.1 L.Aemilius and C.Plotius: L. Aemilius Mamercinus Privernas and C. Plautius Venno were the consuls of 341.

Persuaded most of the Greeks to be his friends, a recapitulation of 77.3, where we are told that Philip made peace with some of the Greeks who had assisted Byzantium.

Was keen to intimidate the Athenians: since Diodorus omits the antecedents to this campaign, above all the declaration of war by Athens in 340 (see note on 77.2), the impression given here is that Philip was the aggressor.

Elatea, a city in the north of Phocis close to the borders of Opuntian Locris and of considerable strategic importance because of its position on the principal road from Thermopylae to Chaeronea, Thebes and Athens. Since Nicaea in the Thermopylae corridor had been occupied by the Boeotians earlier in the year (Philochorus, Frag. 65), Philip was unable to penetrate Thermopylae, but advanced by an alternative route through the Dorian city of Cytinium (Philochorus, loc. cit.). From there one route led to Amphissa, Philip's ostensible objective, but instead he took the more easterly fork and occupied Elatea. This action can only have been intended to intimidate the Athenians, whose territory lay distant by no more than a two or three day's march, as well as the Boeotians, whose friendship for him was beginning to wear somewhat thin.

Resolved to make war on the Athenians: in fact he was merely reacting to the Athenian declaration of war of the previous year, which he had put in abeyance at the time because of his expedition to Scythia. He halted at Elatea to embark upon a diplomatic offensive which continued well into 338 (see note on 84.5 below), and was aimed at keeping the Boeotians on his side and bringing the Athenians to the conference table.

84.2 They were unprepared because of the peace which they had concluded: they had concluded no such peace but had declared war. Philip's absence in Scythia and the Theban occupation of Nicaea will have lulled them into a false sense of security, based on the erroneous assumption that they were now safe from invasion from the north.

When Elatea had been captured: the passage beginning here and continuing to the end of the chapter is based directly or indirectly on the famous description in Demosthenes' speech *On the Crown* (Dem. 18.169ff.), which was much admired in antiquity for its vividness (e.g. [Longinus], *On the Sublime* 10.7).

84.3 The generals sent for the trumpeters: Diodorus is guilty of telescoping events at this point. From Dem. 18.169 it is clear that the news was first brought to the prytanies, the standing committee of the Council in permanent session in the *tholos*. It was the prytanies who summoned the generals.

The people rushed to the theatre: Diodorus is here guilty of anachronism. In Demosthenes' day, the assembly met not in the theatre but on the Pnyx, a hill about $^1/_4$ mile to the south west of the agora. The Theatre of Dionysus was used for meetings of the assembly only exceptionally, chiefly for the review of the ephebes at the beginning of the second year of their training ([Aristotle], Ath. Pol. 42.4). In Diodorus' day, and indeed from the Hellenistic period onwards, the theatre had superseded the Pnyx as the venue.

Before the customary summons from the magistrates: a meeting of the assembly could only be held when summoned by the prytanies, who would first convene the Council to prepare an agenda (see Dem. 18. 170). This step is omitted by Diodorus, whose interest is not in correct constitutional procedure but in the panic stricken behaviour of the citizens. However Demosthenes (loc. cit.) confirms that the people had taken their seats even before the arrival of the Councillors, presumably on the assumption that the emergency communicated by the trumpet signals would necessitate the summoning of an *ecclesia synkletos* (an assembly called at short notice).

84.4 When the generals arrived: the generals had the right to attend meetings of the Council, and could even take the initiative in recommending that an assembly be held, but Diodorus here seems to ignore the role of the Council. It is clear from the corresponding passage of Demosthenes that it was the prytanies, not the generals, who gave a formal report on the emergency and introduced the messenger.

The herald...called upon someone to speak: all citizens who had not been disqualified enjoyed the right to address the assembly, and were invited to do so when the herald put the question "Who wishes to speak?"

84.5 The dispatch of envoys to the other allies: Diodorus is here guilty of anticipation, for the Boeotians were not yet allies. Strictly speaking, he should have written 'the existing allies', who included the recently created Euboean League, the Corinthians and their colonists the Leucadians and Corcyraeans, the Achaeans, the Megarians and the Acarnanians (Dem. 18.237; Aesch. 3.97; Plut. *Dem.* 17.4). In addition Athens had alliances with the cities on the peninsula of Acte (Troezen, Hermione and Epidaurus) (Aelian, *Poik. Hist.* 6.1), as well as with Messenia, Mantinea, Megalopolis and Argos (IG II^2 225; scholiast on Aesch. 3.83, both translated by Harding, no. 89), though as the latter all had alliances also with Philip, the Athenians can hardly have expected much to come from an approach to the Peloponnesians.

A friend and ally of the Boeotians, since 347, if not earlier (see notes on 58.3 and 59.2).

85.2 He persuaded the Thebans: Diodorus offers no explanation for the Theban volte face other than the influence of Demosthenes' eloquence. He could have pointed out that they had been growing increasingly disenchanted with Philip for more that a year, and showed it by expelling the Macedonian garrison from Nicaea in Locris that very year (Philochorus, Frag. 65B). This suggests that they were decidedly uncomfortable with Philip's command of Thermopylae. Moreover they were coming to resent the growth of his power in Thessaly and in the Peloponnese which had been achieved largely at their expense, and deplored Philip's treatment of Theban allies and former allies such as Byzantium, the Locrians of Amphissa and Acarnania, which was threatened by Philip's Epirot campaign of 343/2 and by his alliance with Acarnania's traditional enemy Aetolia (Dem. 9.34; Philochorus, Frag. 56). In addition they can scarcely have shown much enthusiasm for Philip's proposed pan-Hellenic crusade against their long time friend and paymaster Persia, nor can the recent improvement in the position of their traditional enemies the Phocians (see note on 60.2 above) have met with their approval. Furthermore the terms offered them by Demosthenes (sneered at by Aeschines at 3.141) were remarkably attractive and far more favourable than those normally included in an agreement between equals: the Athenians abandoned all claim to the disputed frontier territory of Oropus, they recognised Theban hegemony over the whole of Boeotia, they agreed to pay two thirds rather than the more usual equal share of the cost of the war, and, while yielding the high command by land to the Boeotians, they even consented to the exercise of a joint command by sea, despite the lack by the Boeotians of anything worthy of the name of navy.

They appointed Chares and Lysicles as generals: on Chares, see note on 7.3. On Lysicles, see also ch. 88.1. A third general who fought at Chaeronea was Stratocles (Aesch. 3.143; Polyaenus 4.2.2).

The young men embarked...with enthusiasm: for the Chaeronea campaign the Athenians called up the citizen levy and were not content on this occasion to rely on the usual mercenary troops.

The Athenians..arrived at Chaeronea: Diodorus is telescoping here. The alliance between Athens and Boeotia was concluded late in the year 339, but Chaeronea was not fought till the late summer of 338. After the conclusion of the alliance, the Athenians and Boeotians surprised Philip by marching out in winter contrary to custom, and seized the Phocian city of Parapotamii, which was strategically situated in the Cephisus valley in a narrow gap between Mt. Parnassus to the west and Mt. Hedylion to the east, astride the route from Elatea to Boeotia and Attica (Polyaenus 4.2.14). In addition a mercenary force under Chares and Proxenus the Theban was sent to Amphissa to block the Gravia pass on the route from Cytinium to Amphissa and the Corinthian Gulf (Aesch. 3.146; Deinarchus 1.74; Polyaenus 4.2.8). Philip's occupation of both Elatea and Cytinium was thus effectively neutralised. We hear (Dem. 18.216) of two engagements (the 'winter battle' and 'the battle by the river', presumably the Cephisus), as each side sought to probe the other's defences. Philip succeeded eventually in penetrating the Gravia pass by a trick (Polyaenus 4.2.8, cf. Aesch. 3.146), but no major battle was fought in the first half of 338, and Philip was more interested in a diplomatic than in a military solution.

85.3 Philip sent envoys to the Boeotian League: this was his second attempt to negotiate. In 339, when the Boeotians were debating the proposed switch of alliance from Macedonia to Athens, Philip sent four envoys, Amyntas and Clearchus of Macedonia and Daochus and Thrasydaeus of Thessaly (Plut. *Dem.*18.2, cf. Dem. 18.211), who demanded the evacuation of Nicaea and requested that the Boeotians either participate in the forthcoming invasion of Attica or at least grant him passage through their territory (Philochorus, Frag. 56). This second embassy belongs to 338, after the Boeotians had allied with Athens. Plutarch would also appear to suggest that Philip sent an embassy to Athens, but the timing is unclear. At *Phoc.* 16.1, he mentions the Athenian rejection of overtures 'after Phocion's return from the islands' (340?), but at *Dem.* 18.3, the offer, if indeed it is to be identified with that mentioned in the *Phocion*, came later, after the conclusion of the Atheno-Boeotian alliance. Aeschines (3.148) also refers to Philip's desire for reconciliation in 338, but implies that the projected embassies (to Athens and Thebes?) were not in fact sent. However if Philip did send envoys in 338, it was not in Aeschines' interest to play them down, for if Demosthenes was responsible for their rejection, it would have given Aeschines added ammunition for his attack by blaming him for the failure of Philip's last ditch peace offer. Perhaps Plutarch is guilty of exaggeration in converting Philip's well known desire for peace into a specific proposal.

Pytho, a native of Byzantium and celebrated orator who had spent some time in Athens as a pupil of Isocrates (Zosimus, *Life of Isocrates* 3.90). He had entered Philip's service as a diplomat and spokesman and is best known for his diplomatic mission to Athens in 344 on Philip's behalf, when he complained of a recent Athenian attempt to stir up anti-Macedonian feeling in the Peloponnese and imparted Philip's willingness to consider revision of the terms of the Peace of Philocrates ([Dem.] 7.20; Aesch. 2.125; Dem. 18.136).

85.4 He says in his published speeches: the Demosthenic quotation is from *On the Crown* (18.136), but there the orator is referring to Pytho's embassy to Athens in 344, not to his Theban embassy of 338.

85.5 He proceeded into Boeotia: his penetration of the Gravia Pass (see note on section 2 above) obliged the Athenians and Boeotians to evacuate Parapotamii and fall back on Chaeronea, thereby enabling him to cross the border into Boeotia.

85.6 In the number of troops and in generalship the king was superior: few would dispute Philip's superiority in generalship to his adversaries, led as they were by a composite board of relatively inexperienced Boeotarchs and Athenian *strategoi*. In contrast to Diodorus, Justin states (9.3.9) that the Greeks were numerically superior. We have no independent confirmation of Diodorus' estimate for the strength of Philip's army and no figures at all for that of the Greek coalition. The Boeotians probably contributed the usual 7000 hoplites (see note on 30.4), but Athenian numbers are far less certain. In 394 they sent 6000 hoplites to Nemea (Xen. *Hell.* 4.2.17), and 5000 to Thebes both in 379/8 (Diod. 15.26.2) and in 377/6 (Diod. 15.32.6), while Polybius (2.62.6) refers to 12,000 soldiers (including presumably cavalry and peltasts as well as hoplites) for a full scale mobilisation in 369. (The figure of 20,000 alleged by Diodorus at 15.29.7 to have been called up in 369 is a gross exaggeration.) If the Athenians were able to muster 12,000 troops in 369, they should have been able to call up similar numbers in the emergency of 338, and of this number it would be not unreasonable to put the hoplite component at roughly 10,000. Thus the Boeotians and Athenians should have been able to rely on some 17,000 hoplites of their own for the Chaeronea campaign, and if the Corinthian, Euboean, Megarian, Achaean and Acarnanian contingents are included, a total of up to 25,000 hoplites as an estimate of the strength of the Greek coalition is indicated. How many of Philip's 30,000 infantry were Macedonian hypaspists is impossible to determine, and a fair number will have been allies and mercenaries.

85.7 In numerous pitched battles, against Illyrians, Paeonians, Thracians, Scythians and various combinations of Greek states in Thessaly and in Chalcidice.

Emerged victorious in most of them: the only two defeats he is known to have suffered in pitched battles (as opposed to sieges or ambushes) were both in Thessaly, at the hands of Onomarchus, in 354 (see ch. 35.2).

Iphicrates and Chabrias, as well as Timotheus were dead : on Iphicrates and Timotheus see 21.1, note, and on Chabrias, see note on 7.3. Iphicrates died c. 353 (he was prosecuted in 355 or 354 for his role in the Social War (Nepos, *Iph.* 3.4 and note on 21.4), but was dead by 352 (Dem. 23.130), while Chabrias was killed in the sea battle off Chios in 357 (Nepos, *Chab.* 3.1-3; Plut. *Phoc.* 6.1; cf. Dem. 20.81; see ch. 7.3-4). Timotheus died in 354/3 (see Isocrates, *Antidosis* 101-39, a eulogy by his teacher in commemoration of his death).

Chares: see note on 7.3. He was still alive at the beginning of 324 (Plut. *Mor.* 848E) but dead by the end of the year ([Dem.], *Epistle* 3.31). Diodorus mentions Chares no less unfavourably at 15.55.3, a not unfair comment in the light of what is known of Chares' record. It is curious that Diodorus should compare Philip only with Athenian generals and ignore the Boeotians, who supplied the commander-in-chief Theagenes (Deinarchus 1.74; Plut. *Alex.* 12.3, *Mor.* 259D). This suggests the use of an Athenian source (Diyllus?).

86.1 The battle lines were drawn up: the battle was fought on the plain between the city of Chaeronea and the river Cephisus, which from the point of view of the Greeks offered a safeguard against outflanking on their right by the Macedonians.

On one wing the king posted his son Alexander: Alexander, born in 356, had already been left to govern Macedonia while Philip was absent on his Thracian campaigns of 342-39, and in 340 had defeated the Maedi, a Thracian tribe living in the Strymon valley (Plut. *Alex.* 8.1). Since most of the Macedonian casualties were suffered at the hand of the Theban Sacred Band and were buried by the Cephisus (Plut. *Alex.* 9.1), Alexander must have had charge of either the left wing or of the cavalry which wrought havoc in the Sacred Band when it came into conflict with them.

In age a mere youth: Alexander was at the time of Chaeronea 18 years old.

The most important of his commanders: it is unfortunate that Diodorus does not choose to name them. The most important of Philip's commanders were Antipater and Parmenio: for the latter's presence at Chaeronea we have no evidence, but Antipater, who was subsequently sent to Athens to escort the bones of the Athenian dead (Polybius 5.10.4), may have been stationed on the Macedonian left.

Specially selected men: Diodorus' vagueness and reluctance to use technical terminology can be infuriating. The reference is probably to the hypaspists as a whole, or to the elite *agema* of the hypaspists that was regularly under the personal command of the king. Philip's post on the right wing was the regular place of a Macedonian king on the field, to judge by Alexander's similar position at the Granicus (Arrian, *Anab.* 1.14.1), Issus (2.10.3) and Gaugamela (3.13.2).

86.2 The Athenians divided up their line: since Aeschines informs us (3.143) that the high command on land was held by the Boeotians, Diodorus is here mistaken, and it will have been they who made the dispositions on behalf of the Greek coalition.

Assigning one wing to the Boeotians: since the Boeotians were opposite

Alexander on the Macedonian left (Plut. *Alex.* 9.2), they will have reserved for themselves command of the right wing, the more honorific of the two in the eyes of Greeks.

While they themselves commanded the other: the Boeotians placed the Athenians on the left wing, opposite Philip on the Macedonian right (Polyaenus 4.2.2 and 7; Frontinus, *Strat.* 2.1.9). The other Greeks were posted in the allied centre.

When battle was joined: Diodorus' account of the battle, the only one extant, is unsatisfactory. His lack of interest in battles makes reconstruction difficult and largely speculative. For modern reconstructions, see N.G.L. Hammond, *The Two Battles of Chaeronea (338 BC and 86 BC)*, Klio 31, 1938, pp. 186ff. and W.K. Pritchett, *Observations on Chaeronea*, AJA 62, 1958, pp. 307ff. See also Hammond and Griffith, *A History of Macedonia*, Vol. II, pp. 596-603.

86.3 Alexander...first opened up a gap: so Plut. *Alex.* 9.1, who states that Alexander's struggle was against the Theban Sacred Band, an elite standing force of 300 men formed in 378, maintained at public expense and characterised by pair bonding (cf. *Pelopidas* 18), but this can only have occurred after the gap had been opened up elsewhere in the line.

86.4 The king himself...thrust back the troops opposite: Philip's decisive move against the Athenians can only have been made after Alexander's success. It was perhaps at this point that he deceived the Athenians by implementing a controlled withdrawal, if there is any truth in the story found in Polyaenus (4.2.7) and Frontinus (*Strat.* 2.1.9), according to which the Athenians, scenting victory, began to move forwards and to the left, thereby dangerously over-extending their line till a gap opened up between them and their allies: while the general Stratocles was still shouting "Let's chase them all the way back to Macedonia!", Philip reached higher ground and, turning his men round, attacked and drove the Athenians back. Presumably with the loss of cohesion in the Greek line, the Macedonian cavalry, riding through the resulting gap, cut the Athenians off from their allies and fell on the Sacred Band. The story does however give rise to difficulties. In the first place the successful execution of such a strategy requires advance preparation, and Alexander's success against the Thebans was not a foregone conclusion. Secondly, there was the risk that a retreat by Philip at the time of Alexander's advance might open up a gap in the Macedonian line, unless they were performing a wheeling manoeuvre that needed both meticulous planning and skilful coordination. Thirdly modern research on the topography of the battle-field can find no trace of the higher ground to which Philip is said to have retreated, unless the reference is to the bank of the Haemon, a minor tributary of the Cephisus (Plut. *Dem.* 19.2), which would have blocked any further withdrawal. Finally the alleged remarks shouted by Stratocles are ascribed by Plutarch (*Mor.* 259D) to the Boeotian commander Theagenes, who was not in any way involved in the pursuit of Philip. The authenticity of Polyaenus' story is thus suspect.

86.5 Of the Athenians more than 1000 fell: the figures for the Athenian casualties go back ultimately to the speech delivered by the orator Lycurgus at the trial of the general Lysicles (see ch. 88.1). Such a heavy loss of citizens was taken particularly seriously in an age when most of the fighting was usually done by mercenaries.

86.6 Many of the Boeotians too were killed: no specific numbers are preserved by Diodorus or by any other source. Excavation of the site marked by the famous Lion Monument, traditionally regarded as the burial place of the Thebans (Pausanias 9.40.10) has revealed the presence of 254 skeletons, which are presumably those of the members of the Sacred Band killed in the battle, who may have been buried apart from the other Boeotians as a mark of special honour. (Plutarch's claim at *Pelopidas* 18.5 that all 300 were slain must be an exaggeration). Of the other allied losses, we know only that the Achaeans were mauled so severely that they could credibly offer them as an excuse for failure to participate in the Lamian War fifteen to sixteen years later (Pausanias 7.6.5). For Macedonian casualties no figures are preserved.

87.1 In the course of the carousal: it seems to have been Philip's practice to celebrate victories with (to the Greeks) an excessive display of conviviality. Cf. the victory celebrations to mark the capture of Olynthus (ch. 55.2 and Dem. 19.192ff.). Such incidents contributed to Theopompus' portrait of the king as a regular party thrower and inveterate drunkard (see fragments 27, 81, 162, 163, 225, 236 and 282).
    Leading the revel: Cf. Plut. *Mor.* 715C and above all *Dem.* 20.3, where he tells the celebrated story of how Philip, drunk with unmixed wine, led a tour of inspection around the corpses, chanting the opening words of a Demosthenic decree:

Demosthenes son of Demosthenes of Paeania thus proposes,

beating time to the metrical pattern of the words which in Greek form a trochaic tetrameter catalectic.
    Demades the orator: an Athenian politician famous for his talent in ex tempore speaking (Plut. *Dem.* 8.5). From comparatively obscure beginnings

he rose to prominence through his oratory, and, according to the hostile tradition, through his venality (Hyperides 5.25; Deinarchus 1.89 and 104; Diod. 17.15.3; Plut. *Mor*. 525C and *Phoc*. 30.4). Apart from his role in concluding the Peace which bears his name, he is best known for his successful embassy to Alexander in 335 to intercede for those whose surrender the king had demanded, "in return for the sum of 5 talents from the men in danger" (Plut. *Dem*. 23.5). He was also allegedly involved, along with Demosthenes, in the embezzlement of the money brought by Harpalus in 324 (Deinarchus 1.89). He was sent to Antipater as ambassador in 322 to obtain terms after Athens' surrender in the Lamian War (Diod. 18.18; Plut. *Phoc*. 26.3), and proposed the decree condemning to death the anti-Macedonian leaders responsible for the war (Plut. *Dem*. 28.2). He was put to death by Antipater in 319, on the strength of a treasonable letter which he had written to Perdiccas in 322 (Plut. *Phoc*. 30.4-6 and *Dem*. 31.3-4; Athenaeus 13. 591F). The animosity between the two men was mutual, Demades calling Antipater "an old rotten thread", and Antipater describing Demades as "a dismembered sacrificial victim, nothing but tongue and guts" (Plut. *Phoc*. 1.2).

Who was at that time among the captives: since the Athenians at Chaeronea put a citizen army in the field, many important men fell into Philip's hands. Unlike Demades, Demosthenes avoided capture, only to be accused by Aeschines of running away, as he loses no opportunity for reminding the jury in the Ctesiphon case (3.159, 181, 187, 253). Cf. Plut. *Dem*. 20.2 and *Mor*. 854F, 'as he was running away, a thorn bush caught his cloak, whereupon he turned and said, "Take me alive"'.

87.2 Aren't you ashamed to be playing the role of Thersites: Thersites was a Greek in Agamemnon's army at Troy, described by Homer (*Iliad* 2.212-9) as:

> measureless in his speech, his mind was full of disorderly words with which to provoke the rulers, whenever he thought to raise a laugh among the Argives. He was ill-favoured beyond all men who came to Troy, had bandy legs and was lame in one foot. His shoulders were humped, bent inwards over his chest. Above, his head came to a point at the top, and a thin stubble grew on it.

He is depicted as a rabble rouser and trouble maker who taunts Agamemnon and is struck with a staff on his shoulders and back for his pains (*Iliad* 2.265-6). It is Thersites' buffoonery that Demades wished to bring to Philip's attention on this occasion.

Philip is said to have changed his attitude: so Plut. *Dem*. 20.3 and *Mor*. 715C (without mention of Demades).

Admitted him with all honour to his own circle, perhaps by making him a *xenos* (see note on 54.4). According to unreliable sources ([Aeschines], *Epist.* 12.8, Suda, s.v. Demades), Philip also gave him land in Boeotia.

87.3 He released...the prisoners without ransom: Diodorus is referring only to the Athenian prisoners, whose release without ransom is also mentioned by [Demades], *On the Twelve Years* 9; [Dem.] *Epist.* 3.11; Polybius 5.10.4 and Justin 9.4.4. This was the third occasion on which Philip released Athenians without ransom (for two earlier instances, see notes on 3.6 and 8.5, above).

Sent envoys to the Athenian people: with them went Demades himself, to reassure the Athenians of Philip's good intentions. They in turn dispatched envoys of their own to Philip, who included Aeschines (Dem. 18.282), Phocion (Nepos, Phoc.1.3) and Demades (Suda s.v. Demades) to conduct the negotiations.

Concluded with them both peace and alliance, as previously in 346.This Peace is known in modern times as the Peace of Demades, named from its proposer ([Demades] 9). Diodorus is silent on the terms of treaty, but it is known from other sources that Athens was required to dissolve her Confederacy (Pausanias 1.25.3) and cede the Chersonese to Philip (nowhere specifically stated, but the area was henceforth in the Macedonian sphere of influence). However she retained full internal autonomy (Paus. 7.10.5), as well as control of Imbros, Scyros and Lemnos ([Arist.], *Ath. Pol.* 62.2), together with Samos (Diod. 18.56.6; Plut. *Alex.* 28; Athenaeus 3.99D). In addition, perhaps as compensation for the loss of the Chersonese and as a deterrent to future Atheno-Boeotian friendship, Philip required the Boeotians to hand over Oropus to Athens ([Demades] 9; Paus. 1.34.1). Diodorus fails to explain the reason for Philip's lenient settlement, but it is probable that he was influenced by Athens' determination to continue the war, e.g. by implementing energetic measures for the defence of the city (Dem. 18.248), such as the appointment of Charidemus to take charge of the city's defences (Plut. Phoc.16.2), the dispatch of Demosthenes to collect money (Aesch. 3.159), and the mission of Hyperides to seek assistance from Epidaurus, Troezen, Andros and Ceos (Lycurgus, *In Leocratem* 42). In the light of this intelligence, Philip can only have concluded that, unless he offered acceptable terms, he would be obliged to embark on a difficult, expensive and protracted siege with little hope of sucess without enjoying command of the sea. Moreover, since he had his thoughts on a campaign in Asia to avenge Xerxes' invasion of Greece, harsh treatment of the city which had contributed so much to Persia's defeat would seriously damage the philhellenic image he was cultivating in the Greek world. On learning Philip's terms, the Athenians gratefully accepted, and the bones of the dead were conveyed to Athens by Alexander, Antipater and Alcimachus (Polybius

5.10.4; Justin 9.5.4). The Athenians thereupon conferred citizenship upon Philip (Plut. *Dem.* 22.3) on the motion of Demades ([Demades] 9, and awarded honours to Antipater and Alcimachus (Hyperides, Frag. 77; Tod 181).

He installed a garrison in Thebes: so Deinarchus 1.19; Diod. 17.8.3; Plut. *Alex.* 11.5; Arrian, *Anab.* 1.7.1; Paus. 9.1.8 and 6.5). Garrisons were also installed at Corinth (Polybius 38.3.3; Plut. *Aratus* 23.4), at Ambracia (Diod. 17.3.3) and perhaps at Chalcis (Polybius 38.3.3; Strabo 10.1.8), though at Chalcis this may have been due to Alexander rather than Philip. To the brief information on Philip's Boeotian settlement provided by Diodorus can be added the replacement of the Theban democracy with an oligarchy of 300 (Justin 9.4.4ff.), some adjustment to the constitution of the Boeotian League to weaken Theban influence, notably by the restoration of Thespiae, Plataea and Orchomenus, the three cities previously destroyed by Thebes (Diod. 17.13.5; Pausanias 4.27.10, 9.1.8, 9.37.8), and the removal from Thebes to Macedonia of the bones of Linus (Paus. 9.29.8), presumably a symbolic gesture to indicate that Philip and not Thebes, was now the protector of the Boeotians. In the light of the planned anti-Persian crusade, harsh terms for the arch-mediser were unavoidable.

88.1 The Athenians condemned to death Lysicles the general: the loss of so many citizens required a scapegoat. Of the generals who led the army at Chaeronea, Stratocles is not heard of again, and Chares' presence at Athens is unattested after 338 (his name does appear on the list of prominent citizens whose surrender was demanded in 335 by Alexander, but only in the unreliable lists in Arrian (*Anab.* 1.10.4) and the Suda (s.v. Antipater). His name is conspicuously absent from the eight alleged by Plutarch (*Dem.* 23.4) to be those found in the most reliable authorities. He is next heard of in 334 at Sigeum, his personal possession (Theopompus, Frag. 105; Nepos, *Chabrias* 3.4), whence he went to meet and make his peace with Alexander (Arrian, *Anab.* 1.12.1). In the circumstances it is probable that he did not venture to return to Athens after Chaeronea in fear for his life. Lysicles had the misfortune to be the only, or, if Stratocles too survived the battle, the more prominent of the generals available for prosecution.

Lycurgus, an anti-Macedonian politician and orator (c.390-325/4) of the aristocratic family of the Eteobutadae, who is first attested as one of the envoys who toured the Peloponnese in 342 ([Plut.] *Mor.* 841E), and became one of the most important statesmen in Athens during the reign of Alexander.

Enjoyed the greatest reputation of all the orators of the day: despite this assertion of Diodorus, of the 15 speeches attributed to him in antiquity ([Plut.] *Mor.* 843C), only one still survives, the speech he composed for his prosecution of Leocrates for fleeing the city after Chaeronea in contravention of the emergency regulations then in force.

He administered the revenues of the city for 12 years: Lycurgus' chief claim to fame was his outstanding record as a financier, which enabled him to put Athenian finances on a sound basis after a period of weakness ([Plut.] *Mor.* 852B). Historians disagree on the nature of the position he held: some believe that he held a specially created post with a title along the lines of 'treasurer in charge of the administration' (*epi tei dioikesei*, Hyperides, Frag. 118, cf. *epi ten dioikesin* at 5.28, if indeed Hyperides is there referring to Lycurgus), with a tenure of 3 four year periods: this idea goes back to the Decree of Stratocles, proposed in 307/6, but as the contemporary *Ath. Pol.* makes no mention of the post of treasurer in charge of the administration in its treatment of the Athenian magistracies, it is possible that belief in four year periods of office rests on a misunderstanding both of the nature of Lycurgus' position and of the meaning of the phrase 'from Panathenaea to Panathenaea'. Since the Panathenaea was celebrated every fourth year with special magnificence, the expression has been thought to mean 'for a period of four years', but, as the festival was in fact annual, the expression could equally well refer to a one year period commencing on the day of the Panathenaea (Hecatombaeon 28) and ending on Hecatombaeon 27 of the following year. See P.J.Rhodes, *The Athenian Boule*, Oxford, 1972, pp. 236-7 and *A Historical Commentary on the Aristotelian Athenaion Politeia*, Oxford, 1981, p. 517. On this interpretation, Lycurgus will have held financial magistracies of some kind for 12 years (e.g. Commissioner of the Theoric Fund, Treasurer of the Stratiotic Fund), but not necessarily always the same one. On either view, Lycurgus' period of office lasted from 338/7 till 327/6 or from 337/6 till 326/5, though the natural interpretation of Diodorus' words would suggest the 12 years before the prosecution of Lysicles.

Led a life...exemplary for its probity: so Hyperides, Frag. 118;[Plut.] *Mor.* 842D, 843F, 852B.

As an accuser he was exceedingly harsh: cf. [Plut.] *Mor.* 841E,'some of the sophists said that Lycurgus made out his indictments with a pen dipped in death rather than ink'. As a man of high moral probity, he expected and demanded similar standards in others, and as both patriot and staunch democrat he felt it his duty to prosecute those he deemed guilty of disrespect for the city or for the *demos*.

88.2 The speech with which he prosecuted Lysicles: apart from the passage quoted by Diodorus, only two brief fragments (Frag. 77 and 105) remain.

88.3 Another battle took place in Italy, at Mandurium. See ch. 63.1 and note.

88.4 This man was king of Sparta for 23 years: probably from 360 till 338. See note on 63.2.

Agis...reigned for 9 years: from 338 till 331 or 330. See note on 63.2.

88.5 Timotheus the tyrant of Heraclea: his rule lasted from 353/2 till 338/7. See note on 36.3.

His brother Dionysius succeeded: he ruled from 338/7 till 306/5 (Diod. 20.77.1; Nymphis, Frag. 10) and married Amestris, daughter of Oxathres the brother of Darius III the last of the Achaemenids (Memnon, Frag. 1.4.4; Strabo 12.54.4). Of his three children, two were named for their grandfathers and the third for her mother (Memnon, Frag. 1.4.8). According to Nymphis (Frag. 10), Dionysius grew excessively obese through luxury and overindulgence, but ruled with mildness and humanity.

89.1 T. Mallius Torquatus and P. Decius: T. Manlius Imperiosus Torquatus and P. Decius Mus were the consuls of 340.

Philip was ambitious to become the leader of the whole of Greece: Diodorus omits at this point details of Philip's campaign against the Spartans at the end of 338 (Polybius 9.28.26; Plut. *Mor.* 218F, 219F, 233E and 235B; Paus. 3.24.6, 5.4.9), as a result of which he deprived them of some border territories which were then assigned to Messenia, Megalopolis, Tegea and Argos (Polybius 9.28.7). In 337 he may have become embroiled in another Illyrian war (see note on 93.6 below).

89.2 For the acts of sacrilege they had committed: the reference is to the burning of Greek shrines and temples during the Persian invasion of 480-79 (e.g. Apollo's shrine at Abae in Phocis, Hdt. 8.32; Paus. 10.35.2, and the Athenian acropolis, Hdt. 8.53.2; Diod. 11.14.5; Paus. 1.27.2). In the course of diplomatic exchanges between Alexander and Darius in 332, Alexander also complained of Ochus' unprovoked aggression against Philip in 340, when the Persians sent aid to Perinthus and interfered militarily in Thrace (Arrian, *Anab.* 2.14.5).

He declared to the cities his desire to hold talks: these talks concerned his plans for the future of the Greek states: in the case of those which had opposed him at Chaeronea, he will have dictated his terms for making peace, and with all the states he will have discussed his proposals for the establishment of a Common Peace and details of the new organisation to which he intended to entrust its preservation. The individual states will have been persuaded, cajoled or bullied into participating, though the Spartans were allowed to remain aloof (Plut. *Mor.* 240A; Arrian *Anab.* 1.1.2; Justin 9.5.2).

89.3 A common council was held in Corinth: Diodorus is here allowing his narrative to outstrip events. He is referring to the organisation devised by Philip to keep the peace, which modern historians call the League of Corinth, but he provides no details of its foundation or constitution, and alludes to it here as if it had already been instituted. He seems quite unaware of his failure to describe its inauguration, unless he believes that the meeting he is describing really was the inaugural session. The correct order of events is found only in Justin (9.5.1-2): 'Having settled the affairs of Greece, Philip ordered that ambassadors from all the states should be summoned to Corinth, in order to confirm the current state of affairs. There he imposed the universal law of peace in proportion to the deserts of the individual states, and chose from all the states a council of all, just like a single senate'. Among the sources for the constitution of the League, the most important are epigraphical (Tod 177 = Harding 99, the surviving portion of which contains the oath sworn by the member states, followed by a fragmentary list of participants, and IG IV^2 68 = Harding 138, the constitution of the Hellenic League of Antigonus and Demetrius instituted in 303/2 and thought to be a revival of Philip's original organisation), together with [Dem.]17, *On the Treaty with Alexander*, a speech concerned with alleged breaches of the League which quotes some of the clauses of the original treaty.

He addressed the delegates: the delegates (*synedroi*) were appointed by the member states and sent to represent them at meetings of the *synedrion* or League Council. As duly elected leader, Philip had the right to address the *synedrion* and was charged with the execution of League policy.

On the issue of the war with Persia: though this was uppermost in his mind for a long time, and a useful cohesive force in an organisation that otherwise lacked any common purpose, Philip did not, *pace* Diodorus, broach this subject at the original meeting of the League, which will have been devoted to measures for safeguarding the Common Peace and punishing prospective transgressors (Tod 177, lines 19-22 shows this as the ostensible objective of the League). Philip will have given the League some time to settle down, and did not raise the Persian issue till he saw it working efficiently on more mundane matters. The correct order of events is established from Justin, who informs us (9.5.4-5) that war with Persia became an issue only after the fixing of the contributions of the individual members, which will have been intended in the first instance for use against states which broke the Common Peace.

Elected him general...with full powers: in Greek, *strategos autokrator*. Philip's official title was hegemon or 'leader' (Tod 177, line 2; Arrian, *Anab.* 2.14.4. Cf. *hegemonia*, 'leadership', at *Anab.* 1.1.2 and *hegemon autokrator* at *Anab.* 7.9.5). Diodorus also uses the phrase *strategos autokrator* at ch. 60.5 and at 17.4.9. This may be yet another instance of his use of inaccurate technical terminology, though it is also possible that Philip's title *hegemon* in time of peace but *strategos* when the League was at war. ' word *autokrator* ('with full powers'), if it is to be taken literally, should m(that the holder was given the right to make urgent decisions in time of w without the need to go through the cumbersome mechanism of summonii and securing the approval of the League delegates.

Having worked out for each city the number of troops to be contribute(**to the alliance:** it is clear from Justin's account of the foundation of the Leagu(that military quotas were established for members even before the declaration of war on Persia, though these can only have been for a small standing force sufficient to deal with breaches of the peace in Greece, and totally inadequate for waging an offensive war in Asia. When war was finally declared on Persia, the original contributions will have been upgraded to meet the new situation. The only specific figures for individual contingents to survive belong to the reign of Alexander, when both Athens (Diod. 17.22.5) and Chios (Tod 192 = Harding 107) provided 20 ships, and Thessaly supplied 2000 cavalry (1800 accompanied Alexander to Asia in 334, Diod. 17.17.4, and the remaining 200 joined him in the following year, Arrian, *Anab.* 1.29.4). The Athenian contribution looks remarkably small, but may also have included cavalry (Plut. *Phoc.* 16.5 refers to 'triremes and horses') and money (a very badly mutilated inscription, IG II^2 329, containing the remains of a treaty of some sort between Athens and Alexander, refers to payments of 1 drachma per day for Macedonian hypaspists: it is true that what is legible on the stone does not state that these payments are to be made by Athens, but it is difficult otherwise to explain why such payments would be set out in an Athenian document). Also relevant to the issue of Greek contributions is Tod 177, which ends with a badly preserved list of league members, each with a number attached. This figure has been thought to refer to the number of delegates, or alternatively to the number of votes possessed by each state in the League synedrion, if Philip was indeed responsible for the introduction of proportional representation. It is also possible that the numbers are related to the size of the military contingents provided by the member states. On this interpretation, the most illuminating of the names is Thessaly, with its quota of 10. If there is a link between the numbers and the contributions, 2000 cavlary will have been the equivalent of 10 delegates (or votes), i.e. each delegate or vote was worth 200 cavalry (or its equivalent in infantry or ships, whatever that may have been).

90.1 Section 1 of this chapter describes the death of Timoleon at Syracuse and the posthumous honours which were paid to him.

90.2 Ariobarzanes died after a reign of 26 years: Diodorus omits to mention the identity of either Ariobarzanes himself or of his kingdom. He was in fact a Persian, born into a family reputedly of the highest nobility (Polybius 5.43.2; Diod. 19.40.2), and ruled a principality on the south coast of the Propontis from his capital city of Cios from 362/1 (see also Diod. 15.90.3).

Mithridates...ruled for 35 years: This Mithridates was the second dynast of Cios who bore the name (for the first, see Diod. 15.90.3). He ruled Cios from 337/6 till 302/1, when he was put to death by Antigonus for intriguing with Antigonus' enemy Cassander (Diod. 20.111.4). He was the uncle of a third Mithridates, who in the next century carved out a kingdom for himself from parts of Cappadocia and Paphlagonia, a kingdom which came to be called Pontus. He ascended the throne of Pontus with the title of Mithridates I Ktistes ('Founder') (Diod., loc.cit.; Strabo 12.33.41; Appian, *Mithridatica* 9). Section 2 ends with a brief note on a Roman victory over the Latins and Campanians at Sinuessa (cf. Livy 8.11.11).

91.1 In the archonship of Pythodorus: Diodorus (or his copyist) is careless: Pythodorus was archon under the Thirty in 404/3, the year all good democrats, who refused to recognise nominees of the Thirty, called the year of *anarchia*, when there was no proper archon. The archon of 336/5 was Pythodelus.

Q. Publius and Ti. Aemilius Mamercus: these represent the consuls of 339, but again the names are corrupt. The correct names are Ti. Aemilius Mamercinus and Q.Publilius Philo.

The 111th Olympiad: this ran from 336/5 till 333/2.

91.2 Attalus and Parmenio: Attalus was the uncle and guardian of Philip's latest (and last) wife Cleopatra (see ch. 93.8 and 17.2.3, where the given relationship is incorrect; cf. Plut. *Alex.* 9.4), whose promotion may have owed much to the increased influence that accrued to him from the marriage. Parmenio had long been one of Philip's outstanding commanders, and also happened to be Attalus' father-in-law (Curtius 6.9.18). Hammond and Griffith (p. 680) draw attention to the order in which their names appear, but believe (perhaps rightly) that though Attalus is named as sole commander at 93.8, Parmenio was in fact commander in chief with Attalus as his second in command. Their reasoning is based on the assumption that Diodorus' word order is due to his interest in Attalus as one of the principal actors in the events culminating in Philip's murder (see ch. 93.7-9). However at 17.2.4 Diodorus describes the command as given to 'Attalus along with Parmenio', which, if correct, would suggest joint leadership. Justin (9.5.8) adds a third commander, Amyntas, (perhaps the Amyntas son of Arrhabaeus mentioned by Arrian at *Anab.* 1.12.7, 1.14.1 and 1.28.4), whose father is to be identified with Philip's alleged assassin of this name (Arr. 1.25.1).

With instructions to free the Greek cities: the size of Parmenio's force is unknown: according to Polyaenus (5.44.4), it consisted of 10,000 men, which can only be at best a round figure. The main objective was rather to prepare the ground for the arrival of Philip, planned for later in the year, and to establish a bridgehead to facilitate his crossing, such as was provided for Alexander in 334 at Abydos (Arrian, *Anab.* 1 11.6), though doubtless Philip also gave instructions along the lines specified by Diodorus (see, e.g., Arrian 1.17.11 for Ephesus) when the opportunity arose. For further information on the activities of the advance force, see Diod. 17.7.9-10 and Justin 9.5.8-9).

Enquire of the Pythian priestess: Philip's consultation of the oracle is taken as fact by H.W. Parke and D.W. Wormell (*The Delphic Oracle*, Vol.I, Oxford, 1956, p. 238), but rejected as fictional by the more sceptical J. Fontenrose (*The Delphic Oracle*, Berkeley & Los Angeles, 1978, p. 67) on the grounds that it is a typically equivocal prediction of doom taken favourably by the consultant, similar to the notorious oracle given to Croesus about the consequences of crossing the Halys (Hdt. 1.53.1; Aristotle, *Rhetoric* 1407a 38; Diod. 8.31.1).

The bull is garlanded: the oracle is expressed symbolically in language borrowed from the vocabulary of the sacrifice, which is particularly apt as a prelude to the sacrifices soon to be performed at his daughter's wedding (section 4, below). The animal to serve as the victim varied from (at the humbler end of the scale) a cock, through a goat or sheep to the bull, the most prestigious offering of all, and one especially appropriate for a king.

91.3 The oracle was...ambiguous: The bull might be construed as symbolic of the Persian Empire, with Philip in the role of the sacrificer who would strike it down, the interpretation made by the king himself. Alternatively the bull could be Philip, struck down at the hands of an assassin at a festal occasion. Garlands were worn both by animals about to be sacrificed and by revellers at banquets and other festal occasions, and are thus appropriate to the slaughter of Philip at a marriage celebration. An alternative version of the oracle is given by Cicero (*De Fato* 3.5) and Valerius Maximus (1.3.9), who tell of a warning to beware of the violence of a four-horsed chariot; Philip accordingly dismantled all the chariots in Macedonia and even avoided Lake Harma ("Chariot") in Boeotia, only to fall victim to the dagger of Pausanias, which had a chariot engraved on the hilt. If the story of the bull is a fabrication, that of the dagger is even less probable, for there is no evidence that Philip was superstitious about chariots. Indeed he even placed a chariot (drawn admittedly by a team of two horses rather than four) on his gold staters which were minted to commemorate his Olympic victory in this race.

91.4 The wedding of Cleopatra, his daughter by Olympias, and so the full sister of Alexander the Great.

Alexander the king of the Epirotes, who was the full brother of Olympias, and so the bride's uncle as well as her husband-to-be. For this Alexander, see note on 72.1. Diodorus gives no explanation for Philip's choice of bridegroom, but modern scholars connect the marriage with the deterioration in relations between Philip and Olympias that resulted from his marriage to Attalus' niece (Plut. *Alex.* 9.3-5; Arrian 3.6.5). Because Olympias had returned to her native Epirus, Philip was alarmed that she might try to turn her brother against him, and sought to neutralise her influence by strengthening his own links with the Epirote monarch. Since Cleopatra was the daughter of Olympias as well as of Philip, this plan was not a guaranteed success, but, though Philip had at least one other unmarried daughter available (Thessalonice, born c.352 and so of marriageable age), he obviously decided that the gamble was worth taking, in the hope that Alexander would appreciate the honour being conferred on him by the choice of the daughter who was not only of part-Epirote descent but also of the highest status (as sister to the heir apparent).

91.5 Musical competitions and sumptuous feasts: for Philip's use of competitions and feasts to cultivate the friendship of prominent Greeks, compare the conversion of the Olympia of 348 into a victory celebration for the capture of Olynthus (ch. 55.1-2)

The ties of guest-friendship: see note on ch. 54.4.

91.6 He instructed his...friends to bring...as many acquaintances as they could: clearly this celebration surpassed all his previous festivities in the number of guests present, and was doubtless intended as preliminary to the extension of Philip's network of guest-friendships even more widely.

Demonstrate his affability to the Greeks: as their new *hegemon*, Philip's aim was to consolidate and reinforce Greek enthusiasm for the forthcoming panhellenic campaign in Asia. Affability as one of Philip's memorable qualities is also selected for emphasis at 3.3, 60.4 and 95.2.

92.1 Aegae, the modern Vergina, the old capital of Macedonia before its supersession by Pella in the reign of Archelaus, and still the burial place of the Temenid kings.

Philip was awarded crowns of gold: the award of a crown was one of the methods employed by cities to honour both individuals and states. The Athenians awarded crowns made of various materials, notably olive (for citizens, foreign ambassadors and *proxenoi*), ivy (mostly to honorands connected in some way with Dionysus), and above all gold. The value of the crown depended on the importance of the honorand: the most common gold crowns were to the value of 500 (for citizens) and 1000 drachmai (the usual award to distinguished foreigners).

92.2 Proclaiming that...anyone who plotted against the king...was to be handed over: the public proclamation of a crown was by no means automatic, and, when made, was regarded as a mark of unusually high esteem. The promise to extradite plotters against Philip is best seen as being in accord with the oath taken by the members of the League of Corinth not to subvert the kingdom of Philip and his descendants (Tod 177, Harding 99), itself an extension of the promise to uphold the existing constitutions of the parties to the treaty.

92.3 Neoptolemus the tragic actor, an old friend of Philip whom he had known at least since 348/7, when he was sent by the Athenians to negotiate the release of their fellow citizens captured at Olynthus (Dem. 19.12), and returned bringing Philip's protestations of friendship for Athens (Dem. 19.215). By 346 he was sufficiently close to Philip for Demosthenes to describe him as 'Philip's agent and representative in Athens' and accuse him of selling up and abandoning his native city in favour of Macedonia (Dem. 5.6-8). For the presence of actors in the company of Philip's guest friends, see note on 55.3.

Proceeded to speak the following passage: the words seem to belong to the sung part of a lost Greek tragedy, but the authorship and context are both unknown.

92.4 He remembered the Pythian oracle: see ch. 91.2.

92.5 The twelve gods: the chief Olympian deities Zeus, Poseidon, Hades, Hera, Demeter, Hestia, Apollo, Artemis, Athene, Ares, Aphrodite and Hephaestus.

Enthroned with the twelve gods: the Greek word is *synthronos*, literally 'sharing a throne with', 'sharing in the enthronement of'. The crucial issue is how far, if at all, this piece of showmanship was intended by Philip to lay claim to divinity. The closest analogue to the word *synthronos* is Plutarch's use at *Moralia* 753F of *synnaos* and *synieros* (literally 'sharing the same temple with') in connection with the erection by the sculptor Praxiteles of a statue of his mistress, the courtesan Phryne, in the temple of Eros (and of

174

Aphrodite, Paus. 9.27.5) in her native city of Thespiae, where there is surely no suggestion that Phryne received divine honours. Phryne's statue is called by Pausanias both in this passage and at 10.15.1 *eikon*, not *agalma*, the correct technical term for a statue that is the object of a cult. If *synnaos* is used of a statue located in a temple along with a divine image but not itself the object of a cult, the related *synthronos* should by analogy mean 'carried along with statues of the gods but not itself the object of worship'. Moreover, apart from the dubious case of Lysander, whose Samian adherents are alleged to have deified in his lifetime (Plut. *Lys.* 18.2-5), there is no known precedent for the deification of a living Greek before the time of Alexander, unless one wishes to take into account the aberrant cases of the crackpot physician Menecrates, who identified himself with Zeus and Clearchus the tyrant of Heraclea Pontica, who is said to have called himself son of Zeus and demanded worship from his subjects (see note on ch. 36.3). Philip's behaviour was by contrast remarkably sane, though evidence of his desire for deification has been sought in the placing of his statue in the temple of Artemis at Ephesus in 336 (Arrian 1.17.11), in the erection of an altar to Zeus Philippios at Eresos (Tod 191, l.6, Harding 112B) and in the construction of the Philippeum at Olympia, which housed chryselephantine statues of Philip, Olmpias, Alexander and Philip's parents Amyntas and Eurydice (Paus. 5.17.4, 5.20.4). In the case of Ephesus, there is no evidence either that the statue was erected on Philip's instructions or that it was the object of a cult: since the word used is *eikon*, it is likely that it was no more than a votive statue erected by the Ephesians. At Eresos, the altar was dedicated to Zeus, not to Philip, and the latter's name is in adjectival form ('Philippian Zeus'), i.e. the altar was that of Zeus in his capacity as patron or protector of Philip. At Olympia, though the sheer expense of the material might suggest that the chryselephantine statues were intended to be objects of worship, they are called *eikones*, not *agalmata*, and the edifice in which they were accommodated is termed *oikema* ('building'), not *naos* or *hieron* ('temple'). There is thus no unequivocal evidence that Philip ever took steps to promote his deification, and the carrying around of his statue with those of the twelve gods hints at it rather than advertises it openly. Philip may have recalled the words of Isocrates in the letter he dispatched after Chaeronea (Epistle 3.5: "Be assured that you will achieve a glory that is unsurpassed and worthy of your past actions when you compel...the King currently called Great to carry out your orders. For then there will be nothing left for you except to become a god"). Philip had scarcely achieved this as yet, but in the circumstances may have felt it not inappropriate to take the first steps towards asserting his divinity. Certainly this is as much as his behaviour on the present occasion was intended to suggest.

93.1 He ordered his bodyguards to follow him: the inaccurate use of technical terms in our sources leaves the identification of words like bodyguard open to uncertainty. In Alexander's day at least there were three distinct groups who could be described with greater or lesser degrees of accuracy as having some responsibility for the protection of the king. Firstly there were the Royal Pages, youths of aristocratic birth who were charged with the care of the king at court, especially on the hunt or when he was asleep (Arrian 4.13.1; Curtius 5.1.42). Their official title was *basilikoi paides* ('the royal boys'), but they were sometimes loosely described as *somatophylakes* ('bodyguards'). Secondly there was the elite squadron of the hypaspists ('the *agema* of the hypaspists', 'the royal hypaspists'), the king's footguard which, unlike the other two squadrons, was under the direct command of the king. This group seems to have comprised the sons of Companions, and held a sort of intermediate position in the Macedonian *cursus honorum* between the Royal Pages and the Companion Cavalry (see W. Heckel, *The Marshals of Alexander's Empire*, London, 1993, pp. 244-53). They are occasionally if inaccurately termed *somatophylakes* by Arrian (*Anab.* 1.6.5; 1.24.1; 3.17.2; 4.3.2) and perhaps also by Diodorus at ch. 94.4 below and 17.65.1. Thirdly there were the *somatophylakes* in the strict sense of the term, the elite group of seven men of the highest nobility who held the most prestigious office in the kingdom next to that of the king. In Philip's day the terminology may have been different, and Diodorus' use both here and at 94.3 below of the non-technical *doryphoroi* is unhelpful for clarifying the problem. In the latter passage at least the *doryphoroi* were probably royal hypaspists (see the note on that passage), but if so, these cannot all have been present in the theatre and we must suppose that only a select few were given the honour of escorting Philip on this occasion. According to Justin (9.6.4-7) Philip intended to enter the theatre flanked only by his son and son-in-law the two Alexanders, but changed his mind and came in alone.

93.3 Pausanias who originated in...Orestis: Pausanias was the son of Cerastus (Josephus, *Antiquities of the Jews* 11.8.1) and his homeland Orestis, one of the cantons of Upper Macedonia in the upper valley of the Haliacmon and the Argestaean Plain where Epirot influence was strong. Many of the inhabitants were of Epirot origin (Hecataeus, Frag. 107; Strabo 7.7.5 and 11).

He was a Bodyguard of the king: the word used by Diodorus is *somatophylax* (*doryphoros* at Plut. *Mor.* 170E), but in which sense of the word? As one who was young enough to be the alleged object of Philip's homoerotic attention, Pausanias is unlikely to have been a *somatophylax* in the technical sense of the word, unless his affair with the king took place some years before the murder (see note on section 6 below). His implied age might suggest that he was a Royal Page, as does the story that he was receiving instruction from the sophist Hermocrates (see note on 94.1 below), and he might indeed have been a Page when the affair began. If the other

Bodyguards present were Royal hypaspists (see 94.4, note), he too is likely to have been among their number. It is possible that he was promoted from Page to hypaspist by way of compensation for his abuse at the hands of Attalus (see section 9 below).

Loved by Philip for his good looks: this story concerns one of the few homosexual relationships attested for a king who had the reputation of a rabid womaniser (Theopompus, Frag. 27; Polybius 8.9.2; Justin 9.8.3). Other stories of Philip's homosexual behaviour are his alleged affair with Alexander of Epirus (Justin 8.6.4), perhaps invented to explain his transfer from Epirus to the Macedonian court at Philip's insistence in 351/0, and the arrival at court of two fathers with handsome sons intended to fill the role of catamites (Phrynon of Athens and his unnamed son, Dem. 19.230-4; Lycolas of Trichoneum and his son Physcidas, Theopompus, Frag. 248). However in both these instances the initiative came from the boy's father, not Philip, and in neither case did a lasting relationship develop. Homosexual relationships like that alleged between Philip and Pausanias were rife among the Royal Pages (e.g. that between Archelaus and the pages Crateuas and Hellanocrates, Aristotle, *Politics* 1311B 8ff. and, in Alexander's day, between Epimenes and Charicles, Arrian, *Anab.* 4.13.7), and if Philip did have an affair with Pausanias, it will have begun while the latter was still a Page.

93.4 Willing to submit to the erotic advances of anyone who desired: by the standards of the day, a relationship between a youth and an older man was acceptable and in certain circumstances even honourable, but here the taunt is of promiscuity, tantamount to calling the second Pausanias a *pornos* (male prostitute).

93.6 Pleurias the king of the Illyrians: the date of this battle is controversial. On the assumption that Pleurias is to be identified with Pleuratus, the Illyrian king (of the Ardiaei?) against whom Philip fought in 345 or 344 (see note on 69.7), the role of Pausanias as Philip's catamite and his abuse by Attalus are appropriate for someone who was a Royal Page at the time but who had achieved promotion to Royal Hypaspist by the time of Philip's murder. On the other hand a delay of some eight years between the original insult and Pausanias' vengeance, as required by this chronology, is improbable, and all other aspects of the story suit a date for the rape of Pausanias in 337 or 336. Thus Diodorus' claim in sections 8 and 9 that Philip was unable to punish Attalus because his services were urgently needed admirably fit his appointment as a commander of the advance force about to be sent to Asia, and the reference in section 7-8 to Attalus' influence with the king can be true only after Philip's marriage to his niece in 337. Likewise Plutarch's version, which implicates Cleopatra as well as Attalus in Pausanias' degradation (*Alex*. 10.4), requires that she be of mature years at the time and not the child she must have been in 345. The most natural interpretation of Diodorus' narrative is that Pausanias was outraged not long before Philip's murder: in this event Pleurias should not be identified with Pleuratus (he is regarded by Hammond in ABSA 61, 1966, pp. 245-6, as king of the Autariatae, an Illyrian tribe inhabiting the valleys of the Lim and Tara to the north west of the Ardiaei whom Philip had fought in 345. We must therefore postulate an otherwise unattested Illyrian war in late 337 or early 336, perhaps caused by Alexander's attempts to stir up unrest while living in exile there (Plut. *Alex*. 9.5).

Positioned himself in front of the king: this should indicate that Pausanias fought on foot and was therefore a member of what in Alexander's day was known as the *agema* of the hypaspists.

93.7 Exercised a good deal of influence with the king, suggesting a date after Philip's marriage to Cleopatra.

Handed his body over to his stablemen: Plutarch (*Alex*. 10.4) even involves Cleopatra in the incident, and Justin (9.6.5-6) more dramatically has Attalus personally assault Pausanias.

93.8 Attalus was the nephew of Cleopatra: Diodorus is mistaken about their relationship, as he is at 17.2.3, where he makes him her brother. In fact he was her uncle and guardian (Satyrus, Frag. 5; Pausanias 8.7.7).

Chosen as commander of the advance force: so 91.2 and 17.2.4, where he is said to have shared command with Parmenio. See note on 91.2.

Promoted him to a more honourable position among the Bodyguards: the word used for 'position among the bodyguards' is *somatophylakia*. What Diodorus has in mind is unclear, as there is no other evidence for a hierarchy of grades within any of the groups commonly referred to as bodyguards. Perhaps he has in mind promotion from one rank to another (from Royal Page to hypaspist? See note on section 3 above).

94.1 Eager...to exact vengeance...from the one who had declined to avenge him: Pausanias' murder of Philip rather than Attalus is difficult to explain, at least if Pausanias was behaving rationally. The much briefer accounts of Aristotle (*Politics* 1311B 2) and Plutarch (*Alex*. 10.4) are in basic agreement with Diodorus, and, if correct, would indicate that he was possessed by an obsessive desire not only to avenge his humiliation but to have his vengeance witnessed by as many people as possible.

The sophist Hermocrates: the story occurs also in Valerius Maximus (8.14.4), who calls him Hermocles. No sophist of either name is known at this period, unless an identification is made with Hermocrates of Iasos, an authority on accentuation who was later to teach the poet Callimachus (Suda s.v. Callimachus). Questions of identification apart, the story is suspiciously similar to one told about Callisthenes, who allegedly gave much the same reply to a question from Hermolaus the Page (Plut. *Alex.* 55.2. Cf. Arrian *Anab.* 4.10.3 on Callisthenes' alleged advice to Philotas).

94.3 Having stationed horses at the gates: the reference to horses in the plural indicates a plurality of conspirators, whereas Diodorus' narrative has Pausanias acting alone. However at 17.2.1 (from a different source?) he does state that Alexander punished his father's murderers (cf. Plut. *Alex.* 10.7). Perhaps he has in mind the three sons of Aeropus, Heromenes, Arrhabaeus and Alexander, the only others known to have been accused of complicity in the assassination. Of these, Heromenes and Arrhabaeus were tried and executed immediately (Arrian 1.25.1), whereas Alexander was temporarily spared, only to be put to death in 330 for alleged involvement in the conspiracy of Philotas (Arr. loc.cit.; Curtius 7.1.9; Diod. 17.32.2 and 80.2; Justin 11.2.2).

The bodyguards were standing somewhat apart: the word used here is *doryphoroi*. For the meaning of 'bodyguard' in this context, see the note on 93.1.

94.4 Leonnatus, Perdiccas and Attalus: Leonnatus and Perdiccas were more of an age with Alexander than with Philip, and held important positions in the former's reign. Hence C.Bradford Welles in his note on this passage in the Loeb edition suggests that they were bodyguards of Alexander rather than of Philip. Leonnatus subsequently played a leading role in the downfall of Philotas in 330 (Curtius 6.8.17) and in undermining the introduction of prostration at Alexander's court in 328 (Arrian 4.12.2). After Alexander's death he was appointed satrap of Hellespontine Phrygia (Curt. 10.10.2; Diod.18.3.1) and was killed in battle against the Hellenic coalition in the Lamian War in 322 (Diod. 18.15.3; Plut. *Phoc.* 25.3). Perdiccas, a native of the Upper Macedonian canton of Orestis, commanded the Orestan brigade of the infantry at Thebes in 335 (Arrian 1.8.1), at the Granicus in 334 (Arr. 1.14.2), at Issus in 333 (Arr. 2.8.3; Curt. 3.9.7) and at Gaugamela in 331 (Curt. 4.13.28). After the death of Hephaestion in 324, he became chiliarch of the Companion Cavalry (Arr. 7.14.10) and on Alexander's deathbed received from him his signet ring (Diod. 17.117.3, 18.4.2; Curt. 10.5.4; Justin 12.15.12). He was subsequently appointed regent and met his death in 320 in an abortive attempt to remove Ptolemy as satrap of Egypt (Diod. 18.36.5; Arr. 7.18.5; Paus. 1.6.3; Justin 13.8.10). The Attalus mentioned in the present passage can hardly be Philip's new father-in-law, who was in Asia with the advance force (see 91.2 and 93.8 above), and the only other well known bearer of the name, the son of Andromenes, was closer to Philotas than to Alexander (Arrian 3.27.1). Leonnatus and Perdiccas were too old to be Pages in 336, and too young to be *somatophylakes* in the technical sense. Leonnatus became a *somatophylax* only in 332/1, when he replaced Arybbas (Arrian 3.5.5), and Perdiccas not long before the conspiracy of Philotas in 330 (Curtius at 6.8.17 calls him *armiger*, the Latin equivalent of *somatophylax*: the title is first bestowed on him by Arrian at 4.21.4, with reference to the year 327). By a process of elimination, the three men must have been Royal Hypaspists, just like the bodyguards mentioned at 93.1.

94.5 Perdiccas...ran him through and killed him: it is curious not only that Pausanias was killed immediately and allowed no opportunity to talk but also that those responsible were closely linked to Alexander. Such nuances are ignored by Diodorus, who gives no hint in Book 16 that others may have been implicated in the assassination. Even Aristotle, who is essentially in agreement with Diodorus, fails to consider the possibility that Pausanias may have been used as a tool by others, though this admittedly would not have been germane to his purpose. The motives of the sons of Aeropus, who were put to death by Alexander for alleged involvement in the plot, are unclear, if indeed they were guilty. The name of one of the brothers (Arrhabaeus) suggests a connection with the Lyncestian royal house, which contained two kings of this name (for Arrhabaeus I, see Thuc. 4.83.1; for Arrhabaeus II, Aristotle, *Politics* 1311B 13), and if so, their motive will have been a desire to use the turmoil created by Philip's death to regain independence for their homeland. However the father's name suggests membership of the Temenid dynasty which included two kings named Aeropus. For Aeropus I, see Hdt. 8.139; Satyrus, Frag. 1; Justin 7.1 and for Aeropus II, Diod. 14.37.6 and 84.6; Polyaenus 2.1.17). In this event, the brothers will have had a claim on the throne in their own right. Other suspects mentioned in our sources include the Persians (see the letter of Alexander to Darius at Arrian 2.14.5 and at Curtius 4.1.12), who hoped thereby to put an end to the projected invasion of Asia, as well as Alexander (Plut. *Alex*.10.8; Justin 9.7.1-6) and Olympias (Plut. *Alex*. 10.6-8; Pausanias 8.7.7; Athenaeus 13 557B; Justin 9.7), who supposedly both feared for their position since Philip's marriage to Cleopatra and were believed to suspect him of seeking to remove Alexander as heir. For a more detailed discussion of the identity of the conspirators who instigated or were privy to Philip's assassination, see Appendix B.

95.1 A reign of twenty four years: cf. note on 1.3 above.
Enthroned alongside the twelve gods: see note on 92.5.

95.2 Deployed the most meagre resources...but acquired the greatest

kingdom: repeated from 1.3.

Diplomatic skill and affability: these attributes struck Diodorus as lying at the heart of Philip's qualities as a ruler. Cf. 1.6, 60.4, 89.2, 91.6.

95.5 We shall commence the following book with the succession of Alexander...and...cover all his exploits: following his usual practice, Diodorus here provides a preliminary announcement of his programme for Book 17, which covers the years 336-323.

Appendix A

Philip II and the Transformation of Macedonia

The Macedonia which Philip inherited in 359 was a country divided on both political and ethnic lines, economically and constitutionally backward, situated on the periphery of the Greek world and inhabited by a people who were, in the eyes of the Greeks, barbarians "from whom it wasn't possible in the past to buy even a decent slave" (Demosthenes 9.31). Though endowed with abundant fertile land in the central Emathian Plain and in the coastal district of Pieria that was capable of supporting a large population and rendered the state agriculturally self-sufficient, not all of the low-lying land was cultivable, and parts were too marshy to be productive. Moreover much of the remainder of the country was mountainous and virtually isolated from the heartland by mountain ridges and river valleys. Macedonia was blessed with an abundance of natural resources, of which the most significant were timber and pitch obtainable from the heavily forested mountain slopes and the rich deposits of silver and gold to be found in the various mining regions, but all of these were underdeveloped, and few of the relevant areas were under Macedonian control on a permanent or even regular basis: for lengthy periods many of the mineral producing areas were under foreign domination and open to exploitation by Illyrians, Thasians, Amphipolitans and Chalcidians.

Given the extent of good quality terrain, the Macedonian aristocracy had long excelled in the breeding of horses (cf. Euripides, *Bacchae* 574), which facilitated their ability to field cavalry of the highest quality, but this asset had been sadly depleted as a result of Perdiccas' defeat at the hands of the Illyrians early in 359. The Macedonian infantry on the other hand was late in developing: like most tribal peoples and unlike the city states, such infantry as existed consisted mainly of light armed troops rather than hoplites. To the Greeks, the Macedonian foot was something of a joke, and in 423 could be dismissed by Thucydides (4.124.1) as "a big mass of barbarians".

The advantages brought to Macedonia by the nature of the terrain were counterbalanced by serious disadvantages, of which the most serious was the growth of fissiparous tendencies: though the central districts ('lower

Macedonia') were ruled directly by the king from his capital at Pella, the peripheral areas to the west and north ('Upper Macedonia') were politically fragmented into a number of ethnically based cantons such as Elimea, Tymphaea, Orestis, Eordaea and Lyncus or Lyncestis, inhabited by peoples with strong Epirote affinities, each with its own royal house, which sought to exercise as much independence as the central government was willing to permit. In effect, when the central authority was weak, the cantons went their own way, even to the extent of going to war with the king at Pella, but in times of strong rule from the centre they had to be content with playing a subordinate role. Beyond these principalities lay the territories of fierce barbarian tribes, Epirotes to the west, Illyrians to the north west, Paeonians to the north and Thracians to the east, all of whom were attracted by the prospect of the rich pickings that could be acquired with ease in the course of an invasion through any number of gaps and mountain passes. To the south were the Greek states, ever eager to wring concessions from a Macedonian king whom it was in their interests to keep as weak as possible: Chalcidians, Thessalians, Thebans, Athenians and Spartans had all intervened in the past and might do so again should a suitable opportunity occur. Of these, the main threat at the time of Philip's accession came from the Athenians, who had designs not only on Macedonian timber but on the acquisition of new possessions on the north Aegean seaboard.

Even at home conditions could never be described as settled, and much of the instability was caused by feuds within the royal family. The absence of any clearly established rules for determining the succession and the polygamous lifestyle of the king ensured that there was no shortage of claimants when the throne became vacant. In effect the ultimate choice lay with the army assembly, but the lack of any universally agreed criteria for choosing between the rival candidates meant that there were plenty of aspirants who, in the belief that they had as good, if not a better, claim than the present incumbent, were only too willing to revive it whenever the prospects of success appeared favourable.

Unfortunately for Macedonian kings troubles rarely came singly: bids from rival claimants and revolts of Upper Macedonian principalities tended to be timed so as to coincide with intervention from without. Indeed Greek and barbarian invaders could arrive on the scene during the same campaigning season, each with their own candidate, as Philip found to his cost in the first year of his reign, when Athens backed Argaeus and the Thracians Pausanias (Diod. 16.2.6). A few kings, notably Alexander I (c.498- c.454) and Archelaus (413-399), had survived the odds, if not the assassin's dagger, and had enjoyed some success both in unifying the realm and developing its resources, but the great majority of rulers lurched from crisis to crisis, content merely to survive. Few kings, whether successful or not, died peacefully in their beds.

When Philip came to the throne, he understood the nature of the problem and saw clearly what the remedies were, given the assets that would be available to the ruler of a unified kingdom. What he needed was time, the time in which he could develop and build upon that potential in order to transform Macedonia into the powerful state that it was capable of becoming. To obtain that time, Philip was willing to secure it by any means at his disposal, be it by purchase or by diplomacy, and when it was once secured, he embarked on the transformation that would convert Macedonia from its current lowly status into the leading power in the Greek world, a state both willing and able to play a dominant role on the world stage.

Once the immediate crisis was over, Philip was able to devote himself to the eradication of his country's weaknesses. The Upper Macedonian principalities were integrated into a unified kingdom and their ruling families presumably abolished (they are never heard of again): leading members of those families were conciliated by gifts of land elsewhere in the kingdom (Polemocrates of Elimea, the father of Cleander and Coenus, for example, receiving estates in Chalcidice, Syll.³ 322.5ff.). In addition they received high and honourable positions at court, as can be seen from the considerable influence wielded in Alexander's reign by men such as Perdiccas of Orestis, Leonnatus of Lyncus and Polyperchon of Tymphaea. The Elimaean princely family was also granted the honour of a royal marriage when Philip wedded Phila, sister of Derdas and Machatas (Satyrus, Frag. 5). The levies of the former cantons, which had previously served their own ruler, were now incorporated into the Macedonian army, perhaps with the title *asthetairoi* (see A.B.Bosworth, *Asthetairoi*, CQ 23, 1973, pp. 245-53): certainly under Alexander there were separate brigades from Elimea, Tymphaea and a joint brigade of Orestans and Lyncestians, Diod. 17.57.2).

The military effectiveness of the infantry was greatly enhanced by the introduction of the *sarissa* or long thrusting spear, which gave the phalanx the initial advantage in any encounter with Greek hoplites, whose shorter thrusting spears were less effective and who found it difficult to open up a gap in their more densely packed opponents. Philip further improved the phalanx by enacting a series of reforms mentioned briefly by Diodorus at chapter 3.1-2, aimed at tightening up discipline, achieving greater mobility and quicker march rates and at the rewarding of efficiency by the introduction of a system of competitive rewards.

If the infantry could be enlarged by the incorporation of men from the outlying cantons, the cavalry was augmented by the creation of new Companions. Some of these, like the aforementioned Polemocrates, were Upper Macedonians, others were ennobled Lower Macedonians or prominent Greeks who caught Philip's attention and whose gift of land in newly conquered territories endowed them with both the social status and the economic resources with which to sustain this new rank. Theopompus tells us (Frag. 224) that "Philip collected Companions, some from Macedonia, some from Thessaly and some from the rest of Greece", while another fragment (225) adds that there were even some barbarian Companions. Among those of Greek origin may be mentioned Nearchus son of Androtimus the Cretan, later to be Alexander's admiral (Arrian, *Ind.* 18.10), Medeius of Larissa (Arr. *Anab.* 7.24.4, *Ind.* 18.7; Diod. 17.117.1) and Eumenes of Cardia (Arrian, *Anab.* 7.4.6, *Ind.* 18.7; Nepos, *Eum.* 1.4; Plutarch, *Eum.* 1.1-2), while barbarian Companions are represented by Sitalces, whose name suggests membership of the Odrysian royal house and who served as one of Alexander's infantry commanders (Arr. *Anab.* 1.28.4, 2.5.1, 2.9.3, 3.26.3-4, 6.27.4; Curtius 10.1.1). The estates which Philip conferred on his new Companions will have come from land annexed at the successful conclusion of one or another of his wars, largely at the expense of uprooted individuals or whole communities. Amphipolis, taken in 357 (Diod. 16.8.2), supplied the lands subsequently held in Alexander's reign by Nearchus, Laomedon and Androsthenes (Arrian, *Ind.* 18.4) and presumably allotted by Philip to their respective fathers Androtimus, Larichus and Callistratus. Pydna, captured later in the same year (Diod. 16.8.3), was to provide estates for Metron and Nicarchides (Arrian, *Ind.* 18.5), while the territory of Methone was to be allocated to Macedonians a few years later (Diod. 16.34.4). The more extensive the territory acquired, the greater the number of Companions that could be enrolled. At the beginning of Philip's reign, he had only six hundred (Diod. 16.4.3), but by the time Theopompus described the institution (Frag. 225), they had been increased to eight hundred. By 334, when Alexander crossed over to Asia, he was able to take with him 1800 and still leave some 1500 behind in Europe (Diod. 17.17.3-4).

The once weak Macedonian economy, which had heen improved by the reform programme recommended to Perdiccas III by the exiled Athenian statesman Callistratus ([Aristotle], *Oec.* 2.22.2), was further strengthened by Philip's annexation of various territories rich in precious metals which had been previously worked by other peoples. The silver mines in the vicinity of Mt. Dysorus, which had been operated by Alexander I in the early fifth century and produced for him an annual revenue of 360 talents (Herodotus 5.17), were regained, as were the gold and silver mines in Bisaltia previously controlled by the Chalcidians. Success in the Illyrian war of 358 led to the acquisition of the mines near Damastion, and the annexation of Amphipolis in 357 brought him the Pangaeus mines. Most important of all for Philip was the takeover in 356 of Crenides and its mining district, formerly a Thasian possession, which he proceeded to develop till it produced for him some 1000 talents per year (Diod. 16.8.7). The securing of plentiful sources of precious metals enabled Philip to embark on the minting of coins on a scale unparalleled in Macedonia: his silver tetradrachms minted at Pella and Amphipolis, with the distinctive head of bearded Olympian Zeus on the obverse and, on the reverse, a horseman in Macedonian hat, tunic and cloak, became common throughout the Greek world, while the gold stater, minted at Pella from about 345, bearing on the obverse the head of long-haired Apollo and on the reverse a two-horsed chariot and driver, soon spread all over the Mediterranean. Philip's revenues were further increased when he was appointed *archon* of the Thessalian League, which gave him access to the not inconsiderable revenues of that wealthy country (Demosthenes 1.22, 6.22), and the tribute which was paid by subject peoples like the Thracians (Diod. 16.71.2) augmented his resources to such an extent that they eventually came to impress even the jaundiced Demosthenes (19.90).

With these revenues Philip was able to maintain large armies for lengthy periods, and even possessed units that were sufficiently professional to be described by Demosthenes as a standing army (8.11), with its weapons constantly at hand (18.235), both in summer and in winter (9.50). In addition he employed mercenaries on an unprecedented scale (Diod. 16.8.7), though in fact all his major battles were won for him by his Macedonians, and his mercenaries were mainly deployed as garrisons (e.g. at Thermopylae, Dem. 9.32; in Phocis, id. 19.81; in Thessaly, id. 18.260) or, alternatively, as the main component of forces which he sent to the assistance of pro-Macedonian regimes who requested his aid (e.g. Argives and Messenians, Demosthenes 6.15; Eretrians, id. 9.58; Magarians, id. 19.87 and 29.5). Philip even employed some of his monies to build a fleet, which we first hear of in 353/2 (Polyaenus 4.2.22) and in 351 (Demosthenes 4.22 and 34), though the lack of a naval tradition in Macedonia and the inexperience of his crews ensured that it was never a match for the Athenians. More tangible benefits might have been expected from his ability to afford the services of the most skillful engineers of the day, Polyeidus of Thessaly, the inventor of the torsion catapult, and his pupils Diades and Charias, who constructed for him the machines with which he sought in vain in 340 to breach the defences of Perinthus and Byzantium (see the notes on 74.5). More fruitful for Philip was the investment of vast sums in establishing the wide network of guest friendships which he forged with many Greeks who were politically active in their own cities, and who were won over by the lavish presents which he used as his contribution to the gift exchange which normally cemented such links (see 16.8.7, 54.4 and the notes on the latter passage).

The Macedonian economy was strengthened still further by the consolidation of the frontiers and the adoption of various measures designed to deter barbarian inroads. These included the foundation of military settlements and cities in strategically important areas (Demosthenes 4.48, Justin 8.5.6), which could block off the mountain passes through which marauding troops had traditionally entered the country in the course of their pillaging expeditions, as well as the construction of roads to facilitate the rapid dispatch of reinforcements when required. Such means would discourage Illyrian and Thracian invasions, and Philip's election to the archonship of Thessaly, a country always difficult for foreign armies to penetrate (Thucydides 4.78.2), effectively prevented attack from the south. Only by sea was Macedonia vulnerable, but the Athenians, learning fron the failure of their 359 venture to install Argaeus, were for the most part forced on to the defensive (Diopeithes' aggression in the vicinity of the Chersonese in 342-1 was an exception, but affected only those parts of Thrace that were adjacent to his base).

Both in the frontier districts and in the territories he annexed in the course of his reign, Philip founded cities with the purpose of improving security, civilising turbulent and unruly natives, and developing the mineral and agricultural resources of the area on a scale that had been impossible under less settled conditions. Among Philip's new cities were Celetrum (modern Kastoria) in Orestis, Astraea and Dobera in Eordaea, Doberus adjacent to the Paeonian border, and, in Thrace, Philippopolis (the modern Plovdiv, Theopompus, Frag. 110, Plutarch, *Moralia* 520A), Beroe, Cabyle (Theopompus, Frag. 220; expanded from an insignificant habitation already on the site, Demosthenes 8.44), and, above all, Philippi, on the site of the former Crenides (Diodorus 16.8.6), which, though a mining centre in origin, was also intended to develop the rich agricultural region in which the city was situated. Philip had the plain of Philippi transformed from a forested, marshy underdeveloped area into one of remarkable productivity by cutting down the forests and draining the marsh land (Theophrastus, *Causes of Plants*, 5.14.6). Similar treatment may have been meted out to the land along the Thermaic Gulf, which was subject to periodic flooding when the channels of the rivers Axius and Haliacmon became clogged up with silt (see N.G.L. Hammond, *A History of Macedonia*, Vol.1, Oxford, 1972, pp. 142-9).

Schemes such as these enabled Philip to encourage the change from transhumance to agriculture, from nomadism to the settled way of life of which Alexander reminds his mutinous troops in the famous address delivered at Opis in 324 (Arrian, *Anabasis* 7.9.3-5):

> Philip took you over as nomadic vagabonds, clothed for the most part in skins, pasturing a few sheep on the mountains and fighting unsuccessfully in their defence against Illyrians, Triballians and the neighbouring Thracians. He gave you cloaks to wear in place of animal skins, he brought you down from the mountains to the plains and made you a match in battle against

the neighbouring barbarians...he made you dwellers in cities and civilised you with good laws. He transformed you from being slaves and subjects and made you rulers of those very barbarians by whom in the past you and your profits had been plundered. He added to Macedonia the greater part of Thrace, and by occupying the best positioned places on the sea, he opened up the country to trade. He made it possible for you to operate the mines in security, he made you rulers of the Thessalians who in the past had struck you dead with fear, he humbled the Phocian people...and instead of our having to pay tribute to the Athenians and take orders from the Thebans, it was rather from us that they obtained their security.

The passage is a splendid piece of rhetoric, but, provided that due allowance is made for the exaggeration of earlier Macedonian backwardness, it shows a good appreciation of the transformations wrought by Philip, and provides no more fitting or eloquent testimony to his achievements.

Appendix B

The Death of Philip

The sordid tale of the murder of Philip at the hand of Pausanias, a member of his bodyguard, in revenge for his failure to punish Attalus, who had subjected Pausanias to the humiliations of sexual abuse, is described by Diodorus, our most detailed source for the incident, in chapters 93-4, a highly sensational account which depicts Philip's demise as a fitting penalty for his hybristic behaviour on the occasion of his daughter's wedding, and one reminiscent of the sort of publicity conscious reporting that characterises some of the less reputable of our modern tabloids. Briefer versions also occur in Plutarch (*Alex.* 10.4) and Justin (9.6.5ff.), though our earliest reference is to be found in a passage of Aristotle's *Politics* (1311b3):

> The attack on Philip by Pausanias took place because he allowed
> him to be outraged by Attalus and his henchmen.

The motivation attributed to Pausanias in this story has not on the whole gained much credence in the eyes of modern scholars, whose objections are essentially three in number. In the first place, Pausanias' grievance was against Attalus, not against Philip, who sought to placate him with gifts and a promotion; secondly it was foolish to kill him in a theatre in full view of a large crowd, where the odds on a successful escape were considerably less than they would have been had the deed been done in private. To combat these two objections one might argue that modern scholars have underestimated the effects of rape on the victim, whose humiliation would have increased with the appointment of the perpetrator to the joint command of the advance expedition to Asia Minor (chapter 93.4). Though such advancement might conceivably have transferred Pausanias' wrath from Attalus to Philip, male rape at the Macedonian court, where homosexuality was rife, is unlikely to have been quite as traumatic an experience for the victim as it would be today. One suspects that, if he really took umbrage at and even

189

became mentally unbalanced as a result of the affair, it was not so much because of the rape itself as through outrage at the treatment of his aristocratic body by a gang of stable hands at the opposite end of the social spectrum.

The third implausibility in Diodorus' story is one of date. The assault on Pausanias took place in the course of a war Philip fought with Pleurias the Illyrian king (chapter 93.6), but the most recent Illyrian war of which we have any knowledge is that dated by Diodorus to 344/3 (69.7). If the two wars are to be identified, we are being asked to believe that Pausanias nursed his grievance against Philip for some eight years before deciding on vengeance. However the idea of an eight year grudge may be illusory. The Illyrian king against whom Philip fought in 344 was named Pleuratus (Marsyas of Pella, Frag. 17, Jacoby), but though Pleuratus is similar to Pleurias, must we assume that Diodorus has garbled the name? There were several different Illlyrian tribes against whom Philip fought in the course of his reign and Hammond (*BSA* 61, 1966, pp. 245-6) makes out a good case for making Pleuratus king of the Ardiaei and Pleurias king of the Autariatae. No Illyrian war is attested for 337 or 336, but, by connecting Pausanias' grievance with Attalus' Asian command (93.8), Diodorus certainly implies that it was recent, as does Plutarch when he implicates Cleopatra as well as Attalus in the incident (Alex. 10.4): if she was born around 355 (so W. Heckel, *The Marshalls of Alexander's Empire*, London and New York, 1992, p. 8) she was no more than a young girl in 344. It is easy to postulate an Illyrian war in 337, a year that was, for an active king like Philip, otherwise remarkably free of military activity, and Illyrian hostility is suggested by Alexander's choice of that country, in the aftermath of the Pixodarus affair, as a suitable place to seek sanctuary (Plut. *Alex*. 10.4).

It is thus possible that Pausanias' grudge was of recent origin, and that it was indeed a motivating factor in his decision to kill the king. But even if this was the case, it does not preclude the existence at court of others who had reasons of their own for wishing to see Philip dead and who might have sought to use Pausanias as their tool. Neither Aristotle nor Diodorus gives any hint of the involvement of others, but as their sole preoccupation is with Pausanias, they would have deemed the motives of any other interested parties, had there been any, as irrelevant. Yet even Diodorus preserves tantalising hints of a possible conspiracy: at 94.3 he makes a suggestive reference to a plurality of horses which Pausanias had prepared for his escape and which, were he acting on his own, would have surely served to facilitate the inevitable pursuit, while at 17.2.1 he informs us (from a different source?) that in the first year of his reign Alexander punished his father's murderers. Compare the tradition that among the questions he put to Ammon's oracle at Siwah was whether all his father's assassins had paid the penalty (Diod. 17.51.2, Curtius 4.7.27, Plut. *Alex*. 27.4, Justin 11.11.10).

Pausanias apart, the only Macedonians known to have been executed for complicity in the murder were two brothers, Heromenes and Arrhabaeus the sons of Aeropus, who had links with the Upper Macedonian canton of Lyncus (Arrian, *Anab.* 1.25.1). It is they who are likely to have been the assassins Diodorus had in mind at 17.2.1. A third brother, Alexander (usually called 'the Lyncestian' in our sources (Diod. 17.32.1; Curtius 7.1.5, 8.7.4, 8.8.5, 10.1.40; Justin 11.2.2; 12.14.1) to distinguish him from the homonymous king, was also suspected of involvement but was spared because he was one of the first to hail his namesake as king and because of the influence of his father-in-law Antipater (Curt. 7.1.7; Justin 11.7.1, 12.14.1; cf. Diod. 17.80.2, where there is confusion between Antipater and Antigonus, whose infuence on Alexander in 336 was minimal). On the assumption that the brothers were not just innocent scapegoats, their motives can only be a matter of conjecture. If they really were of Lyncestian origin, and the name Arrhabaeus is one well attested in the royal house of that canton (e.g. the son of Bromerus king of Lyncus in 422, Thucydides 4.83.1, and his putative grandson, Lyncestian king in the reign of Archelaus, Aristotle, *Politics* 1311b 13), the motive will have been one of local nationalism, designed simultaneously to wreak vengeance on the ruler who had stripped the family of its royal estate and to use the probable confusion following Philip's death to restore Lyncestian independence, and perhaps even, in common with Pausanias of Orestis (Diod. 16.93.3) to detach the whole of Upper Macedonia from the domination of Pella.

If however Lyncus was simply the area in which their estates lay, they may have been Temenids with a claim on the Macedonian throne for themselves: their father's name turns up in the Temenid line as that of two Macedonain kings, Aeropus I the great-grandfather of Alexander I (Herodotus 8.139; Satyrus, Frag. 1; Justin 7.1) and Aeropus II, king from 398/7 to 395/4 (Diod. 14.37.6 and 84.6; Polyaenus 2.1.17). Also in favour of a royal lineage for the Lyncestian brothers are Darius' alleged offer of the Macedonian throne to the survivor, Alexander (Arrian, *Anab.* 1.25.3; Justin 11.7.21), surely unrealistic unless he had a Temenid pedigree, and his subsequent execution in the aftermath of Philotas' conspiracy in 330 (Diod. 17.80.2; Curtius 7.1.5-9; Justin 12.14.1): the timing suggests that the king was afraid that Philotas was planning to replace him with the only suitable surviving Temenid. A third possibility would stress the links between the Lyncestian brothers and Amyntas, the son of Perdiccas III and Alexander's cousin, for whom, according to Justin (7.5.6ff.), Philip originally held the regency. However the only source suggestive of such link is Plutarch, who, while describing the situation in Macedonia at the time of Alexander's accession, writes that 'all of Macedonia was festering and looking towards Amyntas and the sons of Aeropus' (*Moralia* 327c). Yet in this passage Plutarch may be doing no more than stating the existence of alternative factions without necessarily implying any connection between the two. Moreover it is difficult to find any convincing reason to explain the Lyncestians' preference for Amyntas over Alexander, whose mother Olympias, as an Epirot, was ethnically akin to the natives of the Upper Macedonian cantons (Strabo 7.7.5, 9.5.11; cf. Hecataeus, Frag. 157), though the identity and nationality of Amyntas' unknown mother might be of relevance in this connection. In addition, if the Lyncestians really did plot to set Amyntas on the throne, his survival for a further year is inexplicable: when he was eventually eliminated (probably in 335, when his widow Cynna was available as a wife for the Agrianian king Langarus, Arrian, *Anab.* 1.5.4), the alleged reason was conspiracy against Alexander, not against Philip (Curtius 6.9.17, 6.10.24). In other words his liquidation did not form part of the purge that marked Alexander's accession, but belonged rather to a later one that was in no way related to the execution of the Lyncestians.

A fourth possible explanation for the brothers' animosity to Philip could be resentment at his treatment of their father, though there can be no certainty that their father was the Aeropus whom Philip degraded from a position of authority for disciplinary reasons: at all events the demotion of an Aeropus for spending an excessive amount of time in the company of flute girls (Polyaenus 4.2.1) seems to have been entirely merited, and even if his sons thought otherwise, their reaction would have been out of all proportion to the triviality of the original offence.

Of the four possible motives, only the first two are in any way convincing. However it is just as likely that they (and perhaps Pausanias as well) were the innocent victims of more important figures lurking in the background, by whom they were selected as scapegoats because their known grievances against Philip lent plausibility to a charge of regicide. The most popular theory in recent times would cast them in the role of fallguys for any one, two, or all three members of the all-powerful triumvirate comprising Alexander, Olympias and Antipater.

There is not the slightest hint in Diodorus that Alexander or either of his associates wished to see Philip dead, and Curtius' account of the circumstances of Alexander's accession is lost. The complicity of Olympias and Alexander is recorded as an undoubted fact (complete with fabricated sensational details) in Justin (9.6.5ff.), and, as a plausible rumour, in Plutarch (*Alex.* 10.4). The alleged role of Antipater is unattested in any ancient source, but his closeness to the new king at the beginning of his reign suggests that Alexander cannot have been involved, if indeed he was, without Antipater's knowledge. Among the possible motives attributed to Antipater by modern scholars have been jealousy of the promotion over his head of Parmenio and Attalus to the command of the advance force sent to Asia Minor, and strong aversion to Philip's alleged pretensions to divinity when he had his statue carried in a procession of those of the twelve Olympian gods (chapters 92.5 and 95.1). To the former charge one could reply that Antipater was passed over for the command in Asia only because Philip was planning to give him, when he left on campaign himself, the regency of Macedonia that he was later to receive from Alexander, and to the latter that the evidence for Antipater's objections to Philip's divine aspirations is based on nothing more than an inference drawn from the article devoted to him in the Suda, which refers to his later disapproval of Alexander's far more grandiose pretensions in the same direction: Antipater, on this interpretation, was more of a religious fanatic than the pragmatic statesman which the rest of his career surely proves him to have been. The speed with which he rallied to Alexander's cause has been viewed by some modern scholars as incriminating, but it is best explained as the act of a patriotic statesman which was necessary if the state was to avoid a period of instability or even anarchy.

The likely motives of Alexander and of Olympias, whose fortunes were inextricably linked, are best taken together. By 337, Philip had accumulated five children by six wives, but of the five, only two were male, and of the two, only Alexander was qualified to succeed to the throne, and had already been marked out as such by Philip. In a polygamous court like that at Pella, there was no official position of queen, and the amount of influence wielded by each of the royal wives depended on other factors. As mother of the heir, Olympias occupied a far more powerful position than any other wife, and, since her main concern was to retain the power she already possessed, she could tolerate the other wives without undue concern. However when in 337 Philip married Cleopatra the niece of Attalus, the situation changed overnight. As Satyrus rightly says (Frag. 5), "he threw his whole life into confusion". Though Satyrus sees the new marriage as one inspired by love, Philip, who was not the sort of king to allow his emotions to go to his head, is far more likely to have been influenced by the need to produce another son before he invaded Asia, as an insurance against the possibility that both he and Alexander might be killed in battle. To Alexander and Olympias, Philip's motives may not have been apparent, the former fearing that he might be supplanted as heir, the latter that she might have to yield precedence to Cleopatra. All of Philip's surviving wives (Phila of Elymaea was probably dead) were of foreign extraction, Illyrian, Epirot, Thessalian or Getic, with no male relative at court to strenthen their position, but not only was Cleopatra from the Macedonian nobility but her uncle stood high in Philip's favour, and was soon designated as one of the commanders of the advance force sent ahead to Asia Minor. If Cleopatra was in herself no threat, her relationship to Attalus made her a formidable rival to Olympias, and any son she might bear would be an equally formidable threat to Alexander.

If Alexander and his mother already had any cause to fear the consequences of the new marriage, an incident that took place at the wedding feast will have strengthened their convictions. When the carousals were well under way, the bride's uncle offered up a toast to the birth of a legitimate heir to the throne. The use of the term 'legitimate' meant in the context of Philip's complicated matrimonial affairs a child born to parents who were both of Macedonian origin. In actual fact, whatever was in Attalus' mind at the time, and since his tongue had been loosened by wine, he may not have been fully in control of his actions, it is doubtful if the Macedonians were much concerned with the birth of pure Macedonian heirs. Kings had married non-Macedonian wives in the past, and a foreign mother had never been an obstacle to the succession: Philip himself was not only half Illyrian (through his mother Eurydice the daughter of Sirras), but, though his father Amyntas III had another wife Gygaea, whose name suggests that she was of Temenid blood (cf. Gygaea the daughter of Amyntas I, Herodotus 5.21.2 and 8.136), it was his three sons by Eurydice who successively held the throne, to the exclusion of Gygaea's three sons. Though Attalus' words amounted to little more than a drunken indiscretion, the effect on Alexander was instantaneous. Enraged at the insult, he shouted, "Do you then take me for a bastard?" and threw his cup at Attalus. This might have been the end of the affair, if not of Alexander's resentment, had not Philip, outraged at this outbreak of unseemly violence on what should have been a happy occasion, drawn his sword against Alexander, only to stumble and fall to the ground. Alexander thereupon transferred his wrath from Attalus to Philip and with the jeering remark, "To think that one who is preparing to cross from Europe to Asia cannot even cross from one couch to another!", prudently withdrew not only from the banquet but from Macedonia. Now a self-appointed exile, he removed his mother from court and sent her to Epirus, where she sought to rouse her brother against Philip. Meanwhile Alexander sought refuge among the Illyrians, who were already hostile to Philip (Plut. *Alex.* 9.4-5).

When sober, Philip came to appreciate the full consequences of his drunken behaviour, and his desire to seek a reconciliation with Alexander proves that it was no part of his plans to discard him, though significantly enough he appears to have made no attempt to patch things up with Olympias. In fact, to counter any attempts she might make to stir up her brother against him, he arranged a marriage between Alexander of Epirus and Cleopatra, his daughter by Olympias.

If Philip and Alexander were now reconciled, the latter remained deeply suspicious of his father's intentions, and when not long afterwards Pixodarus the Carian satrap, desirous of securing allies in a bid to strengthen his far from legitimate title to the satrapy (Diod. 16.74.2), proposed a marriage between his daughter (the younger Ada?) and Philip's mentally defective son

Arrhidaeus, Alexander, despite the fact that the initiative had come from Pixodarus, immediately leaping to the conclusion that Philip was grooming Arrhidaeus for the succession, sent an intermediary to Pixodarus to suggst himself as a more suitable son-in-law (Plut. *Alex.*10). Alerted to the instability of the Macedonian court, Pixodarus withdrew his offer, thus denying Philip the opportunity of securing influence and political support in either Caria or Cappadocia, the homeland of the proposed bride's mother (Strabo 14.2.17). Philip manifested his anger by exiling several of Alexander's close friends, Harpalus, Ptolemy, Nearchus, Erigyius and Laomedon (cf. Arrian, *Anab.* 3.6.5), who had presumably encouraged his involvement in the affair, but Alexander himself emerged unscathed, his position as heir apparent intact. Philip's assurance that he he had in mind for him a grander alliance than that with a barbarian satrap should be accepted as sincere. For the foreseeable future, or at least till Cleopatra should bear a son, Alexander's position at court was safe, though he himself did not necessarily believe it. His misgivings may have been somewhat allayed when Cleopatra gave birth to a daughter, Europa (Satyrus, Frag. 5), not to the son implied by Pausanias' use of the masculine participle in referring to her child at 8.7.7. Yet the later careers of both Alexander and Olympias prove that neither would scruple to resort to murder to rid themselves of troublesome enemies: assassination was employed by Alexander to eliminate Attalus (Diod. 17.5.1-2) and Parmenio (Diod. 17.80.3; Curtius 7.2.22-7; Arrian, *Anab.* 3.26.3-4; Plut. *Alex.* 49; Justin 12.5.3), while Olympias was later to liquidate Cleopatra and daughter (Pausanias 8.7.7; Justin 9.7.12), Philip Arrhidaeus and Eurydice (Diod. 19.11.5-6), and Nicanor the son of Antipater, together with some hundred of Cassander's friends (Diod. 19.11.8). But since Olympias was still languishing in Epirus and did not return till she received intelligence of Philip's death, she lacked the opportunity to incite Pausanias on her own, and if the sex of Cleopatra's child freed Alexander from immediate political eclipse, he may well have believed that the danger to his position had not been averted, only postponed: since a second pregnancy would put him once more at risk, he may have decided, with or without his mother's backing, to eradicate the threat once and for all. Though proof is lacking, it cannot be denied that Alexander and Olympias were major beneficiaries of Philip's death, and on the principle *cui bono?* the question of their complicity cannot be dismissed out of hand.

One other possible suspect remains to be considered. In order to put an end to the trouble on his western border, the Great King had a personal interest in the termination of Philip's life, in the not unreasonable belief that a disputed succession would weaken Macedonia, effect the recall of the advance force from Asia Minor and postpone the threatened invasion for the foreseeable future, perhaps even indefinitely. It would have been a simple matter to send an agent to Macedonia to bribe men like Pausanias and the Lyncestian brothers, especially if they were already rumoured to be disaffected. Persian involvement is indeed stated as a fact in the propaganda letter supposedly dispatched by Alexander to Darius in 332, as quoted by Arrian (*Anabasis* 2.14.4:

> My father was murdered by conspirators whom you organised,
> as you boasted in letters written to everyone,

as well as by Curtius (4.1.12):

> Who is unaware that my father Philip was killed by those whom
> your people had seduced with the hope of a huge sum of money?.

As parallels may be cited the abortive attempt allegedly made by Darius in the winter of 334/3 to send his agent Sisines to tamper with the loyalty of the surviving Lyncestian brother in order to encompass the death of Alexander (Arrian 1.25; cf. Curtius 3.7.11-15), and the suspicion of Persian complicity in the murder in 370 of Jason of Pherae who, like Philip later, had publicly announced his intention to lead the Greeks against Persia (Xenophon, *Hell.* 6.1.12, Isocrates 5.119). However in the latter case, as in 336, there were other suspects with other motives (Xen. *Hell.* 6.4.30; Diod.15.60.5; Valerius Maximus 9.10, ext.2; Aelian Frag. 52), and the case for Persian involvement is flimsy. Suspicions of Persian complicity in the assassination of Philip are no less tenuous. Alexander's letter to Darius, in which the allegation is made, is a crude attempt at propaganda, designed to show both Darius and the Persians in the worst possible light, in order to make credible their alleged responsibility for starting the war. As such the letter contains more than its fair share of distortions and unverifiable charges that include, *inter alia*, the dispatch of troops to Thrace and the claim that it was Darius who instigated the murder of his predecessor with Bagoas serving merely as his tool. Moreover the internal situation in Persia in 336 was far from secure: Darius had ascended the throne only a few months previously (Diod. 17.7.1, to be preferred to the statement to the contrary at 17.6.2), and was not a free agent till the elimination of the king-maker Bagoas. In addition there may have been unrest in some of the satrapies, including two of the richest, Egypt and Babylonia. In the former, the two year reign of the native pharaoh Khabebsha who is attested in papryrological sources, should probably be placed in this period, and in Babylonia the Uruk king list (most conveniently found in J.B. Pritchard, *Ancient Near Eastern Texts Relating to the Old Testament*, ed. 3, Princeton, 1969, pp. 566-7) gives as Darius' predecessor in Babylon a ruler with the native name of Nidin-Baal. In the circumstances, Darius will have been far too distracted by domestic problems to concern himself with events in Macedonia, and if he did find time to do so, he will have noted that his troops under the command of Memnon had little difficulty in containing the Macedonian advance force: indeed they even succeeded in forcing it back on the defensive. All in all Darius had neither the leisure nor the incentive to instigate the assassination of Philip, and if he did, as Alexander was later to allege, boast of having done so, his claim will have been no more than a propaganda ploy to impress the Greeks with the length of the Great King's arm.

In the absence of any detailed and unbiased ancient sources, attempts to determine the identity of Philip's assassins can be no more than speculative. It was undoubtedly Pausanias who committed the murder, and he did have personal motives of a sort, which are, however, decidedly thin. The Lyncestian brothers too may have been involved, as Alexander was subsequently to claim, but if so, too little is known of their background to establish their real motive beyond doubt. The failure of Alexander's propaganda machine to name his cousin Amyntas ought to exculpate him, while, given their more pressing difficulties on the home front, the Persians too should be excluded from the suspect list. There remain Alexander and Olympias, of whom the latter had already suffered political eclipse and the former saw himself as about to follow. Her absence in Epirus makes it difficult for Olympias to have taken the initiative, and though Alexander had both the motive and the opportunity, the choice of venue, in full view of a gathering of the most prominent natives and Greeks, was, for him, something of an embarrassment in revealing only too clearly the instability of life at the Macedonian court. The stage was doubtless selected by Pausanias himself, and if Alexander or his mother were privy to his intentions, they were not necessarily aware of the details. To anyone living at a time so remote from the events, the absence of any new information makes the mystery insoluble.

Bibliography

Diodorus and Other Ancient Sources for the Reign of Philip

Barber, G.L., *The Historian Ephorus* (Cambridge, 1935).

Connor, W.R., *History without Heroes : Theopompus' Treatment of Philip of Macedon*, GRBS 8, 1967, pp. 133-54.

————*Theopompus and Fifth Century Athens* (Washington, 1968).

Drews, R., *Diodorus and his Sources*, AJPhil 83, 1962, pp. 383-92.

————*Ephorus and History Written Kata Genos*, AJPhil 84, 1963, pp. 244-55.

————*Ephorus' Kata Genos History Revisited*, Hermes 104, 1976, pp. 188-201.

Flower, M.A., *Theopompus of Chios: History and Rhetoric in the Fourth Century BC* (Oxford, 1994).

Hammond, N.G.L., *The Sources of Diodorus Siculus XVI* (I): CQ 31, 1937, pp. 79-91.

————*Diodorus' Narrative of the Sacred War*, JHS 57, 1937, pp. 44-77.

Kebric, R.B., *In the Shadow of Macedon : Duris of Samos*, Historia, Einzelschrift Heft 29 (Wiesbaden, 1977).

Markle III, M.M., *The Support of Athenian Intellectuals for Philip: A Study of Isocrates' Philippus and Speusippus' Letter to Philip*, JHS 96, 1976, pp. 80-99.

————*Diodorus' Sources for the Sacred War in Book XVI*, in I.Worthington (ed.), *Ventures into Greek History* (Oxford, 1994).

Martin, T.R., *Diodorus on Philip II and Thessaly in the 350s BC*, CP 76, 1981, pp. 188-201.

Perlman, S., *Isocrates' Philippus: A Reinterpretation*, Historia 6, 1957, pp. 306-17.

————*Isocrates, Patris and Philip II*, Archaia Makedonia 3, 1983, pp. 211-27.

Sacks, K.S., *Diodorus Siculus and the First Century* (Princeton, 1990).

Shrimpton, G.S., *Theopompus the Historian* (Montreal & Kingston/London/ Buffalo, 1991).

Tronson, A., *Satyrus the Peripatetic and the Marriages of Philip II*, JHS 104, 1984, pp. 116-26.

General Works on the History of Macedonia

Anson, E.M., *Macedonia's Alleged Constitutionalism*, CJ 80, 1985, pp. 303-16.

Borza, E.N., *The Natural Resources of Early Macedonia*, in W.L.Adams & E.N.Borza (edd.), *Philip II, Alexander the Great and the Macedonian Heritage* (Washington, 1982) pp. 1-20.

———*In the Shadow of Olympus: the Emergence of Macedon* (Princeton, 1990) (chapters 9-11 cover the reign of Philip).

Dell H.J., (ed.), *Ancient Macedonian Studies in Honour of Charles F. Edson* (Thessaloniki, 1981).

Ellis, J.R., *The Dynamics of Fourth Century Imperialism*, Archaia Makedonia 2, 1977, pp. 103-114.

Errington, R.M., *The Nature of the Macedonian State under the Monarchy*, Chiron 8, 1978, pp. 77-113.

———*A History of Macedonia* (Berkeley, Los Angeles & Oxford, 1990) (chapter 2 covers the reign of Philip).

Greenwalt, W.S., *Polygamy and Succession in Argead Macedonia*, Arethusa 22, 1989, pp. 19-43.

Hammond, N.G.L. and Griffith, G.T., *History of Macedonia*, Vol.2 (Oxford, 1979) (chapters 11-21 cover the reign of Philip).

Hammond, N.G.L., *The Macedonian State* (Oxford, 1989) (chapters 6-8 cover the reign of Philip).

———*The Miracle that Was Macedonia* (London & New York, 1991) (chapters 6-7 cover the reign of Philip).

Hatzopoulos, M.B., *Succession and Regency in Classical Macedonia*, Archaia Macedonia 4, 1986, pp. 279-92.

Lock, R., *The Macedonian Army Assembly in the Time of Alexander the Great*, CP 72, 1977, pp 91-107.

Markle III, M.M., *The Macedonian Sarissa, Spear and Related Armour*, AJA 81, 1977, pp. 323-39.

Montgomery, H., *The Economic Revolution of Philip II: Myth or Reality?*, Symbolae Osloenses 60, 1985, pp. 37-47.

Books and Articles on Philip II

Adams, W.L. and Borza, E.N. (edd.), *Philip II, Alexander the Great and the Macedonian Heritage* (Washington, 1982).

Badian, E., *Philip II and Thrace*, Pulpudeva 4, 1987, pp. 51-71.

Bosworth, A.B., *Philip II and Upper Macedonia*, CQ 21, 1971, pp. 93-105.

Borza, E.N., *Philip II and the Greeks*, CP 73, 1978, pp. 236-43.

Bradford,A.S., *Philip II of Macedon: A Life from the Ancient Sources* (Westport & London, 1992).

Cawkwell, G.L., *Philip of Macedon* (London & Boston, 1978).

Ellis, J.R., *Population Transplants under Philip II*, Makedonika 9,1969, pp. 9-16.

————*The Security of the Macedonian Throne under Philip II*, Archaia Makedonia 1, 1970, pp. 68-75.

————*Philip II and Macedonian Imperialism* (London, 1976).

————*Philip's Thracian Campaign of 352-1*, CP 72, 1977, pp. 32-9.

Fredricksmeyer, E.A., *Divine Honours for Philip II*, TAPA 109, 1979, pp. 39-61.

————*On the Final Aims of Philip II*, in Adams and Borza, pp. 85-98.

Hammond, N.G.L.H., *Philip of Macedon* (London, 1994)

Hatzopoulos M.B. and Laikopoulos L.D. (edd.), *Philip of Macedon* (Athens & London, 1981).

Markle III, M.M., *The Use of the Sarissa by Philip and Alexander of Macedon*, AAJA 82, 1978, pp. 483-97.

Milns, R.D., *Philip II and the Hypaspists*, Historia 16, 1967, pp. 509-12.

Roebuck, C., *The Settlement of Philip II of Macedon with the Greek States in 338 BC*, CP 43, 1948, pp. 73-92.

Ryder, T.T.B., *The Diplomatic Skills of Philip II*, in I.Worthington (ed.), *Ventures into Greek History* (Oxford, 1994) pp. 228-57.

Philip, Thessaly and the Third Sacred War

Buckler, J., *Thebes, Delphoi and the Outbreak of the Third Sacred War*, in P. Roesch and G.Argoad (edd.), *La Béotie Antique* (Paris, 1985) pp. 237-46.

————*Philip II and the Sacred War*, Mnemosyne, Supplement 109 (Leiden, 1989).

Erhardt, C., *Two Notes on Philip of Macedon's First Intervention in Thessaly*, CQ 117, 1967, pp. 296-301.

Griffith, G.T., *Philip of Macedon's Early Interventions in Thessaly (358-352 BC)*, CQ 20, 1970, pp. 67-80.

Martin, T.R., *A Phantom Fragment of Theopompus on Philip II's First Campaign in Thessaly*, HSCP 86, 1982, pp. 55-78.

Parke, H.W., *The Pythais of 355 BC and the Third Sacred War*, JHS 59, 1939, pp. 80-83.

Westlake, H.D., *Thessaly in the Fourth Century* (London, 1939).

Philip and Euboea

Brunt, P.A., *Euboea in the Time of Philip II*, CQ 19, 1969, pp. 245-65.
Burke, E.M., *Eubulus, Olynthus and Euboea*, TAPA 114, 1984, pp. 111-20.
Carter, J.M., *Athens, Euboea and Olynthus*, Historia 20, 1971, pp. 418-29.
Cawkwell, G.L., *Euboea in the Late 340s*, Phoenix 32, 1978, pp. 42-67.
Parke, H.W., *Athens and Euboea 349-348 BC*, JHS 49, 1929, pp. 246-52.

Philip and Athens

Cawkwell, G.L., *Aeschines and the Peace of Philocrates*, REG 73, 1960, pp. 116-38.
———*Notes on the Social War*, Classica et Mediaevalia 23, 1962, pp. 34-49.
———*The Defence of Olynthus*, CQ 12, 1962, pp. 122-40.
———*Aeschines and the Ruin of Phocis in 346*, REG 75, 1962, pp. 453-9.
———*Demosthenes' Policy after the Peace of Philocrates*, CQ 13, 1963, pp. 120-33 and 200-13.
———*The Peace of Philocrates Again*, CQ 28, 1978, pp. 93-104.
de Ste. Croix, G.E.M., *The Alleged Secret Pact between Athens and Philip II concerning Amphipolis and Pydna*, CQ 13, 1963, pp. 110-113.
Dunkel, H.B., *Was Demosthenes a Panhellenist?*, CP 33, 1938, pp. 291-305.
Ellis, J.R., *Philip and the Peace of Philocrates*, in Adams and Borza, pp. 43-59.
Griffith, G.T., *The So-called Koine Eirene of 346 BC*, JHS 59, 1939, pp. 71-9.
Jaeger, W., *Demosthenes*, Berkeley, 1938.
Markle III, M.M., *The Strategy of Philip in 346 BC*, CQ 24, 1974, pp. 253-68.
Montgomery, H., *The Way to Chaeronea*, Bergen, 1983.
Mosely, D.J., *Athens' Alliance with Thebes in 339 BC*, Historia 20, 1971, pp. 508-10.
Perlman, S. (ed.), *Philip and Athens* (Cambridge & New York, 1973).
Pickard-Cambridge, A.W., *Demosthenes and the Last Days of Greek Freedom* (New York & London, 1914).
Ryder, T.T.B., *Demosthenes and Philip's Peace of 338/7*, CQ 26, 1971, pp. 85-7.
Sealey, R., *Proxenus and the Peace of Philocrates*, Wiener Studien 68, 1955, pp. 145-52.
———*Athens after the Social War*, JHS 75, 1955, pp. 74-81.
———*Demosthenes and his Time: A Study in Defeat* (New York & Oxford, 1993).

The Death of Philip

Badian, E., *The Death of Philip II*, Phoenix 17, 1963, pp. 244-50.

Bosworth, A.B., *Philip II and Upper Macedonia*, CQ 21, 1971, pp. 83-105.

Carney, E., *The Politics of Polygamy: Olympias, Alexander and the Murder of Philip*, Historia 41, 1992, pp. 169-89.

Develin, R., *The Murder of Philip II*, Antichthon 15, 1981, pp. 86-99.

Ellis, J.R., *Amyntas Perdikka, Philip II and Alexander the Great: A Study in Conspiracy*, JHS 91, 1971, pp. 15-24.

————*The Assassination of Philip II*, in Dell (see Section 2), pp. 99-137.

Fears, J.R., *Pausanias the Assassin of Philip II*, Athenaeum 53, 1975, pp. 111-35.

Heckel, W., *Philip II, Cleopatra and Caranus*, RFIC 107, 1979, pp. 385-93.

————*Philip and Olympias (337/6 BC)*, in G.S.Shrimpton and D.J.McCargar (edd.), *Classical Contributions. Studies in Honour of Malcolm Francis McGregor* (Locust Valley, New York, 1981) pp. 511-7.

Inscriptions of the Reign of Philip

The Greek texts of the principal inscriptions of the reign of Philip are conveniently collected in M.N. Tod, *A Selection of Greek Historical Inscriptions*, Vol. II (Oxford, 1948) nos. 150-82. The most comprehensive collection of translated inscriptions is to be found in P. Harding, *Translated Documents of Greece and Rome*, Vol. 2: *From the End of the Peloponnesian War to the Battle of Ipsus* (Cambridge, 1985) nos. 61-102. Inscriptions cited in the Commentary are regularly given the numbers assigned to them by both Tod and Harding. Other collections of translated inscriptions appear in the following books:

J. Wickersham and G. Verbrugghe, *Greek Historical Documents: The Fourth Century BC* (Toronto, 1973) nos. 50-75.

M. Crawford and D. Whitehead, *Archaic and Classical Greece. A Selection of Ancient Sources in Translation* (Cambridge, 1983) nos. 321-50.